Skills and Behaviors for Student Teaching

Skills and Behaviors for Student Teaching

A Progress Monitoring Approach

Bethany M. McConnell

BLOOMSBURY ACADEMIC
NEW YORK • LONDON • OXFORD • NEW DELHI • SYDNEY

BLOOMSBURY ACADEMIC
Bloomsbury Publishing Inc, 1359 Broadway, New York, NY 10018, USA
Bloomsbury Publishing Plc, 50 Bedford Square, London, WC1B 3DP, UK
Bloomsbury Publishing Ireland, 29 Earlsfort Terrace, Dublin 2, D02 AY28, Ireland

BLOOMSBURY, BLOOMSBURY ACADEMIC and the Diana logo are trademarks
of Bloomsbury Publishing Plc

First published in the United States of America 2026

Copyright © Bloomsbury Publishing, 2026

Cover design and illustrations by Kathi Ha

Paper textures © iStock.com/Weerayut Chaiwannaand and natrot

All rights reserved. No part of this publication may be: i) reproduced or transmitted in any form, electronic or mechanical, including photocopying, recording or by means of any information storage or retrieval system without prior permission in writing from the publishers; or ii) used or reproduced in any way for the training, development or operation of artificial intelligence (AI) technologies, including generative AI technologies. The rights holders expressly reserve this publication from the text and data mining exception as per Article 4(3) of the Digital Single Market Directive (EU) 2019/790.

Bloomsbury Publishing Inc does not have any control over, or responsibility for, any third-party websites referred to or in this book. All internet addresses given in this book were correct at the time of going to press. The author and publisher regret any inconvenience caused if addresses have changed or sites have ceased to exist, but can accept no responsibility for any such changes.

Library of Congress Cataloging-in-Publication Data is available

ISBN: HB: 979-8-8818-0587-6
PB: 979-8-8818-0588-3
ePDF: 979-8-8818-6782-9
eBook: 979-8-8818-0589-0

Typeset by Deanta Global Publishing Services, Chennai, India
Printed and bound in the United States of America

For product safety related questions contact productsafety@bloomsbury.com.

To find out more about our authors and books visit www.bloomsbury.com
and sign up for our newsletters.

Contents

FAQs xii
Prologue xiii

Part 1: Self-Care 1

Introduction 3
Learning More About You and Your Brain 3
Respond to Your Brain: Listen, Reflect, and Plan 4
Be Kind. Your Brain Is Listening 5
Reflect with a Growth Mindset 5
Plan Your Order at the Brainy Juice Bar 7
Make a Plan 11

1 You Do Not Have Time for This 15
Introducing a Few Student Teachers 16
Simone 17
Kaycee 17
Jasper 18
Quentin 19
Learn Some of the Places Where You Can Find the Time 21
Reflect on How You Spend Your Time with Time Tracking 24
Plan for How You Want to Spend Your Time 26
Weekly Goal Setting 28
Setting Goals for More Time 30
Quentin Is Working for More Deep Sleep 30

2 Rest and Brain Rejuvenation 37
Are You Getting Enough Rapid Eye Movement Sleep (REM)? 38
Your Sleep Schedule 38
Prepping Your Brain for Rest 39
Listen to Sounds That Help Your Brain Relax 40
Wake-Up Routine 43
Nap Time 44

Sleep Goals 45
Simone's Snooze Goal 45
Kaycee's Sleep Goal 47

3 Fuel: Food and Water 51

But First, Water 52
How Much Water 53
What Counts as Water 54
Going to the Well 54
The Water Bottle Trend 55
More Water Equals Less . . . 56
Making Good Food Choices 56
Out and About 58
At Home 58
Snacking 58
Meal Planning 60
Setting Fuel Goals 61
Simone Is Increasing Her Hydration 62
Jasper Is Limiting Junk Food 63

4 Exercise and Movement 69

Why, Accountability, Convenience, and Weekly Goals 69
My Why 70
My Running Era 70
Revisiting My Skiing Era 71
My Yoga Era 73
My Strength Training Era 74
Adaptations and Accommodations to Support Your Movement 76
Your Why 76
Getting Your Accountability 77
Convenience 78
Weekly Goal Setting 79
Virtual Accountability 79
Movement Goals 80
Stepping Up with Kaycee 80
Jasper Is Jumping into a Workout Routine 81

5 Brain-Centering Practices 87

Hope for Your Brain: Having Spirituality 88
Strength Training Your Brain: Meditation 89

Calming Your Brain: Breathwork 90
Telling Your Story: Positive Visualization 91
Retelling a Story: Meditative Stories 92
Dusting Your Brain: Nature Immersion 93
Nature Connection: Grounding 94
Incorporating Nature in Your Day 94
Organizing Your Brain: Journaling 95
Piecing Together Your Brain: Counseling 96
Brain-Centering Goals 98
Kaycee's Journey Through Journaling 98
Deep Breaths Quentin 100

Part 2: Classroom Management 107

6 Assessing Your Classroom Management 109
Connecting with Your Students 112
Culture 113
Organization 114
Rule Reminders and Clear Expectations 114
Provide Specific Behavior Praise 115
Opportunities to Respond and Student Engagement 116
Clear Structure for Behavior Challenges 116
Video Self-Reflection 117
Classroom Management Goals 121
Simone Can See Clear Expectations 121

7 Responsibility = Respect 127
Survey Your Students 128
Family Survey 131
Check Your Biases 133
Finding Individuality in Elementary Students 133
Finding Individuality with Middle Level and Secondary Students 135
What Do Your Students Value 136
Adding Cultural Considerations to Your Classroom 138
Making Considerations for What Is Happening Outside of Your Classroom 140
Give Students Community 141
Take Opportunities to Participate in Out-of-School Events 142
Responsibility and Respect Goals 143
Kaycee Is Adding After-School Activities 144
Quentin's Principal Investigators (PI) 145

8 Routines and Time on Task 149

Give Clear Rules and Expectations 149
Have Clear Consequences 151
First-Then Statements 153
Give Behavior Specific and Varied Praise 153
Scheduling Each Day 155
Introducing Your Lessons 155
Attention Getters 157
Efficient Transitions 157
Prepare for Downtime 159
Have Engaging and Inclusive Seasonal Activities 159
Prepare for the Unexpected 161
On-Task Goals 161
Simone Gives Clear Expectations 162
Quentin Will Give Relevance to His Lesson 163

9 Student Participation 167

Verbal Opportunities to Respond 167
Think-Pair-Share 168
Choral Responding 169
Turn and Talk 170
Quiet Opportunities for Everyone to Respond 171
Whiteboard Responses 171
Hand Signaling 172
Cue Cards 173
Poll Everywhere/Clickers 174
Student Participation Goals 175
Kaycee's Chatter Boxes 175
Quentin's Questioning 176

10 Identifying Appropriate Behaviors for Classroom Success 181

Classroom Umbrella 182
Positive Behavior Interventions and Supports 184
Teaching a Behavior 186
Precorrections 188
Class-Wide Motivation 190
Teacher Versus Student 190
Group Versus Group 191
Self-Monitoring 192
Classroom Reinforcements 193

Appropriate Behavior Goals 194
Jasper Is Dancing in the Rain to Make Connections with His Students 195
Students Versus Simone 196

Part 3: Relationships and Collaboration 203

11 Works Well with Others 205

Learning Your Tendency Is Based on How You Meet Expectations 206
External Accountability 206
Internal Accountability 207
How Do the Four Tendencies Relate to Teacher Collaboration? 208
How Do People's Tendencies Impact Collaboration? 210
How Do the Four Tendencies Impact the Success of Student Teachers? 211
Kaycee the People Pleasing Obliger 211
Simone Upholds Herself and Others 212
Jasper the Resisting Rules Rebel 214
Quentin Questions Your Questions 215
After Your Tendency Quiz 219
Jasper Is Becoming a Reliable Rebel 219

12 Working with Administrators 225

Shadowing My Elementary Principal 226
The Roles of Administrators 226
Overall Responsibilities 227
Playing Fair 229
Making Big Decisions 230
School-Wide Management Systems 231
Crisis Management 231
Positive Behavior Interventions and Supports 232
Positive Interactions with Administrators During Your Student Teaching Placement 233
Administrative Goals 235
Jasper Is Staying Beyond the Bell 236
Quentin Limits Questions to the Principal 237

13 Colleagues, Paraprofessionals, and Other Support Staff 241

Scenario in the Classroom 241
Collaborating with Others 242
Your Mentor Teacher Is Your Guide 243

Co-Teaching as a Partnership 244
Productive Relationships with Paraprofessionals 248
Strategies for Working with Everyone 250
Regular Check-Ins 252
Informal Communications 254
Scaffolding for Teamwork 254
Shared Measurable Goals 255
Roles and Responsibilities 255
Clear Communication 256
Effective Use of Time 257
What to Do When It Is Not Working Out 258
Collegial Goals 260
Kaycee Has an Agenda 260
Simone Is Checking In 261

14 Collaborating with Families 267

Continue Weekly Ongoing Communication 268
Newsletters 268
Positive Phone Calls 270
LAFF Don't CRY with Families 272
Providing Resources Is a Two-Way Street 277
Making Family Goals 279
Kaycee Actively Listens 279
Quentin's Investigative Report 280

15 Healthy Relationships 285

Building Friendships 286
When Friendships Mix 287
Defining Gray Area 288
A Workplace with Gray Areas 289
Being a Novice Teacher while Avoiding Gray Areas 290
When I Was in the Gray Area as a Novice Teacher 291
Avoiding Gray Areas When You Are the Role Model 292
Ways to Avoid the Gray Area When You Are the Role Model 292
When I Was a Role Model in the Gray Area 293
Reporting Someone in the Gray Area 294
In Closing 295
Healthy Relationship Goals 295
Jasper Gets Digitally Literate 295
Kaycee Is Framed for Favoritism on Social Media 296

References 305
Acknowledgments 313
Index 315
About the Author 321

FAQs

Do I have to focus on all goals each week? No, it is ideal for you to work on the skills and behaviors you want to improve. It will be helpful for you to collect baseline data.

Regarding working on goals and improvements, those skill areas are up to you, the reader.

What is baseline data? The 3 to 5 data points will give you a good idea of your typical performance without making any changes. From this, you will create a goal.

What if I do not know how to collect data? There are sample goals along with data trackers to help you learn how to collect various types of behavior data throughout the book. This may help you to learn how to monitor progress with your students.

What if some of these practices do not resonate with me? Here is your reminder: change and growth are uncomfortable. There are several options for improvements that you can make in your daily life and the classroom. Please stay consistent and try new things. Do not stay stuck. Teaching is about lifelong learning. You will learn more about yourself each week, and you are pretty awesome.

Is this book only for student teachers? This book is written for any teacher walking into the classroom. You may be completing your first few rounds of field placements and want to make a strong start, you may be begrudgingly switching grade levels this year, or you simply need a fresh start in the classroom. Focusing on the most important person in the classroom—you. Specifically, this book will support student teachers during a 15-week segment of student teaching. These concepts can also be helpful for any teachers who want additional insights from a mentor during the most memorable year of their teaching career.

Prologue

This book blends practical strategies with insights from research in cognitive psychology, reflexive practice, and culturally responsive teaching. While not an over-cited scholarly text, I have included references for foundational thinkers whose work supports the practices described. Consider this an informational and reflective workbook that provides guidance on progress monitoring, designed primarily to help you meet your educational needs. You may recall from your assessment course that you start with pre-assessment data to inform your instruction. You will learn more about these key teacher skills and collect your baseline data. Here is a simple breakdown of what you need to know: at the beginning of each part, you will start with a pre-assessment to gain a deeper understanding of your routines and behaviors. Your pre-assessments will provide you with more information about your teaching behaviors.

Once you learn more from each chapter, you can decide what evidence-based skills you would like to focus on to improve your teaching. Once you identify a specific behavior, you will collect baseline data on that teaching skill. Your baseline data consists of 3 to 5 data points of specific skills you want to improve. Your baseline data shows the average time or number of actions you complete in a determined timeline. This data will help give you insight into your status without the evidence-based teacher skills. For example, in Chapter 11, you will learn more about active whole-group student participation in the classroom. You will start collecting baseline data to determine how many times you currently call on your whole group of students for responses. The baseline data will help you determine your desired progress, allowing you to estimate how soon you anticipate meeting those goals. This is the first of many times you will read this: teaching is about making progress. Start small with each skill. You can discuss appropriate progress and efficient timelines for your goals with your mentor teacher.

With each chapter, you can collect baseline data and identify the progress you want to make. The baseline data will help you determine your current status and identify short- or long-term goals you want to achieve during your student teaching (Wang, Husu, & Toom, 2025). Your goal must be measurable, observable, and achievable. Next, you monitor progress toward mastery. What does progress look like for you? How much time do you need to see improvements? How will you know if you have met your goal? This is the beauty of teacher decision-making. You will have reflective questions throughout each chapter to consider, helping you make informed decisions about your progress during student teaching. By following this process of collecting your data and measuring progress, you are practicing analyzing data and making decisions for your students.

As you read the weekly topics, you will collect tools from the evidence-based toolkit to support your behaviors and routines. These are the supports that will help you to succeed in the classroom. Throughout each chapter, you can experiment and reflect on what works best for you. As you collect data on yourself, you can monitor your behaviors to determine what works and what does not. Please remember that you have developed your current routines and habits over many years. Some routines work for you, but you may notice some areas where you would like improvement throughout your day. Be kind to yourself as you go through this process. You can change routines by setting alarms on your phone as reminders or wake-up calls.

Nonetheless, some skills can take time to change. *This is your announcement that you can shift your priorities each week.* All that I ask is that one of the priorities is you! My goal for you is to have the love and passion you had for teaching when you first declared your major. I want you to have this excitement for teaching for years to come. I know that is a feeling that is not measurable. Despite that, I want you to remember your why when you have difficult days. I want to share some secrets, wrapped in evidence-based practice, that will help you stay in this career for many years. Start telling yourself, "Keep going, you got this!"

This book contains three parts, five chapters per part, totaling 15 organized chapters, so you can read one to two chapters each week while you are in your field placement. Part I focuses on the most important person—you. You need to focus on yourself before taking time for others. You may not be accustomed to that, so be prepared to reflect on your self-care routines. Part II highlights positive and engaging classroom management. What are the expectations for your classroom? How are students working together? Lastly, in Part III, you will focus on building positive relationships with others by building strategies through "Getting Along 101." It is essential to develop the skills of getting along and relationship building, so you can apply simple techniques to foster healthy relationships with your colleagues, administrators, staff, and parents.

This interactive book includes tools and resources, as well as themed boxes to help you reflect and jot down ideas that will benefit you in the classroom and on your self-care journey. Please complete these parts; taking notes will help you hold yourself accountable and make these ideas stick. Below is a chart summary with descriptions of how to use these image boxes throughout each chapter.

Share your progress on Instagram. Tag me: @dr.mcconnell.s_progress

Prologue xv

Outlines for the Resources Throughout the Book

This Box Contains	What to do
Think About It. There are reflective questions throughout the chapter that help you to think about what you just read.	Put down some of your thoughts. If you are unsure, you may need to reflect on the questions and come back with a response.
Add Your Ideas. Review the examples to refer to when you need ideas. Add in your own ideas and examples that relate to your classroom.	Use the samples and research provided to add some examples that apply to you. Take pictures and refer to these statements when you need support.
Inclusive and Culturally Responsive Practices Ideas relevant to the chapter and connecting to inclusive practices are also included. These considerations address various cultures, races, abilities, religions.	Apply these examples as they fit into your classroom and lifestyle. Some examples may be new, so you must check your bias and model different practices.
Chapter Recap There is an outline at the end of the chapter to review several key concepts and summarize the big ideas from the chapter.	Skim over your notes from the chapter and summarize the critical points in these reflections. Your answers will help you determine your goals.
Collaborative Thinking These are questions to encourage you to get ideas and brainstorm with your peers and mentors.	Find mentors whom you admire and ask them questions about these topics. You may have a different person to talk to for various issues. Share ideas with your peers as well.

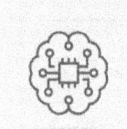 **Technology Checkpoints** This is a list of various websites, free apps, etc. to help you to bring more technology into the classroom.	Review these summaries and sample the activities, videos, and lessons to see how they can enhance your lessons.
 **Teacher Decision-Making** This is an opportunity for you to reflect on all the topics discussed and consider your next steps.	Take this time to assess your progress across all topics for which you are collecting data. Use this time to recognize where to focus your improvements and, at times, let things go.
 **Next Steps.** These are the same questions that you will be asked at the end of each chapter to help you think about your next steps.	As you learn new material, think about what skills you want to add to your weekly progress monitoring. Answer these questions honestly. What is working? What do you need to change?
 **Weekly Reflection** Reflections are at the end of each chapter, so you can journal some thoughts.	Take this opportunity to respond to these questions and statements. Highlight what is working and jot down some of your thoughts.

Part I

Self-Care

Introduction

Chapter Outline

Learning More About You and Your Brain	3
Plan Your Order at the Brainy Juice Bar	7

Learning More About You and Your Brain

First off, thank you for choosing to teach. I appreciate you. Many students question the profession because their family members ask, "Are you sure you want to go into teaching?" or "Is it worth having *summers off* with all that you have to do during the school year?" Perhaps you have even been in classrooms with teachers who have said, "Kids these days are just unbearable to deal with." Even though the teaching profession does receive some negative attention, you persevered through the coursework that has brought you to the next step of student teaching.

For some individuals, their initial interest in becoming a teacher stems from a love of working with children. For others, you love the content you teach so much that you want to spend your days positively influencing future generations. The reason I am here is because of my passion for providing equal educational experiences for students from all backgrounds and abilities. My teaching slogan is "I am here for inclusion and to make a magnitude of positive impact." You can quote someone you admire or make your own statement. Just write down your reminder of why you chose teaching, which can help you through those tough days. As you read along, you will see the thinking person image below for you to reflect on and answer the questions. I encourage you to take the time to use the book when you can read and write answers to the questions.

 **Think About It.**

Write your teaching slogan. Why are you here?
I am here because . . .

?
?
?

Next, thank you for showing up for yourself. By prioritizing yourself, you are taking proactive steps to prepare for a long career in education. Additionally, you are modeling self-care for your colleagues and your students. *By getting this far, I believe in you and your ability to share the love of working with students and the content you teach.* I want you to make it, and I want you to be as excited as you are today as a teacher as you are 20 years from now. Staying in education is one goal I have for you. My goal is to decrease the percentage of quality teachers who leave the education profession due to burnout. You have chosen a rewarding career, and each school year, you will witness your efforts in your students' growth and progress.

I have worked in the education system for over 20 years, and in recent years, I have heard similar narratives of burnout from my college students, who have not yet graduated. Therefore, it is not surprising that a recent McKinsey report found that 38% of younger teachers (ages 25–34) are considering leaving their profession due to the demanding workload (De Smet et al., 2022). You are going into a high-stress, high-needs job, and working on the tools you need to be an effective teacher in the classroom. I hope I am not the first to tell you, it does not have to be this way. In these chapters, I will share some secrets I wish I had learned years ago about the human brain and how the brain handles stress. I want to discuss how stress occurs in your brain and what small things you can do daily to manage your stress response. Many of these concepts are defined through current research, but come from the brain's evolutionary natural response: fight, flight, or freeze. I am still working through some of these challenges. I need to revisit and work on eliminating some bad habits and negative thought patterns each week. Progress takes time, so be easy on yourself. You are working with a brilliant brain. Your goal is to wake up each morning and make progress every day. I believe in you. You got this!

Respond to Your Brain: Listen, Reflect, and Plan

As a teacher, you make an average of 1,500 decisions in a day (Levin, 2008). This places a significant cognitive load on one human being. Then, you factor in primal instinct

concepts you learned previously in your psychology courses. Your brain is trying to keep you alive, and it signals your body to go into response mode. Through this, your brain is firing signals to either fight, flight, or freeze. If your instincts are to fight like a woolly mammoth is attacking you, you will always live with that high response. You hear the voices of other teachers in the staff lounge stuck in negative statements like, "I do not get paid enough to deal with this." This causes you to enter a negative spiral, prompting you to revert to a response mode and forget the skills and tools you have learned throughout your career, which are essential for listening, reflecting, and planning. In this first section, I will break down some critical functions of the brain and what science tells you to do to calm these receptors in your brain so that you can address the actual situations in front of you. Calming your brain and your body does not solve your problems, but it does help you to identify appropriate strategies and behaviors to cope with the day-to-day challenges of teaching (Carroll, Hepburn, & Bower, 2022).

Be Kind. Your Brain Is Listening

Many people use the buzzword stress. Uncovering how your brain is trying to help you limit stress is vital. If you do not recognize what is happening, you can end up in a cycle of unhealthy, negative thoughts. Your Reticular Activating System (RAS) is at the base of the brain. It is like the school security officer or secretary filtering out unnecessary visitors into the school. It is the gatekeeper of important information (Willis & Willis, 2020). RAS is paying attention to what you are telling yourself. So, as an example, if you start the day by saying, "Ugh, it is Monday, and I am so tired. It will be a struggle to make it through the day." Guess what? Your brain has heard this, and now it is just looking for things to prove that it is the Monday-est Monday ever. You will continue to see things that remind your brain that Mondays are hard.

However, as you begin your student teaching placement, I want to challenge you to think differently. Pick an object or a visual symbol, maybe an apple, and every time you see an apple, you say—"I am a great teacher who listens, plans, and reflects." Train your brain to look for good things and connect them to positive phrases. Start to visualize the good things that are coming your way. This strategy is not just magic; it is your RAS building an environment that filters good examples for your brain to shape these good things to happen in your life (Robbins, 2023). The moral of the story is that if you are looking for apples, you will find apples. If you look for a bad day, you will find one. So, use a positive narrative around your brain; your brain is listening. So when you see your visual symbol throughout your day, you can identify that you are exactly where you are meant to be.

Reflect with a Growth Mindset

The scenario above is an exercise from my friend, Mel Robbins. She has taught me strategies to develop a growth mindset. You must exercise your brain like any other body part, or it will gravitate to its protective role of a security officer, ready for fight, flight, or freeze. I want you to model this growth mindset in your classroom meetings with your colleagues. Sometimes, I refer to this as my rainbows and sunshine mindset. In other words, it is essential to enter the classroom each day with an optimistic mindset (Jennings & Greenberg, 2020). I tell myself, "What if it works out?" However, you can see progress if you take a positive "not yet" approach when gaining new skills. Are you starting to understand that you must exercise your brain just as you exercise your body? The chart below contains several ways to shift your narrative from a fixed mindset to a growth mindset.

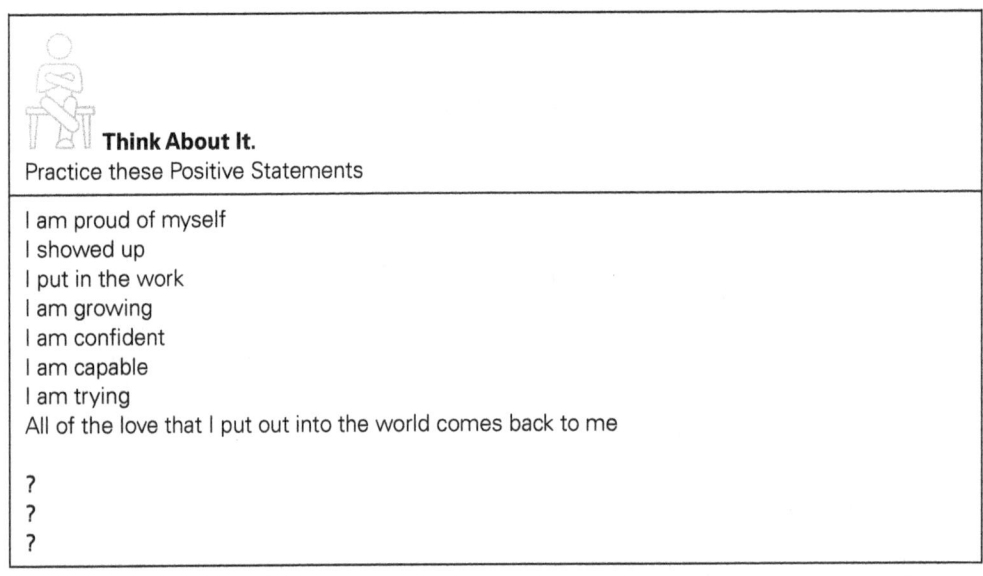

Think About It. Practice these Positive Statements
I am proud of myself
I showed up
I put in the work
I am growing
I am confident
I am capable
I am trying
All of the love that I put out into the world comes back to me
?
?
?

Negative narratives can be challenging to shift. This could be a narrative you have heard your whole life, or it is the approach of some social group members. Mindset-like beliefs are present as early as kindergarten and first grade (Cain & Dweck, 1995). So you may have to work hard to undo your fixed mindset, but let your motivation be the model you are for your students, hardwiring their brains to go out into the world with a growth mindset. Remember, your brain responds with fight, flight, or freeze. Because you need to be present each day and focus on effective teacher decision-making, you must **listen, reflect, and plan**. What is your go-to phrase when you are facing a difficult situation? Better yet, what would your friend tell you? I have started sharing specific praise on Post-it notes and using the "Remind App" to send messages to my students throughout the week. You will see my Post-it notes as you continue to read, and you will see some examples of specific praise in Chapter 8. Write down a positive statement on the Post-it notes for motivation. Let me be your cheerleader if you still have a slump of negative thoughts. Think of one of your statements of encouragement or borrow one of mine from the list below. Remind yourself that every day is a new day. You may have made a mistake yesterday, and today can be different.

⊕ **Add Your Ideas.**
Catchphrases to flip your script to a growth mindset

What are the fixed phrases you use?	Replace it with a growth mindset statement
I am so bad at this.	I'm still learning this—it takes time to get better.
I will never figure this out.	I haven't figured it out yet, but I'm going to keep trying different strategies.
Everyone else has this figured out.	I'm on my path, and I'll get there too.
I keep making mistakes.	Mistakes mean I'm trying and learning—everyone helps me improve.
Everything is so hard for me.	This is challenging right now, but with effort and support, it will get easier.
Today was the worst.	Today was tough, but tomorrow is a chance to start fresh and try again.
•	
•	

Plan Your Order at the Brainy Juice Bar

Now, let's move on to the next steps of why it is essential to maintain a clear and positive mindset when working in the classroom each day. These may be friendly reminders from psychology class or buzzwords about stress on TikTok. However, your brain does so much more than fight, flight, and freeze to protect you. Let's review these concepts from educational psychology to remind you of the intricate responses of the brain. Some natural reactions to others or habits you continue are simply the brain's way of protecting you from harm. It is your job to recognize and reflect on what chemicals and neuroresponses you need to increase and decrease to get your brain working in your favor each day. These chemicals and neurotransmitters are like supplemental juice drinks, with a direct correlation to how your brain responds, depending on the juice you order each day.

Now it is time to put your brain to work and get the brain juices flowing in your favor. You can do this with some minor adjustments. Below is a chart that breaks down some of the main chemicals and neurotransmitters, their primary responsibilities, and how they respond to stress and pleasure. I will break down examples as they apply and use these terms so that you understand what happens to your brain when you are under stress. It is complex! So, you need to realize that you need to take a proactive approach to understanding your brain and how to help you make healthy choices to regulate stress.

Skills and Behaviors for Student Teaching

Think About It.
Brain Juice: Summary of Chemicals and Neurotransmitters in the Brain

Neurotransmitters/ Chemicals in the Brain	Job	What it Does in the Brain	Keyword mnemonic to help immediately recall of vocabulary
Increase these Chemicals/ Neurotransmitters			
Serotonin "feel-good" neurotransmitter	Regulates mood, anxiety, and overall sense of well-being.	Higher serotonin levels are linked to decreased stress and anxiety. It is produced in the brain and intestines. Imbalances in Serotonin are linked to physical and psychological health problems; depression, anxiety, sleep issues.	"Keep a positive tone Sara"
Dopamine neurotransmitter "Pleasure Center"	Regulates pleasure and reward, which can help reduce stress by improving motivation and resilience; reinforcing behaviors drive motivation	There are increases in dopamine when you achieve goals or experience pleasurable activities, lowering feelings of stress.	"Dopey's Mine"
Endorphins "Nature's Pain Killer"	. . . act as natural painkillers and mood elevators often released during physical activity, stress, or pain.	. . . help diminish the perception of pain and produce euphoria, helping reduce stress.	"Dolphin helping the pain"

Oxytocin "love hormone"	. . . reduces stress by promoting social connections and feelings of calm; it promotes a sense of well-being	. . . when released, promotes feelings of safety and calmness and decreases cortisol (stress hormone)	"You are my oxygen"
	Balance these Chemicals/ Neurotransmitters		
Norepinephrine (Adrenaline) Fight-flight-freeze response	. . . balanced levels help regulate mood, attention, and stress responses.	. . . moderate levels help improve focus and resilience to stress, but chronic stress can lead to high levels, contributing to anxiety	"Porcupine fight"
Melatonin	. . . regulates the sleep/wake cycle and promotes relaxation.	. . . signals the body that it is time to rest, reducing stress by helping regulate the sleep-wake cycle	"Mellow Lemon Jello Chill"
	Reduce this Chemical		
Cortisol (Reduction)	. . . primary stress hormone, released in response to stress. While it is necessary for survival, chronic elevation of cortisol levels leads to stress related disorders.	Managing cortisol levels through relaxation techniques helps reduce prolonged stress and its adverse effects.	"Always defending in court"

Dopamine is the driver mechanism that allows you to experience pleasure. Dopamine is the neurotransmitter responsible for the sensation of joy and pleasure that your brain experiences. These can be moments, such as winning a lottery ticket or savoring ice cream. Your brain craves these dopamine hits each day. Sometimes, you get into routines where your brain spots the ice cream shop before you do, and all you can do is think about treating yourself. Is a little ice cream now and then harmful? No, but what can be detrimental is if your brain responds too much to unhealthy pleasure centers and you get to a point where you are unable to control these excessive behaviors: eating, vaping, gambling, drinking, and so on. The brain craves these hits of familiarity. Another contributor to dopamine is from the various apps on your cell phone. From scrolling through reels and playing games to direct messaging, your brain is on autopilot, just hitting those buttons. You can spend hours entertained on your cell phone with limited social interaction. If I am not monitoring myself, I do it too, and am guilty as charged.

Skills and Behaviors for Student Teaching

© iStock.com/wowomnom

 **Add Your Ideas.**
Unhealthy Dopamine Hits if Overused

Bingeing TV	Smoking
Excessively playing Video Games	Hating on people
Sugar	Checking phone for texts
Drinking	Searching for likes and comments on social media
Gambling	Impulsive shopping/ buying
•	•
•	•

 **Think About It.**

Excessive or binge tendencies. How do you know if you are excessive or bingeing? Review this checklist over the next week and reflect on your ability to control these activities.

Do these activities get in the way of other things you would like to be doing?
Do you avoid social interactions to engage in these activities?
Do these activities interfere with your work or productivity?
Do you rely on these habits to function each day?
Are these activities getting in the way of your progress?

?
?
?

If you have answered yes to one or more of these questions, you may need to address them with a professional. However, some people are able to adjust their habits with awareness and replace them with new, healthier options. Finding healthy ways to get better options for dopamine hits each day is essential (Talbott, 2021). Think about lessening how much you vape or cutting back on your social media intake. Try replacing it with other similar, rewarding activities. Below is a list of activities that produce dopamine and joy for most people. Try some of these activities this week. When you start these activities, try to savor them. Reflection is vital for behavior change (Schön, 1983). Take pictures or write in a journal about how they made you feel. Relishing in a moment helps to recognize the benefits of your healthy choices and rewires dopamine receptors. Send a photo to someone who would appreciate your efforts. Do not be hard on yourself. I did not know how to avoid burnout until much later in life. Changing yourself for the better is a journey. You got this! If you are concerned about an unhealthy habit, consider consulting a doctor or a professional to discuss it. Talking is the most essential part. Find your person who casts no judgments. This person could be a friend, partner, or parent.

Think About It. (Circle a few you are interested in and sample)	
Schedule exercise classes	Set small goals each week
Take ice baths/ cold showers	Do something kind for someone else
Foods: Almonds, bananas, poultry (Chapter 3 provides a longer list)	Limit sugars
	Journal
Start your day with 5 minutes of sun exposure, fresh air, and a walk	Make a list of accomplishments
Get adequate sleep (7–9 hours)	Make a plan to have lunch with a friend
Give yourself something to look forward to	

Make a Plan

You must increase the usage of all the chemicals and neurotransmitters outlined. Nevertheless, the job of cortisol is to notify the brain anytime it perceives stress. It activates the amygdala, which signals your body to prepare for the fight, flight, or freeze response. This is the body's natural response to save you from actual harm. Remember that your brain's job is to keep you alive, not help you feel good (Mohapel, 2025). However, as teachers, the best first steps include listening, reflecting, and planning. The issue is that your body has taken over, and you need to regain control of the situation to let your body know there is no danger. Say to yourself, "I've got this!"

As you move forward with a positive approach, I want to remind you to look for small and manageable improvements to make progress. Start with a visualization that motivates you while these weeks continue. Think about the end of the semester. What do you want to say as you walk across that stage to get your diploma? Picture it; picture yourself in the cap and gown, with your loved ones in the stands and friends sitting in rows nearby. What will you think . . . you are alive, sleep deprived, and you have been wearing these same dried-out daily contact lenses for over a month now; or do you want to hold that diploma and say, "You've got this! You've made it! You have grown and progressed, and you are a better version of yourself." I always told myself, "It will be different when . . . and I will have more time when . . ." Guess what never happened? My priorities changed only when I looked honestly at how I spent my time and set clear goals about how I wanted to spend it. I want the same opportunities for you. Why? Because teaching holds a magnitude of impact. If you are making progress and are healthier, so are your students. So, it is time to set clear goals and figure out how to make progress.

© iStock.com/Vanz Studio

Along the way, you will have difficult days in the classroom and in your personal life. I would love to sugarcoat this, but as I mentioned, life happens. Things will go differently from what was planned. Prepare for these days with options to help you navigate and regulate your emotions. Below is a first aid kit with some sample tips recommended by the experts and some routines that have helped me when I felt stuck. For example, when I am mad at myself and disappointed with how a situation is unfolding, I go for a walk. Returning to the situation I see, "it is not that deep." Brainstorm some items that have helped you in the past. Next, create your own first aid kit to be readily available. When you want to doom scroll or spiral into a negative Snapchat, refer to your first aid kit. You cannot always go outside for fresh air when stressed. Nevertheless, if you are overwhelmed and need a break, chances are you have students who could use a break too. Perhaps add some yoga stretches so everyone can benefit from your "brain break" in the classroom. If you do not have many ideas or examples, do not worry; Part I is full of examples supported by research that can help you to improve a negative mindset.

⊕ Add Your Ideas.

Expert Recommendations for when you Feel Overwhelmed		
When you FEEL:	Expert recommendation in CAPS with more tips below	Personal quotes What to Tell Your Brain
like everyone hates you	SLEEP • Close your eyes and take a deep breath of fresh air	Remember, it's not that deep • •
like you hate yourself	Take a SHOWER • Listen to a waterfall	Think of one good thing you did today
like you hate everyone	EAT • Treat yourself with a yummy snack	Pause the caffeine and get some water • •

In summary, understanding how your brain works, maintaining a growth mindset, and planning for balance are all foundational for you to limit stress as a student teacher. If you are not quite sure how this applies to you, keep reading. This workbook is meant to guide you through the student teaching process. You will reflect on your teaching within each section and focus on progress, not perfection. Push yourself to try new activities. Try to break a cycle or a bad habit that is wasting your time. Regardless, keep going and focus on your why as you get into the classroom each day.

1

You Do Not Have Time for This

Chapter Outline

Introducing a Few Student Teachers	16
Learn Some of the Places Where You Can Find the Time	21
Reflect on How You Spend Your Time with Time Tracking	24
Plan for How You Want to Spend Your Time	26
Weekly Goal Setting	28
Setting Goals for More Time	30

The previous section provided context for the importance of what is happening in your brain. It sets the groundwork for you to understand that the topics uncovered in Part I are worth your time. Throughout the Introduction, you sampled some reflections and tips that you will continue to see throughout the book. Before you say, "I do not have time for this while I am student teaching," let me remind you that when you graduate you will have a similar amount of time as you do now. Making time for yourself is crucial as it promotes personal growth. It is essential to incorporate these skills into your teaching practices now so that they stick once you are the lead teacher in the classroom (Nagro & deBettencourt, 2019). Ensure you are taking manageable steps toward success. To stay in the field of education while avoiding burnout, you need to make minor adjustments. Before starting any changes, you might already say, "I do not have time for this."

Have you ever heard the catchphrase "The only person you can change is you"? That is undoubtedly true, but if you change your behavior, other people will tend to follow. Your role as a teacher is so important because you have a group of 5 to 105 students you see in a day, plus consider 55 colleagues you interact with weekly. Modeling these skills improves the moods of the students in your classroom and the adults in your building. This book focuses on how you can monitor your daily habits and teacher behaviors to make progress.

When discussing teacher behaviors, consider any action, from drinking water to calling on students or giving students specific praise. The picture many people often think of is negative behaviors teachers observe in the classroom. An example of this is talking while others are talking.

You will monitor your behavior(s) and habits to reflect on the changes you want to make.

Doing this lets you reflect on the positive outcomes or changes that follow. Some differences may be minor, such as thinking, "I see progress within myself," to your most significant ah-ha moments in teaching, sharing statements like, "I cannot believe how well they did when working together!" Push yourself to adjust your routines. Change does not happen overnight, so do not feel you must work on everything simultaneously. However, some of these recommendations and supports just might be the makeover you need. Caution—happiness and lighthearted humor are some of the effects noted after reading this book.

© iStock.com/nisi.

Introducing a Few Student Teachers

Let me start by saying you are not alone in your uncertainties. I have worked with student teachers for many years, and the same routines and stressors that I faced as a student teacher over 20 years ago are still the dilemmas that my student teachers address today. To help you navigate some of your difficulties, I will share examples of student teachers like yourself. I will use their stories to help you associate with common challenges that student teachers face while working toward their teacher certification. I will be sharing the experiences of these four student teachers throughout each chapter. Identify who you connect with most.

Simone

Simone is 22 and finishing her last semester of student teaching. She teaches 2 ninth-grade algebra classes, one remedial math course, and one geometry class. Simone is a self-starter and keeps her to-do lists organized. Simone benefits from daily routines. She has experienced these difficulties in the college classroom in previous years as well. She typically displayed a visceral response when changes to due dates and assignments occurred. Unexpected changes to the school schedule, like fire drills and students leaving early for sporting events, challenge her routine. A goal that she really needs to focus on is supporting students who are struggling in their math classes.

© iStock.com/Alina Kotliar.

Kaycee

Kaycee is a 21-year-old student teacher working in a first-grade classroom. She teaches in an urban setting and is striving to meet the diverse needs of her students at the school. Kaycee is a straight-A college student who struggles to say no to others. She is a bit of an overachiever, so she tends to go above and beyond, even if it means putting others' needs before her own. For example, while student teaching, she started helping with the spring play and fifth-grade reading competitions. These are all great resume builders, but sometimes they come at the expense of Kaycee's health and well-being. When the weekend rolls around, Kaycee crashes, and she does not have the time to write the resume or look for a job. While working with students, she needs to improve her differentiation of instruction.

18   Skills and Behaviors for Student Teaching

© iStock.com/Visual Generation.

Jasper

Jasper is completing his first semester of student teaching in a middle school, sixth-grade ELA/Social Studies Learning/Emotional Support setting. Jasper is 24, a college baseball player and a future middle school social studies teacher. He pushes into general education classrooms to support three different general education teachers throughout the day. During three additional class periods, students visit his classroom for progress monitoring and mini-lessons to review and preview the content of their various classes. It is a joy to

© iStock.com/ChrisGorgio.

observe Jasper at the school. He likes to keep his lessons fun and engaging. Sometimes, this comes at the expense of implementing state standards and preparing students for state tests. The students have built a quick connection with him, and he is making a difference because of his relationships with his students. He is still learning to organize the classroom and his day. He struggles to balance his practice schedule and meet all the students' needs and his mentors' expectations.

Quentin

Quentin, who identifies as a scientist, is a post-baccalaureate student majoring in secondary chemistry and biology. He worked in a lab for a few years before recognizing how much he enjoyed teaching and mentoring students. Quentin teaches three biology classes and one chemistry class with his mentor teacher each day. He now identifies that his true happiness lies in helping other students fall in love with science. He treats all of his students like scientists when he teaches. One of his struggles is classroom management. He focuses so much on the lesson that he forgets his audience does not always love science as much as he does. In Quentin's first few observations, his mentor teacher always provided him with specific feedback and encouraged him to make changes in his lessons. There appears to be a slight disconnect, as Quentin shares that he spends hours at night planning the perfect lessons.

© iStock.com/Eva Almqvist.

> **Think About It.**
> Which student teachers do you relate to most? What routines are easy for you to implement each day? Name one "glowing" teacher skill you had this week. Name one "growing" skill you are ready to work on.
>
> ?
> ?
> ?

Perhaps you connect with Jasper when you are in the classroom, but in your planning, you feel more like Kaycee. Through these examples, you will develop ideas to improve your craft of teaching. In each chapter, you will read how the student teachers are handling these situations as they work to make progress each week. If you already have your fists up defending your time, I need you to track your time. Please take one week to summarize each hour of your day. How are you spending your time? Some of these hours might be shared with loved ones, taking care of children or family members, or working a second or third job to help you pay the bills. I have been there, and I understand. But what if I told you that you may spend too much time preparing materials for your lessons? Or you are not being practical with how much sleep you are getting? With data collection and reflection, your mentor can share advice on where you could be more realistic about spending less time preparing for your lessons.

On the other hand, some people could be spending too much time in a spinning whirlwind of social media, binge-watching TV, and reaching higher levels with online games. Some of these standard outlets may be your way to de-stress. Time tracking helps you manage your time and visualize how much time you spend on various activities (Ahmady et al., 2021). You can then look at how you spend your time and evaluate what activities are necessary and enjoyable, and which are unhealthy time wasters. For example, exercising just 20 minutes a day is a proven mood boost (Weinstein et al., 2024). If the activities you identify as stress relievers are taking up more time and do not help your mood, consider cutting back and trying different evidence-based activities.

The habits you have now are part of your routine, so without much thought, you follow your schedule each day. The new concepts, or tweaks, recommended in the coming chapters have an evidence base and support overall happiness and progress. Examine how you currently spend your time and identify which of your existing behaviors no longer promote joy, allowing you to make room for positive changes. Do not worry; I pride myself on finding hacks and productivity. Do you need an example? I time myself when I grade papers. Yes, I give myself enough time for each student and set an alarm to avoid getting sidetracked, which cuts down on hours of grading. Writing a book should make me feel more competent in sharing my research. However, I must state, I am not a medical doctor, or as my son reminded me when he was 4, "I am not a band-aid doctor." This is my disclaimer: I am not an expert in everyday health, sleep, or nutrition. I am using research to connect my experience with improving my lifestyle by replacing unhealthy behaviors with healthier options, which I apply as an educator to build positive experiences in the classroom. Please consult your physician if you are facing medical issues or have concerns about your health.

Learn Some of the Places Where You Can Find the Time

Did you know there are 168 hours in a week? Thanks to Laura Vanderkam, I now know this. If I thought about it, I could have figured it out. What Laura taught me was how to spend my time more productively and focus on what matters (Vanderkam, 2022). That is a significant amount of time, and guess what? Everyone has the same amount of time every week. The difference is how people choose to spend their time. Please read that again—wait, I will just write it again. People get to decide how they spend the majority of the 168 hours of their week. It is easy to rule out hours of sleep and commute time. Those times are already determined. So, beyond completing 40 hours of work and 52.5 hours of sleep, I have 75 hours for the activities I choose to do.

When my student teachers have difficulty finding the time, I encourage them to track their week. It is time to recognize your priorities and make informed decisions about how to spend your time. Kaycee struggled with time management during her first few weeks of student teaching. After some pushback and ongoing email chains, I told her to track her time for a week. We then met to discuss and reflect on how she spent her time each week. Kaycee learned she was spending too much time helping with the reading competition. She kept saying "yes" to the added responsibilities and found that she spent more time preparing students for the next reading competition. Therefore, she said "no" to herself when she had no time to prepare for class or apply for jobs.

Quentin shared that he only sleeps 4 to 5 hours on school nights. After learning more about how Quentin was spending his time, he realized that he spent more time researching how to teach the lesson than he was preparing for the lesson itself. Quentin learned more about what he needed to do differently to get more sleep (see Chapter 2). After talking with his mentor teacher, he had a better execution plan for preparing for his lessons. With effective communication and productive planning, these teachers could use time well and meet their weekly teaching goals.

Here is a sample of Quentin's week. I will refer to the chart in Chapter 2 and show the changes Quentin made to get more sleep at night.

Quentin's Chart

	Sunday	Monday	Tuesday	Wednesday	Thursday	Friday	Saturday
5:00 a.m.							
5:30 a.m.		wake	wake up	wake	wake	wake	
6:00 a.m.							
6:30 a.m.		Commute		Commute	Commute	Commute	
7:00 a.m.		Arrive	Arrive	Arrive	Arrive	Arrive	
7:30 a.m.		Prep	Prep	prep	prep	prep	
8:00 a.m.	wake	Lab	Lab	Lab	Lab	Lab	wake
8:30 a.m.							
9:00 a.m.	Breakfast	Bio 1	Bio 1	Bio 1	Bio 1	Bio 1	Gym
9:30 a.m.	w. GF						
10:00 a.m.	Travel	Bio 2					Travel
10:30 a.m.	home						to GF
11:00 a.m.		Lunch					place
11:30 a.m.	gym						
12:00 p.m.		Bio 3					Go to
12:30 p.m.							Football
1:00 p.m.	WATCH	Prep	Prep	Prep	Prep	Prep	Game
1:30 p.m.	TV						
2:00 p.m.		Chem	Chem	Chem	Chem	Chem	
2:30 p.m.							
3:00 p.m.		Grading	Grading	Grading	Prep	Grading	Have
3:30 p.m.							dinner
4:00 p.m.		Prep	Prep	Prep	Gym	Prep	with GF
4:30 p.m.	Commute				Commute	Commute	family

Time						
5:00 p.m.	walk the dog		Grading Commute	Nap		Nap
5:30 p.m.	Commute Nap	Gym Commute Nap	Nap		prep	
6:00 p.m.	dinner w fam		class		prep	
6:30 p.m.						GO OUT WITH FRIENDS
7:00 p.m.	Prep class		group work		Football	
7:30 p.m.	Study for exam					
8:00 p.m.			eat w friends	study	OUT WITH FRIENDS	
8:30 p.m.		eat				
9:00 p.m.		prep	plan			
9:30 p.m.	planning					
10:00 p.m.						
10:30 p.m.						
11:00 p.m.						
11:30 p.m.			Facetime with GF	Facetime with GF		
12:00 a.m.	WATCH TV					
12:30 a.m.						
1:00 a.m.	Bedtime					
1:30 a.m.						
2:00 a.m.	Bedtime	Bedtime	Bedtime			
2:30 a.m.				Bedtime	Bedtime	
3:00 a.m.						
3:30 a.m.						Bedtime
4:00 a.m.						
4:30 a.m.						

Reflect on How You Spend Your Time with Time Tracking

Now it is your turn; create a grid on a spreadsheet or fill in the chart below with a pen or pencil. Before you say anything, something will always happen to add hours to your week. The term I use with my students is that life happened; therefore, I could not get something done. But if you time track for another week, you will find similar instances of life happening. If this is not the case for you, try tracking another week to get consistency. So, how do you time track? Keep the chart on your desktop all week and take a few minutes out of your day to quickly summarize what you did from one hour to the next. You could also handwrite right in this book with colored pencils or pens to fill in your days.

Feel free to color-code your activities. Yes, I know that most teachers have a coding system for everything. Color coding may help you analyze how much time you spend in each life category (Vanderkam, 2011). Analyze your chart. How much time are you spending with your friends and family? How many hours are you spending on schoolwork? If you have a mentor, you could ask them, "What is a reasonable amount of time to spend planning and preparing for my lessons?" You may find that you spend many hours planning meetings, but only a small portion of the time is actually spent planning during the first half of the 60 minutes allocated. You need my "Do not go into a meeting without an agenda policy" (see Chapter 13 for my reasoning). Perhaps you are co-teaching (good for you; it is one of my favorites), and you spend time together in the morning planning, but most of your time talking about the show "Outer Banks." This work could have been completed at another time, allowing you to attend that very early cycling class. It is time to take control of your time and start spending it wisely. Fill in each hour of your time, and reflect on where your time is going.

Time	Sunday	Monday	Tuesday	Wednesday	Thursday	Friday	Saturday
12:00 a.m.							
12:30 a.m.							
1:00 a.m.							
1:30 a.m.							
2:00 a.m.							
2:30 a.m.							
3:00 a.m.							
3:30 a.m.							
4:00 a.m.							
4:30 a.m.							

(Continued)

(Continued)

Time	Sunday	Monday	Tuesday	Wednesday	Thursday	Friday	Saturday
5:00 a.m.							
5:30 a.m.							
6:00 a.m.							
6:30 a.m.							
7:00 a.m.							
7:30 a.m.							
8:00 a.m.							
8:30 a.m.							
9:00 a.m.							
9:30 a.m.							
10:00 a.m.							
10:30 a.m.							
11:00 a.m.							
11:30 a.m.							
12:00 p.m.							
12:30 p.m.							
1:00 p.m.							
1:30 p.m.							
2:00 p.m.							
2:30 p.m.							
3:00 p.m.							
3:30 p.m.							
4:00 p.m.							
4:30 p.m.							
5:00 p.m.							
5:30 p.m.							
6:00 p.m.							
6:30 p.m.							
7:00 p.m.							
7:30 p.m.							
8:00 p.m.							
8:30 p.m.							
9:00 p.m.							
9:30 p.m.							
10:30 p.m.							
11:00 p.m.							
11:30 p.m.							

 **Think About It.**

As you chart your week, compare how you spend your time. What are some excellent ways you spend your time? What are some unhealthy time wasters?

?
?

Plan for How You Want to Spend Your Time

I completed a time tracker at the beginning of the new year. It helped me frame my New Year's resolutions. Yes, I make goals for the new year. I usually wait a few weeks for the holiday celebrations to settle down and for the new semester to start so that I can think about what changes I will make. I know what you are thinking; just jump right into it! Did you know most people quit their resolutions by week 3? January 15 is National Quitters' Day (Norcross, Mrykalo, & Blagys, 2002). So, if I do not start right away, I will make it past National Quitters' Day. (See, that's the humor I was talking about). I like to get a baseline of where I am and set realistic goals. I need to know where I am starting from and where science tells me I should be. So, for some of these goals, if you are realistically beginning at zero, exercising for two days is progress. Researchers suggest most adults need 6 to 8 hours of sleep; so if you get 3 hours of sleep each night, increasing your sleep to 5 hours is making progress. Telling yourself you will get 8 hours of sleep is unrealistic and will set you up for failure. I am just looking for you to make progress.

Do you see what I am getting at with this? My goal for you is to find ways to make progress to be better, happier, and healthier. That can feel overwhelming. I know it was for me. You can see the hashtags #happy and #blessed in commercials and from your followers on social media. But here in the real world, you just need to prioritize healthy behaviors that help your brain and limit unhealthy behaviors that do not help your brain. When you make small goals, you will see progress as you move forward each week. If you are looking at your time tracking chart and like how you spend your time, then that's awesome—you have figured this out. But if you are one of those people who say, "I don't have time," when you do not know how you are spending your time, here is your chance right now to sort out how you spend your time and how you can get started spending your time differently.

Before making exceptions about this or that happening, please take my personal experience—there will always be something. This week is the perfect time to reflect on your week and analyze what you would like to do differently. What sections are you happy about? Reflecting on Quentin's chart, he is happy to report that he does not spend much time on social media or gaming. Just reading the introduction helped Quentin drop the video controller and get control over how he spends his time. One chunk of lost time that Quentin started to notice was the hours he spent in his car. With 6 hours in the car each week, Quentin would like to find a podcast to listen to that will help him get engaging ideas for science lessons with teens. Honest visuals like this help people see how they spend their time and ways to make space if they need more time.

Inclusive and Culturally Responsive Practices.

Consider what hobbies you value and where you want to live. This will impact your commute and your ability to spend time with friends and family. In other cultures, individuals prioritize more time spent eating with friends and engaging in leisure activities. Commute times are longer, particularly in US cities, as we rely on personal vehicle transportation. Start to shape how you want to spend your time now!

Use your time tracking chart to see how you spend your time to be realistic about the goals you will set for yourself in the weeks ahead. Keep your typical schedule. From this, you can gauge the areas you need to modify in your personal and work life. You can review each section to consider how you are spending your time and what realistic goals you need to set for yourself. Remember to be honest with yourself; you do not have to tackle everything. Progress is not linear. It is okay to hit speed bumps and plateaus. Pick the items you need to prioritize. There are some areas that you may not be ready to address at all. I believe in you and your ability to do great things.

Think About It.

Now is the time to reflect on your week. How did it look? What do you like about it? What nonnegotiables can you not change (your work commute)? Where are there some time slots where you want to make some changes? How are you using downtime during your day? What are your strengths in time management and organization? How can you capitalize on your strengths?

?
?
?

 **Add your Ideas.**

Some Ways to Save You Time

Time your grading—See how long it takes to grade your above and below-average students' papers. Use the average to set up a timer to grade each paper. You do not have to be rigid with this, but it will help you to pace yourself.

Teacher's Helper—Talk with teachers who bring their kids to school early or mentor students who have free time during their day. Have these students complete tasks in your room. They can cut out materials, run errands around the building, or put smiley faces on graded work.

Write it down—When you have questions for your mentor or your meeting group, write your questions on a Post-it note. Share your questions before meetings so that your mentor teacher and other members can prepare and benefit from your questions.

Start a Folder with Valuable Resources—Label these documents clearly. You may not be able to use the materials now, but they could save you hours of research and planning. Your future self thanks you!

-
-

Weekly Goal Setting

How is it going? Did you make any instant changes that have impacted how you spend your time? If so, you did a fantastic job creating space for new priorities. Feel free to move on to the next topic, and know that you can always jump back here to time track again so that you can analyze how you spend your time and make space for new and exciting activities. If you are not ready to commit to writing a goal, remember where to come when you say, "I do not have any time."

Sometimes, I catch myself slipping into old habits. I know this because I know my daily and weekly goals that I try to maintain. As my weeks get busy, I cut myself short; these are the times I need it the most. Reflecting on my previous week, I know I have not made it to yoga; this week would have been better had I gone to yoga. I then look at my calendar for the following week and book the class. I know I hate canceling, so I will go. I may also ask my friend to go with me. Even letting her know I am going to yoga makes me feel accountable. If you set goals, you will see progress and get a dopamine hit for meeting those goals. These practices help your week to go smoothly. As you continue setting goals, I want you to picture a healthier you. As you read the examples of other student teachers just like you, my goal is that you find practices that work just for you. Student teachers need to continue to practice, observe, and set goals for implementing evidence-based teaching strategies while they are still getting feedback from mentors (Peeples et al., 2018). This strategy starts in Part I with setting goals for a better you. Do you need help with writing a goal? That is okay; a sample chart for you to fill out with each chapter will help guide you through the goal-setting process. If you are unsure how to set a goal, you can look at the examples set by my student teachers as models.

Strategies for Developing SMART Goals
Make your goal detailed and SPECIFIC. (Who? What? Where? How?) HOW will you reach this goal? Make your goal MEASURABLE. Add measurements and tracking details. I will measure/track my goal by using the following numbers, methods, or benchmarks: Make your goal ACHIEVABLE. What additional resources will you need for success? Items I need to achieve this goal: • How I'll find the time: • Things I need to learn more about: • People I can talk to for support Make your goal RELEVANT. List why you want to reach this goal—how does it relate to your personal values or long-term plan? Make your goal TIMELY. I will know I've reached my goal when TIMELINE: When would you like to achieve this goal?

Specific: What is the Target Behavior?	
With what materials or conditions?	

Measurable: How well must the skill be performed? (Criteria)	**Achievable:** What modifications or accommodations are needed for success? Making the time?
How will the skill be measured? And how often?	Any additional research? People to talk to?
Relevance: Why is meeting this goal important?	**Timely:** What is considered mastery for this goal? **Timeline:** When would you like to achieve this goal?
What other assessments or data will help assess progress toward the goal?	What are the next steps in this goal area?

Setting Goals for More Time

Would you like to make better use of your time? Then, what parts of your schedule do you like, and what areas need to change? Remember, you are decreasing anxiety and refreshing your emotional regulation when you reach your goals. Only you can convince yourself that it is worth doing. And it takes time. You have started a routine that I assume has worked through college, and your body gets used to a rhythm (especially sleep routines) even if they are not ideal. So, do not get frustrated if things do not change within one week. It has taken you several years to craft the 2:00 a.m. bedtime and 3-hour nap schedule. What is one small, realistic step to work on for the next 3 months? Are you still trying to figure out where to start? After you review Quentin's goal, continue to the blank charts at the end of Chapter 5 where you can outline your own time management goals.

Quentin Is Working for More Deep Sleep

Examine Quentin's schedule to see how he made changes and consciously decided to dedicate more time to sleep. He learned he was spending way far too much time preparing for his lessons. He was averaging 3 to 4 hours of sleep a night. Then, he would take a long nap when he got home from school. His modification was to stop taking naps so he could get a better night's sleep (as explained in Chapter 2). But there was more to this adjustment log. After conversations with his mentor teacher, he realized that he was spending far too much time researching and preparing for his classes at night. He got stuck brainstorming so many ideas that he could not commit to any of them. He and his mentor teacher agreed that he would research his lesson plans during his prep period, and once the teacher approved his ideas, he would move on to writing the lesson plan based on the agreed-upon materials. See Chapter 13 for examples and strategies for difficult conversations. Right now, you can just focus on how Quentin adjusted his planning. He set a limit on his planning time to have more time for a bedtime routine and a good night's sleep. By shifting the time Quentin spent on planning, he got more sleep at night and did not need to nap when he got home from school.

Quentin's Chart

Making SMART Goals	
Baseline Data **Sleep Journal**	
Monday	3 hours of research/ planning lesson
Tuesday	4 hours of research/ planning for lab

Thursday	2 hours of preparing Chem test for students
Friday	6 hours of grading and giving feedback
Specific: What is the **Target Behavior**?	
Collecting data on hours of planning for classes, Quentin will spend an average of 3 hours planning and preparing for his classes out of 4 days of recording data during the week.	
With what **materials or conditions**?	
Given the Planning period and end-of-day preparation, Quentin will use that time for research.	

Measurable: How well must the skill be performed? (Criteria)	**Achievable:** What modifications or accommodations are needed for success? Making the time?
3 hours planning and preparing for his classes.	Quentin will focus on planning time at school and save a small amount of time in the evening for finalizing lesson plans.
How will the skill be **measured**? And **how often**?	Any **additional research**? People to talk to?
Record hours spent preparing and grading 4 days during the week. Quentin can review the concepts with his mentor teacher by completing them at school.	He has made more plans with friends and more time for the gym so that he avoids the long naps.
Relevance: Why is meeting this goal important?	**Timely:** What is considered mastery for this goal? **Timeline:** When would you like to achieve this goal?
Quentin is starting to lose his love of science by getting caught up in preparation. He needs to let good be good enough.	After 3 of 4 weeks of 3 hours of planning for 4 days, Quentin will reach mastery. Quentin would like to meet his goal in 2 months.
What other assessments or data will help assess progress toward the goal?	**What are the next steps in this goal area?**
Quentin will keep a check-in/ check-out time on his calendar.	Once Quentin reaches mastery, he will focus on incorporating more technology to his lessons.

Here is Quentin's first week of his intervention. Please note that these changes did not happen in one week. He had some good days and some days when he reverted to his previous habits. But the point is to continue to make progress over time. In his reflection, he noted that he had more time for activities with his friends and to study and prepare for job interviews.

Skills and Behaviors for Student Teaching

	Sunday	Monday	Tuesday	Wednesday	Thursday	Friday	Saturday
5:00 a.m.							
5:30 a.m.		wake					
6:00 a.m.			wake up	wake	wake	wake	
6:30 a.m.		Commute		Commute	Commute	Commute	
7:00 a.m.		Arrive	Arrive	Arrive	Arrive	Arrive	
7:30 a.m.		Prep	Prep	prep	prep	prep	wake
8:00 a.m.		Lab	Lab	Lab	Lab	Lab	
8:30 a.m.							
9:00 a.m.	wake	Bio 1	Bio 1	Bio 1	Bio 1	Bio 1	Gym
9:30 a.m.		Bio 2					
10:00 a.m.	Travel						Commute
10:30 a.m.	home	Lunch					
11:00 a.m.							Science
11:30 a.m.	gym	Bio 3					Fair
12:00 p.m.							
12:30 p.m.	WATCH	Prep	Prep	Prep	Prep	Prep	
1:00 p.m.	TV						
1:30 p.m.		Chem	Chem	Chem	Chem	Chem	Awards
2:00 p.m.							
2:30 p.m.		Grading	Grading	Grading	Prep	Grading	Commute
3:00 p.m.							
3:30 p.m.		Prep	Prep	Prep	Gym	Prep	Visit
4:00 p.m.	Commute				Commute	Commute	with GF
4:30 p.m.							

Time							
5:00 p.m.	walk the dog				Nap	prep	GO OUT WITH FRIENDS
5:30 p.m.		Commute		Grading	Nap		
6:00 p.m.	dinner w fam	prep	Commute	Commute		prep	
6:30 p.m.		Science fair	Kickball	Nap class	Study		
7:00 p.m.	Prep class					Football	
7:30 p.m.	Study for exam			group	Apply for Jobs		
8:00 p.m.		dinner		work		OUT WITH FRIENDS	
8:30 p.m.			dinner	eat			
9:00 p.m.		Study	Facetime with GF	w friends			
9:30 p.m.				Bedtime	Bedtime		
10:00 p.m.		Bedtime	Bedtime				
10:30 p.m.							
11:00 p.m.							
11:30 p.m.							
12:00 a.m.	WATCH TV						
12:30 a.m.							
1:00 a.m.							
1:30 a.m.	Bedtime					Bedtime	
2:00 a.m.							
2:30 a.m.							
3:00 a.m.							Bedtime

 **Chapter Recap**

Student teacher introductions
- Simone, Middle School Math—works hard to meet her expectations.
- Kaycee, first grade—always putting others' needs first.
- Jasper, Middle School ELA and History, athlete likes to make learning fun.
- Quentin, HS Chem and Bio—Wants his students to love science.

Find the time
- Use a Time Tracker
- Analyze your time

Figure out how you want to spend your time
- Be realistic about your goals.
- Find ways to save time.
- Cut out things that are a waste of time.

Weekly goal setting
- Find your baseline—where are you currently
- Make sure your goals are measurable and observable
- Identify supports to help you be successful
- What is a reasonable goal and timeline
- Figure out when and how you will assess your progress
- Identify next steps, what will you do after you meet this goal

 **Collaborative Thinking.**

Questions to ask your mentors/peers

How much time do you spend preparing for your lessons when teaching a new topic? What do you consider an average time for planning each week?

How do you stay organized with time management? Documents?

What are some productive ways you add time to your day?

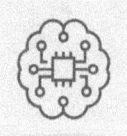 **Technology Checkpoints.**

Dropbox: A file-sharing application allowing for easy collaboration on projects. Dropbox lets you easily share documents for editing or getting signatures and provides storage.

Evernote.com: Evernote is an app that keeps track of all of your notes, to-do lists, schedules, deadlines, projects, and goals . . . all in one place.

Sleep Monitor: These tools can help give you an idea of a night's sleep. They can monitor different aspects of your sleep such as total hours, minutes spent in each stage, heart rate, movement, and breathing patterns.

Pomodoro Timer: The Pomodoro timer uses intervals to help structure work or study tasks into manageable time frames. Typically set to 25 minutes, the timer will then alert you once the interval is over and allow for a short break.

Minimalist Phone: These phones are designed to reduce screen time by eliminating features such as games, social media, and other distracting apps. This concept is also available as an app.

gTasks: A Google app that lets users create to-do lists and manage tasks.

Habitica: For the gamer who wants help managing tasks and productivity, Habitica uses rewards and points when a task is completed or a goal is achieved. You can use Habitica to complete assignments, develop a habit, or make a to-do list manageable.

 **Teacher Decision-Making.**

Are these steps working? Are you seeing the benefits? Make sure that you are making modifications and adaptations to make more improvements in your life, not more difficult. Take a minute to reflect on your self-care. Add some deep breaths to your day and recognize the changes worth making for your overall health.

 **Next Steps.**
What is working? . . .
What is not working? . . .
What do I need? . . .
What am I proud of? . . .
What do I need to let go of? . . .

 **Weekly Reflection.**

Use the space below to jot down some notes. I will use the term "glow and grow" moments for you to refer to "glow" to refer to positive things that are going well in your teaching, and "grow" for areas in which you need to work on. Listen to me telling you that you have this, and I believe in you. I am encouraging these minor changes because you are a quality educator, and students need teachers like you in the field for years to come.

2

Rest and Brain Rejuvenation

Chapter Outline

Are You Getting Enough Rapid Eye Movement Sleep (REM)?	38
Your Sleep Schedule	38
Wake-Up Routine	43
Sleep Goals	45

Now that you see how you are spending your time, it is time to start reviewing the evidence-based activities that will help you decrease cortisol levels (stress) and increase dopamine (joy). The first and best use of time is getting enough sleep. Sleep is the MOST critical piece of a self-care routine you can have. Are you getting enough sleep? How much sleep do you need? What do sleep researchers suggest? For this week, I want you to go to bed at a reasonable time every school night. I will start at 11:00 p.m. Think of yourself like a baby. If you have ever put a little one to bed, chances are there are little routines they love that prepare them for bedtime. Find a sleep routine you can be excited about starting tonight. Watch a repeat of your favorite show, use lotions and potions, brush your hair, and take a calming bath.

I strongly encourage you to avoid technology one hour before bed. As I mentioned in Chapter 1, the blue light on your phone and tablet tells your brain it is daytime. By avoiding blue light, your brain picks up on the natural cue that it is time to start getting ready for bed, which can promote deeper sleep (Shechter et al., 2020). I suggest reading a little bit. Perhaps you can complete your "Add your Ideas" and "Weekly Reflections" in this book. Getting to bed earlier lets you figure out how much sleep you need to feel truly rested. Are you getting up before your alarm? Remember, waking up and getting out of bed physically are two different goals. Do you naturally wake up without the buzzing of an alarm? So what time is that? Most adults need 6 to 8 hours of sleep. For me, it is 7.5 hours of sleep. So yes, every night, I give myself time to relax into sleep mode so that I can be awake by 6:30. The amount of time you need to sleep could be your long-term goal, or you may want to cut out technology 1 hour before bed.

>
> **Inclusive and Culturally Responsive Practices.**
> Individuals with difficulty regulating their emotions may need to focus on their nightly sleep. There is a high correlation between sleep and regulating moods. Consider for yourself and your students that sleep is an excellent priority for your mental health (van der Helm et al., 2010). If you notice one of your students having difficulty regulating their emotions, ask them (or their parents) how much sleep they are getting.

Are You Getting Enough Rapid Eye Movement Sleep (REM)?

Sleep is crucial for your brain health, so allow time for deep sleep! You need to go through four sleep cycles each night without interruption. The first two cycles are relatively brief, transitioning your brain from the busy day to preparing for the vital work ahead. In stage 3 (deep sleep), your brain supports your health, hormones, and growth (Walker, 2017). Therefore, there is a clear connection between fluctuating sleep cycles and mood disruptions commonly experienced by college students (Gau and Yin, 2020). Teachers need all the Stage 4 (REM sleep) they can get. During this time, your brain processes memories and emotions, which connect to big ideas and focus throughout your days. So, instead of spending 40 minutes getting ready in the morning or too long preparing outfits for spirit days, shape your week to protect the important work your brain does during REM sleep. If you find yourself stressed, overwhelmed, and fatigued, getting enough sleep may be the best choice you can make to turn things around.

Your Sleep Schedule

Once you recognize how much sleep you need, adjust your bedtime based on when you need to get out of bed in the morning. It is time for you to do some simple math. Say you must be out of bed by 6:00 a.m. to prepare for your day, and you need 7 hours of sleep for your body to feel rested. Then you must fall asleep by 11:00 p.m. to get 7 hours of sleep. So starting at 10:00 p.m., you need to have your phone away and start winding down that busy, anxious brain. Think about what you can do to help yourself in the morning. Pick out your outfit, pack your lunch, and have your water bottle filled in the refrigerator. Spend some time on your leisure activities, and watch a show. However, if you really must do schoolwork, keep it light. For example, cut out materials for a bulletin board or give positive feedback on students' journal entries.

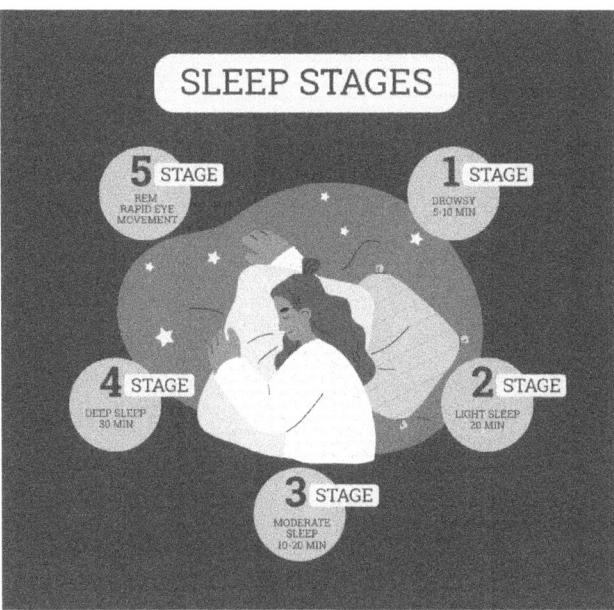

© iStock.com/Kudryavtsev Pavel.

Think About It.

What are some routines you have before bed? What are some unhelpful steps you need to swap for positive steps? What is something mentioned that you would like to add?
?

?

Prepping Your Brain for Rest

No technology. I said it once and will repeat it: put your phone away from your bed and leave it alone until you shut off your alarm in the morning. Not only does the blue light mess with your circadian rhythm and melatonin levels, but you are also filling your brain with distracting content right before bed. It is toxic. You need to tell your brain you are ready for bed. Does this not affect you? Yes, that TikTok hack for teachers is fantastic, along with all the relatable daily occurrences that happen to teachers. However, sleep is more important than anything you watch on social media at midnight. Building these habits changes your brain chemistry. Staying up late rewards your brain through immediate gratification. This can be through socializing, gaming, or using your cell phone. Regardless, it makes these habits more difficult to change. Alternatively, you see posts or messages from a frenemy

© iStock.com/Arina Gladyisheva.

posting that she just passed her teaching exam, reminding you that you still need to register for the exam and study. So, you swirl into anxiety because what if you do not pass? The best thing you can do for yourself is get a good night's sleep. That is where real progress happens.

For me, this includes not checking email in the evenings. I had one very negative experience with a colleague in which this berating email set me into a self-deprecating tailwind of blame. So now, I remind myself that no problem cannot be solved tomorrow. Additionally, I would not give a response reflecting my best self and could sound unprofessional. Everyone has checkout vices, but it is essential to have a bedtime routine that transitions your brain into sleep mode at least 1 hour before bed.

Inclusive and Culturally Responsive Practices.

Many Europeans adjust the temperature in their bedrooms to signal to their brain that it is time for bed. The actual decrease in body temperature can help regulate the sleep routine and promote deeper sleep throughout the night (Hirshkowitz et al., 2015).

Listen to Sounds That Help Your Brain Relax

Is your brain still buzzing from the day? Sample with some relaxing noise color. Most are familiar with the term white noise, which is most popularly known for drowning out sound to help individuals fall asleep. Sound color has picked up in the research world as a way to help as background noise to help to prepare to sleep. Color analogies are a mix of light and the frequency characteristics of different noise types. Feel free to experiment with the sounds that work best for you. Like any new skill, listen to your sounds well before you are ready to go to bed. It is unhelpful to figure out the right noise color when it is midnight on the night before your first day of school.

I have a bedtime song. "Thank you for being a friend" (the theme song from Golden Girls). Golden Girls is the show I turn on before bed because I am familiar with all of the storylines, and my brain is not interested in staying awake to find out what happens. So, shows you have already seen can be a safe way to wind down at night. By the time I hear the end of the opening song, "the card attached would say thank you for being a friend," I am typically asleep. Fortunately, I do not struggle to fall asleep. My sleep issue is that I sometimes wake up in the middle of the night. I know I must do a little extra to stay asleep if I have a busy week.

Do you need a sound transition for bed? Try listening to a boring podcast. Yes, they make dull podcasts for you to listen to to help you fall asleep. If I wake up in the middle of the night, I have a boring podcast on standby. I have two different approaches. If I need to calm down, my go-to is "Get Sleepy." These calming episodes have stories told by narrators with calm and soft voices. You can put yourself into a character, strolling along the beach or hiking in the mountains, and you put your worries back into the earth and relax into a sleepy state. You may be someone who needs to spend your awake time with purpose. You could listen to "Freakonomics," where you learn more than you want to know about objects in your everyday life or quirky human behaviors. Not to say you would bore yourself to sleep, but the calming, nonthreatening details about everyday life can get you back to dreamland.

© iStock.com/IrynaDanyliuk.

⊕ **Add Your Ideas.**

Write down a good sleep routine that suits your schedule.

Prep for morning	☐ ☐ ☐ ☐

No Tech _____ Before Bed

Must-do list:	☐ . ☐ . ☐ . ☐ .

One Great thing that happened today

If I wake up in the middle of the night, I will

When I get up in the morning, I will tell myself:

Morning Must-do list:	☐ ☐ ☐ ☐

Think About It.

Ask a family member about a routine you used to have before bed when you were younger. Maybe you had a habit or something from childhood, like calming music or sleeping in the dark. This could be a good reset to help you to get to bed. What routines can you reintroduce to help you prioritize your sleep?

?
?
?

Wake-Up Routine

Light is naturally put on this earth to tell your brain it is time to get up, so use light to help you get up in the morning. Your circadian rhythm, fueled by melatonin, helps regulate your sleep cycle. Light triggers your melatonin levels, so we use light in the morning to signal that it is time to get up. Add artificial light to your life for those with a long and dark winter. Getting up is a significant struggle, so I investigated alarms that light up when they go off. The one I use also has birds chirping. Although on the first morning I woke up, I thought I was in the pouring rain getting attacked by birds. After adjusting the settings, I found this a lovely, peaceful way to wake up. If you do not want to invest in an alarm, turn on a low light as you get out of bed and start your morning routine. Please note that I never said to reach for the phone.

Do not hit snooze. Think about the domino effect. Do what you need to convince yourself to get out of bed; consider the Mel Robbins countdown. Once that alarm goes off, give yourself a countdown: 5, 4, 3, 2, 1—get out of bed. By hitting snooze, you are putting your body back into sleep mode, which must go through the sleep cycle (Robbins, 2023). So, when you hit snooze, you just put yourself into a fog for the rest of the day. It is your brain trying to complete a sleep cycle. Instead, tell yourself that you are ready for the day, and if you need sleep, you will nap later. Get ready for the day and thank yourself for all the preparation you did the night before. Do you see how this is working? All you have to do is get out of bed and start your morning routine, and you will find that you have momentum, just like the dominoes falling in a chain reaction. What are some things you can tell yourself to just get out of bed? Add some statements of your own and see what works for you.

 **Add Your Ideas.**

Statements to help me to get out of bed.

- I can nap later, just get out of bed now
- Juno needs a morning walk. We both will be so happy if we do not have to rush
-
-

Remember that your brain is listening, so start your day with positive self-talk. It might be the Monday-est Monday ever, but you need to tell yourself you will see progress and have control over that change. Remember, your brain listens to you all day long. It even listens to the voices in your head. It hears you think, "Ugh, I am tired," or "I know my classroom management strategies are a flop, and I should not bother." Unfortunately, your brain believes what you tell it. Flip the script and start your day by telling your brain positive greetings. Here are some ideas for finding an authentic statement that helps you change your narrative and turn a bad day into a joyful one. Review the thought bubbles and write down some of your phrases to help start your day.

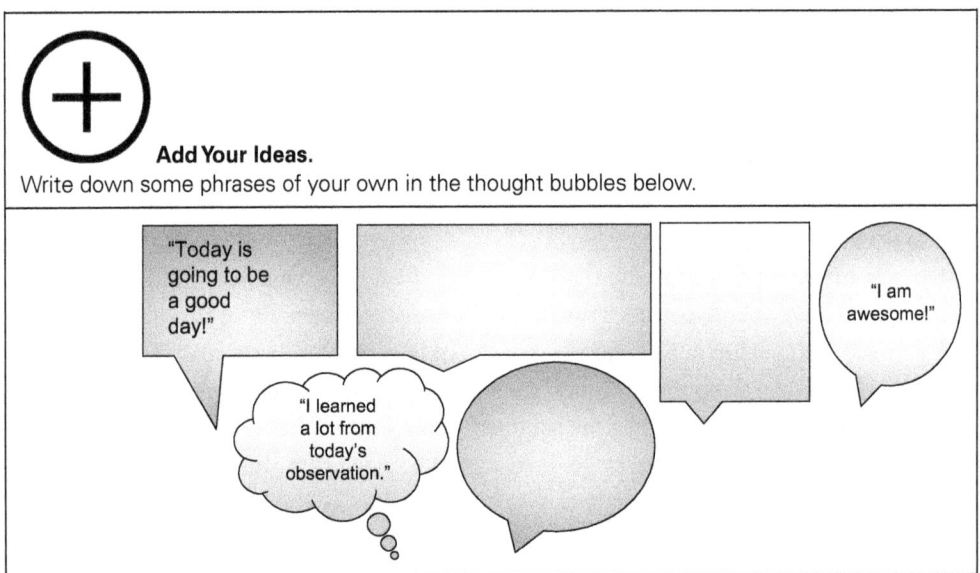

Nap Time

Did you promise yourself a nap this morning? If you are in a kindergarten classroom and buzzing around the room, answering 100 why questions before lunch, you may need a nap before you can have a productive evening. So when you get home, treat yourself like a toddler and nap. Try this: have a cup of coffee, and set your alarm for 20 minutes. Get yourself rested and take a nap. By the time your alarm goes off, the coffee has kicked in, and you can finish your day with purpose. Thirty-minute naps are very healthy for rejuvenation (Hsouna et al., 2019). If you are still unable to function, you should revisit your sleep habits. For me, I rest with my legs up the wall. This inversion gets the blood flow in the opposite direction. It helps shift your sympathetic (fight, flight, or freeze mode) into your parasympathetic (rest and digest mode) nervous system (Xi et al., 2019). This rest is the best for me when I do not get enough sleep. If you are not getting enough sleep, it is time to examine your bedtime routine and return to the beginning chapters. What must you do to give yourself enough sleep each night to be ready to lead in the classroom?

© iStock.com/SM photography.

Sleep Goals

How is your sleep routine? Did you make any instant changes as you read this chapter that have impacted your sleep quality? If so, awesome job. If this is good enough for you, move on to the next topic, and know that you can always jump back here and set clear goals. If you are not ready to commit to writing a sleep goal, remember where to come when you are feeling angry; sleep is a great place to start.

Are you still thinking you need to make more sleep changes? Then what do you like, and what needs to change? Remember that you are decreasing anxiety and refreshing your emotional regulation when you get more sleep. Only you can convince yourself that it is worth doing. Furthermore, it takes time. You have a circadian rhythm, and your body gets used to your sleep rhythm even if it is not ideal. So, do not get frustrated if things do not change within one week. It has taken you several years to craft the 2:00 a.m. bedtime and 3-hour nap schedule. What is realistic for you to work on for the next 3 months? After reviewing these goals, you can create your own goal at the end of Chapter 5 with the blank goal charts provided.

Simone's Snooze Goal

Simone is a snoozer. She has difficulty getting out of bed in the morning. She has made some modifications to encourage her to get up in the morning by getting things ready before bed. She is thriving in her bedtime routine, so she is taking the time to make mornings more motivating. Once she gets out of bed, she gives herself a High-5 in the mirror (recommendation from Mel Robbins and the High Five Habit). She also tells herself, "You can thank me later, Simone!" She did some research and found an app that has alarm music. After reviewing her baseline data, she determined that getting out of bed within 8 minutes of her alarm going off is progress.

Simone's Chart

Making SMART Goals **Baseline Data** Monday—30 minutes to get out of bed Tuesday—10 minutes to get out of bed Thursday—5 minutes to get out of bed Averaging 15 minutes to get out of bed.	
Specific: What is the Target Behavior?	
Simone will get out of bed within 8 minutes of her alarm going off.	
With what **materials or conditions**?	
Given the phone alarm.	
Measurable: How well must the skill be performed? (Criteria)	**Achievable:** What modifications or accommodations are needed for success? Making the time?
8 minutes of alarm going off, 4 out of 7 mornings a week.	Complete evening routine: clothes ready, lunch packed, waterbottle filled. Morning Mantra and Mirror High Five
How will the skill be measured? And how often?	Any additional research? People to talk to?
Simone will note when her alarm goes off, calculated against when her feet hit the floor. Everyday	Find a good alarm app to wake up to Simone will talk about progress with her sister. She will be proud of Simone's growth. Simone always had 5 alarms to get out of bed in the morning.
Relevance: Why is meeting this goal important?	**Timely:** What is considered mastery for this goal? **Timeline:** When would you like to achieve this goal?
Simone is wasting too much morning time lying in bed, letting her brain wander.	6 weeks of getting out of bed within 8 minutes for 4 out of 7 days of the week. Simone would like to meet this goal in 2 months.
What other assessments or data will help assess progress toward the goal?	What are the next steps in this goal area?
Reflect in a journal on how she is feeling. Check the watch alarm app.	Simone will adjust her goal to 3 minutes once she meets this goal.

Kaycee's Sleep Goal

Kaycee's vicious sleep cycle is different. Remember how she is the "say yes" girl and is so busy perfecting the school play? Kaycee spirals to the point that she cannot calm down at night, and if she does fall asleep, Kaycee finds herself wide awake at 2:00 a.m. with visions of costumes and props dancing in her head. For Kaycee, she has decided she needs a bedtime routine. She also needs some modifications if she wakes up at night. See Kaycee's data and some anecdotal notes to see how her changes improved her routine.

Kaycee's Chart

Making SMART Goals **Baseline Data** Sunday 12–3 Asleep [woke and thought about what would happen if I fell asleep in the principal's office before my interview] Asleep 4–5 Tuesday—Wide awake 1:00 a.m. to 3:00 a.m.; Slept 3:30 to 7 (Slept in, no time for breakfast) Thursday—10:30 p.m.: I slept until 1:00 a.m., then thought about what my mentor teacher said about my lesson. She must hate me. I will never get a job in this school district. Friday—3:30 to 6: I told myself, "Good job, you did not sleep in. Happy Friday!" Averaging 5.5 hours of sleep.	
Specific: What is the Target Behavior?	
Kaycee will go to bed at 11:00 p.m., averaging 6 hours of sleep four out of 7 nights a week.	
With what **materials or conditions**?	
Given 11:00 p.m. Bedtime, she will get 6 hours of sleep.	
Measurable: How well must the skill be performed? (Criteria)	**Achievable:** What modifications or accommodations are needed for success? Making the time?
6 hours of sleep 4 out of 7 nights a week.	Complete evening routine: Screen away 1 hour before bed, complete gratitude journal. Meditation on Spotify if she wakes up
How will the skill be measured? And how often?	Any additional research? People to talk to?
Kaycee will use a sleep App to measure hours of sleep. Everyday	NA
Relevance: Why is meeting this goal important?	**Timely:** What is considered mastery for this goal? **Timeline:** When would you like to achieve this goal?
Kaycee needs to prioritize sleep. It is adding a whirlwind of stress to her life.	6 hours of sleep 4 out of 7 nights a week for 4 weeks. 6 weeks
What other assessments or data will help assess progress toward the goal?	What are the next steps in this goal area?
Reflect in a journal on how she is feeling. Refer to sleep app and chart on calendar.	Kaycee will work on better weekend sleep once she reaches this goal.

These are just examples. Remember to frame your goal around your baseline data. Refer to the "Technology Checkpoints" examples to find ways to measure your goal. Maybe you do not want to measure your sleep. Perhaps you just want to ensure you have a good bedtime routine each night. That is great. Give yourself a paper checklist or set an alarm with a phone to-do list. Maybe you just want to put your phone away 90 minutes before bed. To encourage this habit, you can lock your phone or change your settings. Whatever your efforts, I am excited as you become a teacher who makes progress. Please continue to the next topic for self-care: fuel, but remember to keep your bedtime routines and track your progress. I believe in you and your ability to do great things. Keep going—you got this!

 **Chapter Recap.**
Use your time tracker from Chapter 1 to learn more about your sleep routine
Learn more about your sleep cycle.
- Hours of sleep I need _____
- The more hours of sleep lead to deep sleep and brain recovery

Healthy morning routine
- Avoid hitting snooze—it just makes getting up harder
- Have a motivational morning routine that gets you out of bed
- Drink water first

Get into a bedtime routine
- No screens before bed
- Prepare for the morning so you can get out the door faster

Experiment with sounds that can help you sleep
- Turn on reruns of your favorite show (you know what happened it should not keep you up)
- Listen to relaxing nature sounds or music that is calming to you
- If you get up in the middle of the night, have a podcast ready to get you back to sleep

Nap if you need to
- 20–30 minutes can help reset for a productive evening

 **Collaborative Thinking.**

Questions to ask your mentors /peers
What do you do to ensure you have a good night's sleep?
Have you noticed my screen usage? How would you compare me to the average user, who uses screens for 3 hours daily?

Technology Checkpoints.

Mintal Sleep Tracker: Mintal is an sleep tracking app that can give you a detailed look at your sleep habits and patterns. Mintal can track sleep disruptions like snoring, sleep talking, and apnea tendencies.
Sleep monitor: These tools can help give you an idea of a night's sleep. They can monitor different aspects of your sleep such as total hours, minutes spent in each stage, heart rate, movement, and breathing patterns.
Control your screentime: Exposure to the background light of screens is known to be disruptive to sleep. Limit screentime, especially before bed, in order to get a good night of sleep.
Sleep checklist: These checklists can help establish a calming bedtime routine. Customize your sleep checklist with things like no screentime, reading a book, glass of warm milk, or meditation.
Calming alarm: These alarms offer a more gentle wake-up call by using calm sounds and a slowly brightening light mimicking the sunrise. You can find calming alarms in stores, online, or as an app on your phone.
Bedtime stories: Another thing you can add to your sleep routine to promote mindfulness and help calm down for a good night of sleep. These can be found as podcasts to listen to or short stories to read by yourself.
Naptime body scan: Body scans are a form of meditation to help calm your body before sleep. Often used as a guided meditation, you can find one you like by searching YouTube.

Teacher Decision-Making.

Are these steps working? Are you seeing the benefits? Make sure that you are making modifications and adaptations to make more improvements. Do not make your life more difficult. Take a minute to reflect on your self-care. Add some sleep to your schedule and reflect on the "glowing" health moments you have had this week.

Next Steps.

What is working? . . .
What is not working? . . .
What do I need? . . .
What am I proud of? . . .
What do I need to let go of? . . .

Skills and Behaviors for Student Teaching

Weekly Reflection.

Use the space below to jot down some notes here. Reflect on the changes you have made and the progress you see. Listen to me tell you, "You have got this, and I believe in you." I am encouraging these minor changes because you are a quality educator, and students need teachers like you in the field for years to come.

3

Fuel: Food and Water

Chapter Outline

But First, Water	52
Making Good Food Choices	56
Meal Planning	60
Setting Fuel Goals	61

This chapter highlights both food and water consumption. Like every other chapter, I will use the research to describe healthy habits and routines to help you become a person who makes progress every day. I will only discuss healthy food choices, thrifty options for convenience, and tricks to drink more water. If you have specific nutritional or medical needs, be sure to consult your doctor.

I only really paid attention to my nutrition once I saw how it impacted my life. I had to experiment with food options and research digestion because, after most meals, I did not feel well. My stomach would feel bloated when I ate pizza. I was queasy after eating ice cream. After allergy testing and sampling, I learned more about my gut health. It is not just about what to eat but when to eat and drink. I also learned more about the gut-to-brain connection. Did you know that certain foods can trigger stress and cause more issues with digestion? This chapter is more about learning how to reduce stress when eating. I have included tips for cost-efficient food preparation, which ends with good choices for digestion. This chapter may help you to build goals around healthier eating routines, but not necessarily weight loss.

When I was student teaching I got into a food routine and stuck with it. These habits also followed me into the first few years of teaching. I would pop two waffles into the toaster, grab a frozen juice bar, and be out the door. This routine followed me into my first years of teaching. It was not until I was pregnant with my son that I thought about my daily food choices or my water intake. Fortunately, the recent popularity of water bottles has supported the hydration trend. Interestingly, I had my gallbladder removed in my second year of teaching. Now, learning more about gut-to-brain health, I sometimes wonder if I had monitored my eating and regulated my stress levels, would I have made more progress in

© iStock.com/AnnaSivak.

my relationship with fuel (food and water)? I cannot go back, but I urge you to reflect on your food and water habits to make healthy decisions about your consumption.

But First, Water

Remember when we talked about sleeping and waking up in the morning? You may have gotten enough sleep but still want to stay in bed. Well, there is a reason for this. When you wake up, a sleepy chemical called adenosine is still in your brain (another brain juice). It takes approximately two hours for this chemical to wear off. When you drink coffee or other caffinated beverages, it blocks the adenosine (Reichert, Deboer, & Landolt, 2022). Plus, caffine increases cortisol levels, which builds anxiety. There are better ways to start your morning than this. When welcoming students to your room each morning, the last thing you need is a groggy, stressed feeling. I am not telling you to cut caffine; just delay your first sip for an hour after waking up. Set the stage for your day and make time for water.

When I started running and adding more physical activity into my life, trainers, running friends, and influencers all talked about drinking more water. I saw significant changes in my daily life based on drinking more water. It is essential to start each day with a glass of water. There are many reasons for this: (1) after sleeping all night, your body is dehydrated, and (2) caffine helps to increase cortisol levels (stress juice). By considering steps one and two, you are helping to aid digestion with the food you are about to consume throughout your entire day (Bowden & Sinatra, 2020). By starting the day with water, I have learned that I feel less stressed when I delay that first cup of coffee. Therefore, it is important to make water convenient and something that you think about when you are planning your day. Do you need a simple change to minimize your morning stress? Ensure you have enough time to drink water before breakfast.

 **Think About It.**

How much water do you drink in a day? What symptoms of dehydration have you ever noticed (dry tongue, eyes, skin, headaches, dark urine)?

?

?

?

How Much Water

Adults should drink eight 8-ounce glasses of water a day. Another calculation you can use is to drink half of your body weight in ounces of water. Many trainers suggest 100 ounces of water daily if you are in the workout world. If you are working out or running, add more water to supplement the sweat you lose. Again, collect the data and observe your body. Does your tongue feel dry throughout the day? Do you have dry skin? Perhaps you have unexplained headaches.

You may need to drink more water. Collect the data in the chart below and observe how you feel.

© iStock.com/Natalia Darmoroz.

What Counts as Water

Dietitians suggest low-fat and low-sugar drinks can also count toward water intake. So, yes, your morning coffee could count toward your total ounces for the day. To feel healthier, measure your weekly water intake as your baseline. As you reflect on your feelings, you can consider additional drink options to reach your daily water intake. I will include hot tea in my daily water intake each day.

Think About It.

Good beverage choices	Moderate these choices
Water	Alcohol
Herbal teas	Fruit Juice
Coconut water	Milk
Vegetable juice	Energy drinks
Sparkling Water	Soda, Coffee, black tea
	(Anything with Caffeine)
?	Fake Sugars (stevia)
?	
?	?
	?
	?

Going to the Well

Some individuals may need to make water consumption convenient. You will only take a short walk to get water unless you live in a country without potable water. For me, I pair getting more water with adding more steps. I would always go to the filtered water fountain 100 yards away from my office. I often find myself chugging 30 ounces of water along the way. It was a way to add steps to my day and get more water. I would call this "going to the well." In the teaching world, I realize that bladder holding is often necessary, and there are only certain times teachers can go to the bathroom during the day; consider when to chug water and when you can take bathroom breaks. Consider chugging some water before you get to work so you can hit the bathroom before your day starts. Another opportunity to drink water is during lunch. That way, you can hit the restroom before you continue the rest of your teaching day. It is vital to stay hydrated throughout your day. Avoid waiting until the evening to chug all of your water. Waiting to drink water will make you miss out on the benefits, and chugging water at the end of the day will only wake you up in the middle of the night to go to the bathroom. You must consider when to drink water based on when it is convenient to go to the bathroom.

The Water Bottle Trend

In a world of Yeti, Owala, Stanley, and Hydroflasks, use those cups to refill your water throughout the day. Keep track of how many times you fill it. Make sure you have easy access to water. When my family goes camping, I buy two giant water jugs to ensure we have enough water for the trip. Even when we stay in a hotel, I will purchase water jugs to ensure I can have water. Now, yes, sometimes I get a case of water just because it is difficult to reuse or take my water bottle (i.e., skiing). You may be the type of person who needs to see the ounces go down each hour and have the motivation markers to "keep going," or "almost there." Find a strategy that motivates you to get enough water each day. Collect the data and observe.

Think About It.

How much water do you think you drink each day?	How much water do you drink each day?	What are some other beverages that you drink that count as hydration?	What are some beverages you can supplement as healthier choices?

What are some of your barriers to drinking enough water?

?
?

Brainstorm some solutions to those barriers.

?
?
?

© iStock.com/Irina Popova.

More Water Equals Less . . .

American restaurants serve more significant portions of food than what is needed for a typical lifestyle. The body gives cues when you are full. Nevertheless, many people, especially teachers, eat too fast during lunch breaks, leading to overeating before their body has time to signal a full stomach. Drinking water first helps you fill your stomach, so you feel full after a reasonable portion of food. Another consideration is that you are consuming other beverages that are less healthy than water. If you are dehydrated and thirsty, you can drink your beverage. So, if it is coffee time, you will consume more caffeine, which dehydrates you and increases cortisol levels (stress hormone). It may be happy hour, and you have yet to consume enough water; with happy hour prices, you may end up drinking more adult beverages than you typically do. Therefore, it is essential to plan accordingly. Avoid going into situations where you are dehydrated.

You may be expected or required to avoid certain foods or limit your daily calorie intake. Please follow your specific medical guidelines. In this section, I will talk about balance. My focus for talking about food is to focus on foods that are good food choices and fuel your body. I highlight whole foods versus processed foods. There are simple ways to have snacks and meals prepared for each week. Are you making good choices or the appropriate portions? One way to gauge your food routines is to create a food journal. Check the tech options for some great food journals. There is something about jotting down everything you eat in a day. Am I eating because I am hungry, or am I bored, or am I just dehydrated? How is this affecting your mood, or the time you have dedicated to meals?

Making Good Food Choices

Nutritional experts have shifted from the food pyramid to the food plate. One thing that is so valuable about the plate is learning about appropriate portions of food at each setting.

Revisiting the theme of balance is necessary when discussing the foods eaten daily. As you write in a food journal, take note of your patterns. What foods do you crave throughout the day? What snacks do you enjoy? How are your portions? Teaching is a busy job; you must ensure you have the energy to be on and make good daily decisions. In this section, I will uncover balanced options.

Many fruits are healthy options and provide a great source of vitamins and minerals. A trick to consider is always to clean your fruits as soon as you get home. Food preparation helps with the convenience of grabbing a clean apple before you walk out the door in the morning. One great thing about fruits is that they are an excellent replacement for someone with a sweet tooth.

I can only imagine how many cupcake parties and holiday treats are given to teachers each year. Under certain circumstances, eat the cake. However, if you are watching what you eat, save the cake for later, or give those treats to a student helper who enters your room at the end of the day. Some of my favorite and affordable fruits include bananas and clementines. Check out some examples throughout the chapter for some cost-effective, healthy food options.

Vegetables are also essential to include in your day. If your school has a salad bar, this would be a great way to get a healthy lunch daily. I could eat salads on most days. Think about adding various proteins to your salads to add some variety. As mentioned earlier, you do not necessarily need to do food prep, but adding some extra chicken or taco meat to the mix can help you make easy salads for lunch throughout the week. I never pass up fiber at a restaurant. Broccoli and brussels sprouts are my favorite, but I do not like the aromas when cooking them in my house. So, when these are side options or appetizers, I add them to my order instead of french fries. I do not mind warming them in the air fryer, but that is the extent I am willing to take. Again, remember convenience. Clean your veggies when you get home. Frozen vegetables are another cost-effective and relatively healthy way to get your ABC vitamins. Think of leafy greens as the most nutritious option. If you do not like the taste, consider masking vegetables in a yummy smoothie with honey and yogurt.

I only really understood the power of protein once I started running and lifting. Protein is everything. It gives energy when the body burns calories when you are buzzing through a busy school day. When charting my foods, I often found that I needed to eat more protein. When I am hungry, I typically need more protein. Are you catching a trend? Do not take my word for it. So many valuable apps are out there to track your food patterns and help you decide what else your body needs. Yogurt is an excellent source of protein. There are also a variety of nuts that provide a good source of protein. Another healthier protein option is chicken. It will be up to you to decide on food options that fit your lifestyle. Please seek out additional resources for a balanced diet. Now, I am moving forward with fun

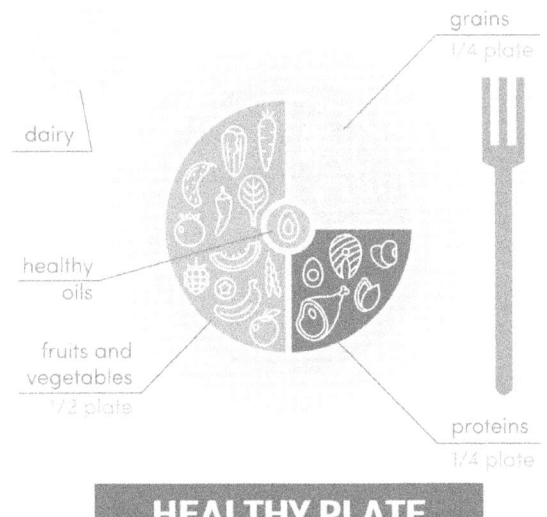

© iStock.com/marina_ua.

hacks and efficient ways to swap unhealthy foods for healthier choices and get good food for less at the grocery stores.

Out and About

We live in a country where everyone can supersize, buy one meal, and get extra sides for less. Restaurants encourage consumers to eat more. Do not get sucked in that the giant popcorn is the better deal at the movie theater. Stay ahead of the game. Before going to a restaurant, look up your dinner options and plan your eating. Plan your dinner order before you are finally seated and starved. You will end up ordering appetizers and getting the greasy sides instead of the fresh veggie choice. Plan an appropriate portion of what is suitable to eat. As you portion your meal, you can think, I will eat the rest for dinner tomorrow. This means no cooking. Now, you may need to add some salad to make it a complete meal, but there is nothing more exciting than having leftovers as an additional meal that requires no cooking. Another way to save on takeout is to consider when you order. There is a Chinese restaurant right next to campus that has a lunch special until 3:30. On the days I get out early, I pick up dinner by 3:30, and of course, I order extra, even if it is just rice and grilled vegetables to add to the extra chicken I made earlier in the week.

At Home

Refrain from using a giant plate when getting your meals and snacks. You realize a typical portion of cereal is two cups. If you fill a typical bowl, you end up with three to four cups of cereal. The same goes for dinnertime. When you put your food on a large plate, or if you or, on a cafeteria tray, you naturally fill the space. When filling the space, you eat way more than the average adult needs. Shifting to snack time, put your snacks into a small bowl. Sitting and watching Netflix with a whole bag of potato chips is deadly. Before you know it, you have binged on a series of shows and a bag of ruffled potato chips, and you are thirsty from all the salt, so you added a can of soda or two. It is essential to take note of your less favorable food choices that you want to change. Remember that minor tweaks can lead to larger changes in your behaviors.

Snacking

Unless you have a healthy relationship with food, your brain naturally gravitates to unhealthy food choices. So, while you may still be hungry, it is because you eat larger portions of foods that do not fuel you through the day. Planning out and journaling your meals is so important. If your cupboards only have junk food, and your refrigerator has no prepared fruits or vegetables, you will choose junk food. Just like you make water convenient, you need to make healthy food choices at home and at school. Here are some reminders of foods that are good for the neurotransmitters and chemicals (brain juices) in your brain. Consuming foods and beverages rich in these vitamins and ingredients can help you improve your cognitive function and decision-making. Swap out unhealthy food choices you tend to reach for when you are hungry, bored, or tired. Instead of chips, swap crunchy veggies and hummus. This takes planning before you go to a restaurant and while you are at the grocery store. Friendly reminder: If you are still hungry, try protein.

© iStock.com/Mark Skitsky.

Think About It.	
Brain Juices	**Foods to increase in your diet**
Dopamine neurotransmitter "Feel Good" Juice	Consuming foods rich in tyrosine (Meats, eggs, legumes)
Endorphin Chemical "Nature's Pain Killer" Juice	Chocolate Spicy foods
Oxytocin "love hormone" Chemical	Eggs Bananas Salmon Nuts Legumes
Balance these Chemicals/ Neurotransmitters	
Norepinephrine (Adrenaline) Fight-flight-freeze response	Lean meat Almonds Avocado
Melatonin "Sleep regulation"	Cherries Gogi berries Warm milk

Reduce this Chemical	
Cortisol (Reduction)	Fermented foods Kombucha Sour Kraut Yogurt *Limit caffeine intake*

Think About It.	
Favorite Snacks and Replacement Foods	
Ice Cream Swedish fish • • • • [Think of some examples you can have ready]	Yogurt with an Oreo Frozen Grapes

Meal Planning

Plan your days. Make Mondays easy—you can buy lunch at the school. Bring a to-go container and get an extra food order for another day this week if it is a healthy meal. School lunches are the most accurately priced meals you can get anywhere. Theme your days to think less and keep it simple. Taco Tuesday, beef, chicken, quesadilla (make extra taco ingredients for a taco salad the next day). Pasta bar Wednesday, have pasta and protein (meatballs or chicken) Thursday leftovers. Pizza is for Friday; get extra. It makes a great and easy lunch; add a side salad. Have a potluck once a week at school. Have your teaching team pull together a potluck once a week. You can rotate each week to see who is bringing the big-ticket items. Again, be ready for leftovers. If I were a college student again, I would go to the football tailgates with to-go containers to round up leftovers. I hate it when food goes to waste.

Many student teachers have mentioned they do not use their meal plan as much when teaching. Consider your best meal options before the semester starts. Is there a way to adjust your meal plan? Instead of getting a large meal plan can you use more money for your grocery bill? You may need to plan differently. You should capitalize on the weekend

© iStock.com/A-Digit.

meals at the cafeteria and take some leftover containers to fill with extra meals for the week. Being thrifty is not always glamorous, but it can save you money and time.

I hope these ideas got you thinking. I know it is a lot to digest . . . but there are some fun and easy ways to make food and water intake easier. Be prepared. So, perhaps your fuel goal is less about how much food you eat and more about having potluck dinners once a week. You do not have to turn every topic into a goal; sometimes, knowing your current food and water intake is healthy. These goals below will give you a good idea of where you could improve.

Inclusive and Culturally Responsive Practices.
Consider the additional food and drinks available in the classroom for snack time and party days. Be sure to survey your students to understand dietary restrictions, food allergies, religious diets, or cultural food practices. Be sure to offer snack options so all students feel included and excited about sharing snacks. Ask the students about their favorite snacks.

Setting Fuel Goals

Does this topic spark your interest? What do you like about your food and water habits, and what needs to change? What did you decide to change about your fuel intake? Did you make any instant changes that have improved your digestion? If this is your case, way to go. Sprint to the next chapter (Movement), and know that you can always skip back here and make clear goals for yourself. That is fine if you are not ready to commit to writing and collecting data on that goal. Remember, to reset when the holiday parties are filled with sugar and carbs, please revisit Chapter 2 for some good, healthy eating tips.

Remember, you decrease cortisol levels and increase healthy digestion by making good food choices. You are the only person feeding yourself (I hope). The food routine you have developed over time will not change in a week. So, do not get frustrated if things do not change immediately. Food is tradition, so whenever you think of going to the movies, you can smell the buttery popcorn and thirst for the supersized soda. Prepare yourself for making healthy fuel choices. Think about manageable adjustments for the next 3 months. Once you have reviewed the student teachers' goals, you can go to the end of Chapter 5 and use a blank chart to make your own fuel goal.

Simone Is Increasing Her Hydration

Do you remember our student teacher Simone? She completes everything, checks the checklist, and has zero unread messages in her email. She has a routine for success, BUT that routine is limiting her time for water intake. She diligently works through her prep periods and uses the end of the school day to tutor students. Her mentor teacher and university supervisor see that she has it together. However, they do not see that by the end of the day, Simone has a major headache, completes her homework, and chugs unlimited fountain soda at the restaurant where she works in the evenings. After seeing her peers with the new water bottles, she wonders how they manage to stay hydrated when there is no time for bathroom breaks in high school. She refills her coffee at lunch and plugs away. After charting her water intake, Simone recognized there were ways to sneak more water into her life.

Simone's Chart

Making SMART Goals
Baseline Data   Simone's water intake   Tuesday—24 oz water   Thursday—18 oz lemonade   Saturday—8 oz Hot tea, 12 oz water
Specific: What is the Target Behavior?
On a 24-hour day, Simone will drink 48 oz of water each day.

With what **materials or conditions**?	
Within a 24-hour day, Simone will pair water with other favorite drinks.	
Measurable: How well must the skill be performed? (Criteria)	**Achievable:** What modifications or accommodations are needed for success? Making the time?
48 oz of water	• 16 oz of bottled water on the way to school • No coffee until she gets to school. • Bathroom breaks before students arrive • 16 oz of water throughout the morning • 2nd cup of coffee after lunch. • 16 oz of water throughout the afternoon • Enjoy a fountain soda at work
How will the skill be measured? And how often?	Any additional research? People to talk to?
Simone will collect data by filling in the water intake on her watch. Everyday	What else counts as water? What are good supplements to soda?
Relevance: Why is meeting this goal important?	**Timely:** What is considered mastery for this goal? **Timeline:** When would you like to achieve this goal?
With journaling, Simone has identified what could be triggering her headaches. After a week, she noticed that most of her headaches had subsided due to increased drinking water.	36 oz of water 12 oz lemonade; for 5 out of 7 days of the week. Simone would like to meet this goal in 3 weeks.
What other assessments or data will help assess progress toward the goal?	What are the next steps in this goal area?
Reflect for themes of feelings in the journal.	Simone will increase to 48 oz of water 12 oz lemonade.

Jasper Is Limiting Junk Food

Jasper is examining his food routine. As a college athlete, he has little time and even less money for his nutritional needs. Conversely, now that he is student teaching, he does not have time to go to the dining hall, and the $5 meals at the drive-thru are draining his wallet and his energy. Jasper will go to the dining hall and get two salads to have in his room throughout the week.

Jasper's Chart

Making SMART Goals Baseline Data						
2 out of the 14 meals were salad						
B: 2 slices of toast with peanut butter and banana, coffee	**B:** Poptarts with whole milk	**B:** Smoothie— protein powder	**B:** Bagel with cream cheese	**B:** Pancakes with syrup	**B:** French toast with syrup and berries	**B:** Breakfast burrito (eggs, cheese, sausage)
S: Chocolate chip cookie	**S:** Doughnut	**S:** Potato chips	**S:** Ice cream cone	**S:** Pretzels with cheese dip	**S:** Snack cake	**S:** Muffin **L:** Steak and Eggs
L: Turkey and cheese cobb salad	**L:** Chicken wings with fries	**L:** Hamburger with a side of fries	**L:** Grilled cheese sandwich and tomato soup	**L:** Sandwich with a side of fries	**L:** BBQ pulled pork sandwich with coleslaw	**S:** Popcorn and soda
S: Soda/ Chips	**S:** Candy bar	**S:** Milkshake	**S:** Trail mix (with chocolate)	**S:** Energy drink	**S:** Nachos with cheese	**D:** burgers with a side of onion rings
D: Pizza with fries	**D:** Taco salad with all the fixings	**D:** Spaghetti with garlic bread	**D:** Fried chicken with mashed potatoes	**D:** Fish and chips	**D:** Takeout Chinese food (sweet and sour chicken, fried rice)	**S:** Sundae with toppings
S: Ice cream sundae	**S:** Brownie	**S:** Cake	**S:** Cookies	**S:** Cupcake	**S:** Chocolate mousse	
Specific: What is the Target Behavior?						
Eat 5 salads a week out of 14 meals (lunch and dinner).						
With what **materials or conditions**?						
Within a 14-meals throughout the week Jasper will get an extra salad from the cafeteria at school to make a salad.						
Measurable: How well must the skill be performed? (Criteria)				**Achievable:** What modifications or accommodations are needed for success? Making the time?		
5 out of 14 meals each week must include salad				Meal prep 2 proteins Salad at the salad bar Complete the food prep plan on Sunday		
How will the skill be measured? And How often?				Any additional research? People to talk to?		

Jasper will collect data by completing a food log.	Research good salads. Snap Julia (Chef cousin)
Relevance: Why is meeting this goal important?	**Timely:** What is considered mastery for this goal? **Timeline:** When would you like to achieve this goal?
Jasper needs to be ready for baseball season; working out won't matter he is not eating the right foods.	3 out of 4 weeks of meeting the salad goal will be considered mastery Jasper would like to meet this goal in 2 months.
What other assessments or data will help assess progress toward the goal?	**What are the next steps in this goal area?**
Reflect with a journal and Prep Chart.	Once he meets this goal, he will focus on grams of protein.

Think About It.
Jasper's Meal Plan Idea

Meal Prep	❏ Rotisserie Chicken ❏ Lettuce from the salad bar ❏ Taco meat from Dad's house ❏ Clean apples and oranges ❏
Weekend Leftovers from the Student Union	❏ Fried Chicken ❏ Lo Mein ❏ Lasagna (salad) ❏
If he needs to buy out, he will get a salad with protein.	

These are just examples. Remember to frame your goal around your baseline data. Refer to the "Technology Checkpoints" examples to find ways to log your food and drink, along with great tools for meal prep. It could be that you do not want to measure your fuel. Perhaps you just want to add some new recipes to your food menu. I can appreciate that. Make a paper menu and create a grocery pickup with new food options. Maybe you just want to drink more water. You could add a reminder as an alarm on your phone or watch. These changes deserve a sticker for encouraging you to become a teacher who is making progress. Please continue to the next topic for self-care: movement. Do not forget about your bedtime routines and fuel intake. Collect data to measure your progress.

Chapter Recap.

Learn the gut-brain connection
- Fuel = food + water

Water and the importance of hydration
- Start your day with a glass of water
- Delay coffee so adenosine (sleepy brain juice) can wear off
- More water can help curb overeating

How much water
- 8 eight-ounce glasses or half your body weight in ounces
- Add more to account for sweat loss
- Factor in what else you drink, and what counts as water
- Good vs. in moderation beverage chart

Making water consumption easy
- As teachers, know good times to drink water in relation to bathroom breaks
- Avoid heavy water consumption in the evening
- Get a fun water bottle

Good food choices
- Food plate as visual portions and nutritional guidelines
- Keep a food journal
- fruits/veggies
  - Clean and prep so they are ready to eat
  - Consider what is provided at your school when planning lunches
  - Add an easy protein to make a meal
  - Order extra at restaurants and cafeteria for leftovers and easy meal sides
  - Consider frozen options

Power of protein
- Provides energy and helps keep you full

Eating healthy out and about
- Plan ahead—look up the restaurant online and decide on your order beforehand. Think leftovers and healthy sides.

Staying on track at home
- Small plates keep portions reasonable
- Pay attention to serving sizes
- Replace your favorite snacks with a healthier option

Healthy snacking
- Keep prepared fruits and veggies on hand
- Limit junk food
- Make healthy swaps like carrots and hummus for chips and dip
- Still hungry? Go for protein

Meal planning
- Examples of lunches for the work week
- Utilize leftovers

Collaborative Thinking.

Questions to ask your mentors /peers.
What are some of your favorite healthy food recipes?
How do you balance drinking enough water with bathroom breaks?
What are some inexpensive healthy snacks, meals, and party foods you enjoy?

Technology Checkpoints.

NOOM Food App: NOOM app logs food but also helps you understand why you eat the way you eat. NOOM focuses on the psychology behind eating habits and tendencies.
Log your meals: By using old fashioned paper and pencil or new food tracking apps, logging your meals can help keep you accountable and more aware of your eating habits.
Log your water: Logging water intake, whether with a physical journal or app, can let you see just how much fluid you are getting throughout the day.
Grocery pick up: One of the best things to come out of the pandemic, grocery pickups help save money and time. It helps you stick to your lists and avoid impulse buys.
Lose It!: Lose It! is an app that you can use to track weight, calories, nutrition as well as intermittent fasting.
My Fitness Pal: Another calorie and activity tracker that provides insight into macros and other nutrients. There is a recipe library and weekly meal plans available through this app.

Teacher Decision-Making.

Are these steps working? Are you seeing the benefits? Make sure that you are making modifications and adaptations to make more improvements in your life, not make it more difficult. Take a minute to reflect on your self-care. Swap some good food choices for processed foods and recognize the changes worth making for your overall health.

 **Next Steps.**

What is working? . . .
What is not working? . . .
What do I need? . . .
What am I proud of? . . .
What do I need to let go of? . . .

Weekly Reflection.

Use the space below to jot down some notes. Reflect on some habits that you have that you are grateful for. Listen to me tell you, "You have got this, and I believe in you." I am encouraging these minor changes because you are a quality educator, and students need teachers like you in the field for years to come. In what areas do you need to grow?

4

Exercise and Movement

Chapter Outline

Why, Accountability, Convenience, and Weekly Goals	69
My Why	70
Adaptations and Accommodations to Support Your Movement	76
Movement Goals	80

Why, Accountability, Convenience, and Weekly Goals

Exercise has so many benefits for your mental and physical health. To be a successful teacher, you need effective ways to minimize stress. It is easy to say, but it is essential. As I shared the charts in the Introduction, exercise is one highly effective way to minimize stress (Gao & Yin, 2020). To put it into scientific terms, you need to decrease cortisol levels, increase serotonin, and find healthy ways to get dopamine hits. I did not realize the demands that this profession would take a toll on my decision-making and mental health. I was training my brain to live in stress mode. In my last year of college, my professor put up a slide I can still see today: "Find other ways to manage your stress beyond alcohol." It took me 21 years of being 21 to understand what she meant. As someone who played sports year-round throughout high school, I spent quite a few years just chilling and not making time for exercise. This chapter will discuss moments that led me to my years of fitness goals. I have completed various forms of fitness in the past 12 years. Nevertheless, with each skill, I kept a theme within each "Era." Within each Era, I had a why, accountability, convenience, and weekly goals for each skill.

People work out to stay in physical shape. I missed the opportunity to gain mental fitness. I thought playing in the yard and splashing at the pool with my kids was enough. When I learned more about the buzz of how regular exercise is good for mental health, I took action. To get into a regular workout routine, I needed to create a routine I could follow. In this chapter, you will read more about my why, accountability, convenience, and weekly goals that help me get into regular workout routines. Hopefully, you can connect to this framework to build a workout that enables you to maintain a mental health routine.

My Why

In my early 30s, I had an epiphany moment at a family reunion. We were competing in a family relay. Because I was the only one willing to get in the water, I had the swimming portion of the triathlon. I was swimming like my 16-year-old self, not wanting to disappoint my team, especially my 6-year-old son. My team won the relay, but I was still panting 30 minutes after the race. Seriously, this was a huge eye-opener. Just because my clothes fit does not mean I am in good physical health. I looked in shape, but my heart, lungs, and brain said otherwise. My lack of confidence in my physical fitness helped me to change my habits immediately. I always felt rushed. I told myself there was no time for the gym. As I continued to hear more about how physical activity would help my mental clarity, this would be time well spent. For me, exercise was for my mental and physical health. This is my why. Here is a brief run-through of activities I have started since graduating from college and how these activities can be relevant for teachers. I encourage you to start a routine before completing your degree so that exercise becomes a healthy part of your life.

My Running Era

So, I started running the week after my family's Olympic championship. I did not love it, but I loved how it made me feel afterward. These endorphins helped me to feel confident, optimistic, and motivated to keep running. For me, running was cheap and accessible. Once my kids got to school, I would go into town and hop on the local trail. I needed more accountability for my runs as the temperatures got cooler. So, I joined my local running club's "Couch-to-5K" group. It was perfect; it felt like I was on a team again. My best friend came with me, and we signed up for a group that met several times a week. Joining this group came with added skills I learned about myself and running.

As we got closer to the 5K, I asked the trainer if we could have a half-marathon training group. Planning my next race before completing my first made me an official runner. Ultimately, I asked her if I could pay her to hold me accountable for running. I did many things I thought I could never do: run in 11 degrees, tackle 9 miles on a Saturday morning, and be consistent 4 days a week for 3 months. I wish I could have found running earlier in life because I love the community it has brought. If you are a runner, you will find that 5Ks are great local fundraisers, and this is an opportunity for you to get out into the community. Unfortunately, my knees want me to walk, and for now, that is okay. I just need to find a walking club to hold me accountable. Step counter competitions using a fitness app could help.

© iStock.com/Route55.

As a teacher, simply adding steps to your day is progress. Take the long way to the photocopier or to pick your students up from lunch. Be silly! If you are in the elementary grade levels, get moving when your students are moving. Chances are, more students will "dance like nobody is watching" if you do it too! Even in middle or high school, put yourself out there. Do not be afraid to have a dance session brain break. Tell your students you are going to a wedding and you would like to learn a few new moves. Continue reading to learn more about accountability through technology.

 **Think About It.**

I never thought I would consider myself a runner. Yet now, I pay to run LOL. Is there a sport or activity that you never gave a chance? List some exercises or sports that you might consider trying.

?

?

?

Revisiting My Skiing Era

If you experience the four seasons, it comes with benefits and transitions. If you are a teacher, you know that smooth transitions are critical. I am learning in my adult life that I need to prepare for these seasonal transitions. I know I need to get outside in the winter.

Fortunately, I grew up less than an hour from the ski slopes, and my dad signed me up for the ski club. This outdoor sport turned into something that I love to do. When I skied in high school, I did not even take a break to eat my packed hoagie, sports drink, and bag of chips.

Once my kids could walk, I figured it was time to teach them how to ski. In the meantime, I also realized how valuable these days outdoors were for me. I loved the feeling of letting go. Seeing the true joy in my daughter's eyes as the snowflakes hit her face. All this energy motivated me to make skiing a part of the winter routine. With the first winter of Covid, I knew I needed a way to get outside during the winter. Now, skiing is my way of getting through the cold months. This weather option is an excellent mental trick. I would be happy if we had mild weather and sunshine so we could safely travel to school and work, but if we get any snow, it is a chance to ski. Once my kids learned the basics of skiing, they became my accountability partners for getting some fresh air and physical activity in the winter.

Skiing can be expensive, but consider chaperoning the school's ski club. Who knew chaperoning a bus with 50 teenagers was a readily available position in most school districts?

You may be able to ski for free. A used pair of skis may be a valuable investment in your mental health. For me, the price of used skis to get through the winter months is priceless. Another bonus is that it allows me to connect with students not typically in my classrooms. This often bridged conversation and helped me to work with more students to build inclusive environments for my students.

© iStock.com/krugli.

 **Think About It.**

What sport or activity did you play in your childhood or even through high school?

Brainstorm some ways you could bring play back into your life (summer leagues, coaching, group workouts).

?

?

 **Inclusive and Culturally Responsive Practices.**

Special education teachers!! Find ways to connect with students who are not in special education. For example, sponsor a club (i.e., ski club), coach sports, or an extracurricular activity. This is a way for you to include students who are not in your classroom much, and it lends itself to students not in special education who stop into your room. In high school, people will stop saying "those kids." They will be the students, just like in any other class.

My Yoga Era

It took a year of my friend encouraging me to try yoga, but I always felt like I needed to be more coordinated to attend an organized class. Therefore, I never wanted to exercise in front of people until I had an opportunity to exercise in the dark. Unless you have experienced it, not many people say, "Oh yeah, hot yoga, that sounds awesome." Nevertheless, I loved the idea of a great workout, stretching, and mental clarity—in the dark—where no one could judge my upward dog position, or my fall when I tried the thread the needle pose. I loved how my feet and sinuses felt, and my brain fog lifted. After that first class, I have been to yoga at least once a week for the past 4 years. When I go on vacation, I am the girl who looks for a yoga class. In my senior methods course, we take the opportunity to attend a free yoga session before our class starts. I always make it optional, but everyone loves to join the class. Yoga is excellent for any classroom because it is meant to be shared with fun, patience, and encouragement (Casses, 2025). Add yoga poses to your classroom. Tree pose is a great way to build balance. Mountain pose is a terrific way to work on visualization and brain-centering.

© iStock.com/Rudzhan Nagiev.

 **Think About It.**

Organized classes were a deal breaker for me, and this was just an excuse my brain was telling me. What are some deal breakers you have been telling yourself? In what ways do you need to be more flexible (in a figurative sense)?

?

?

My Strength Training Era

Remember that skiing I loved so much? Well, one of my adventurous days, and indeed one of my favorite days of skiing, led me to a wreck that left me unable to lift my arm for weeks. I refused to get it checked, and after some research, I learned that lifting helps with bone density (Benedetti et al., 2018). I needed to figure out where to start, and then a friend linked me to a fitness instructor who posted four 30-minute videos each week. I love this idea! I can complete a workout at home in less than 30 minutes. Once again, I love how this made me feel—muscles were a bonus. Talking about strength training with students has helped me to join conversations with students about different exercises. This allows me to connect with students regardless of the sport they play. It is great to talk to students about the benefits of lifting. As a mentor, you can also highlight that lifting is an athletic activity that does not require physical contact. Additionally, lifting is excellent for mental health. There are even benefits to having strength from lifting and mood boosts.

 **Think About It.**

In what ways can you get motivated for your mental health? What is a reminder that can get you moving each day/week?
?
?

As you can see, I have had quite a journey with a range of exercise and fitness. I genuinely wish I had started this journey earlier in life. It would have helped me to find healthier ways to cope with stress and meet some great people. I cannot look back. I can only pass along Dr. Kline's wisdom, which I wish I had listened to sooner: "Find good habits to relieve stress." As you read through the description of each activity note, I did not particularly enjoy getting ready or moving. Still, through reflection, I love the effects of movement. Now, it is time for you to think about ways to move your body and relieve stress. Continue with a writing exercise to get you thinking about ways to get motivated about movement. You could create a goal to take time to find what you like doing.

© iStock.com/Viktoria Nevzorova.

Inclusive and Culturally Responsive Practices.

Think about movement in your classroom. It may look different for some of your students who have physical disabilities. How will you move around the room inclusively? How can you alter movement and transitions so that students with physical differences still get movement and feel included in your room?

Adaptations and Accommodations to Support Your Movement

Your Why

As I mentioned previously, I was motivated to be healthy to fit my definition of being in shape. To be honest, I have another looming fear of growing old. As I see people hovering around on scooters, watching cholesterol, and having knee replacements, I just want to avoid those experiences if I can. I recognize that some components of health are genetic, such as certain diseases. However, I can start a lifestyle to prevent these problems. It is just the special educator in me, but my approach to most activities is preventative maintenance. Think about your why as a motivational tool to keep you moving (Sinek, Mead, & Docker, 2017). What is going to get you going each week to keep making progress? Go back through your reflections in this chapter to find what you like doing and get an opportunity to try new things.

Think About It.

What is your why? What is going to get you moving each week? What can you think about and reflect on to help you decide to move each week?

?

?

?

Think About It.

Neurotransmitters/ Chemicals in the Brain	Movement that Helps Brain Function
Dopamine neurotransmitter "Pleasure Center"	Hobbies Exercise Making and achieving goals
Endorphins "Nature's PainKiller" Juices	Exercise (Cardio) Laughter Meditation
Oxytocin "love hormone" Chemical	Physical touch (e.g., hugs) Socializing Quality time with loved ones Snuggling pets
Balance these Chemicals/ Neurotransmitters	
Norepinephrine (Noradrenaline) Fight-flight-freeze response	Exercise Adequate sleep Mindfulness practices
Melatonin "Sleep regulation"	Adequate sleep Sun exposure Avoiding blue light before bed
Reduce this Chemical	
Cortisol (Reduction)	Exercise, Mindfulness, Meditation, Breathing techniques

Getting Your Accountability

Nobody else cares if you work out. Conversely, if I have a running group meeting at 6:00 a.m., they will text me if I am not there. In my head, I cannot let them down. There are so many ways to be held accountable. Perhaps you have a super anxious dog that loves to go on walks. I cannot get over the routine my dog nephew has, and he knows precisely when it is time for a walk. You may need your watch to buzz to remind you to take steps, or a competition notification that your brother just hit 10,000 steps. Find the people who will care if you show up or not. Maybe you must tell yourself, "I will thank myself later if I lift those weights. My arms are going to be ripped during tank top season." Figure out who your accountability person is and tell them that you need a cheerleader.

Another way to build accountability is to join a class. You may have a friend who has already attended a class and could recommend one. Have this friend hold you accountable. Also, I tell myself that if I attend, they get paid more. It is a crazy little mental trick that the

Skills and Behaviors for Student Teaching

© iStock.com/Kudryavtsev Pavel.

instructor cares about if you attend. I talk to my students about my running goals. By sharing, I learn more about students who run (sometimes I have even gotten great running and nutritional advice). I get encouragement when students ask me about upcoming races. For my husband, when he pays for a gym membership, he will make sure he gets his money's worth.

Think About It.

How can you hold yourself accountable? Who are the people who are counting on you to live a healthy lifestyle? Find a way to let them know that their encouragement matters.

?

?

Convenience

The most critical piece to making this work is convenience. So, laying out your workout clothes the night before or having sneakers in your car always makes your walk more comfortable. Ask your gym teacher or new fitness instructor in town to have class first thing in the morning, right in your school gym. You and your new teacher pals can decide on a monthly payment for the instructor to teach at your school. Do whatever is convenient for you. I need the time options for exercise to be convenient. I need to know that I can exercise at various times throughout the day.

> **Think About It.**
>
> What are your hurdles? How do you jump over them? How do you need to make movement convenient?
>
> ?
>
> ?
>
> ?

Weekly Goal Setting

There is something about charting my progress that gives me a sense of accomplishment about my work. If you set goals, you will see progress. Setting small goals and seeing that progress is a beautiful hit of dopamine. Meeting goals goes deeper than your why. Your why is more of a big picture, like looking stunning in your bridesmaid's gown. However, the short-term goal setting is the weekly visual you see along the way, as the bride annoyingly counts down the days and the minutes to the big day. When you set goals, as you will for many skills throughout this book, I urge you to think about something to get your heart rate going and clear your brain space for a healthy lifestyle. Through these various examples, you may get some ideas to help you figure out a weekly routine that works for you.

Virtual Accountability

With technology today, there are plenty of options for virtual workouts on the beach, cycling through Milan, or working out to YouTube videos from your favorite athletes. Your motivation may come from video games where you can dance with a friend or kickbox with an enemy. There are competitive ways to earn points and level up without even realizing that you are working out. Most watches have step count competitions so that you can challenge family members, coworkers, and friends to various step challenges each week. Finding an appropriate routine for movement may take some exploring, but so many companies offer low monthly subscriptions, or one of your television accounts already has various workout episodes.

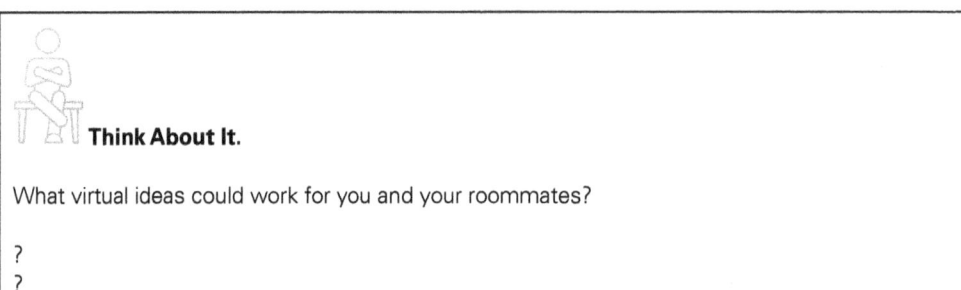

Think About It.

What virtual ideas could work for you and your roommates?

?
?

Movement Goals

Are you still motivated to make a movement goal? Consider your why, get some accountability, and make movement convenient each week. I am excited that you are making this a priority! On the other hand, changes in your movement may not be for you right now. If you are all set with your exercise, you can always sprint back to this chapter if you need to get back on track. If you become stressed, remember that taking an extra walk is a significant way to relieve stress. If you are ready to set movement goals, I hope you are jogging in place while you waited. As you think about the introduction. you will see that natural changes happen to the chemicals and neurotransmitters in your brain when you exercise. However, de-stressing may not be your why. Take some time to reflect and answer why this matters to you. Like a sleep routine, your exercise routine, or lack thereof, did not happen in one week. Take some time to build attainable goals. Once you have looked over the goals shared by the student teachers, move to the blank chart end of Chapter 5 to create your own movement goals. Look at some examples to get your ideas going.

Stepping Up with Kaycee

Starting with Kaycee, as you recall, she needs to take more time for herself. However, after tracking her days, she recognized that she had some time in her day for movement. She spends much time in small group instruction, so she often sits on the floor or in tiny chairs to be at the same level as her students. When asked about a time when movement was fun, she immediately thought about the weekly competitive dance group she had participated in for 10 years. Once Kaycee started student teaching, she stopped wearing her watch because she was embarrassed by the limited number of steps she took each day.

After thinking about the importance of movement, she said, "I am adding steps to my day." She then chatted with the play director to see if she could add choreography with several dance routines to the play. She set up a simple choreography routine and had eight students practicing three times a week. She also added dance to her brain breaks in the classroom. She started doing short dance routines with music to get her students moving. Adding dance to her day motivated Kaycee to move and competitively step more each day. Bonus effect: Since Kaycee started dancing, she has found that she is more interested in water, and has improved her sleep each night.

Kaycee's Goal

Making SMART Goals Baseline Data	Thursday: 7,000 steps Saturday: 5,000 steps Tuesday: 12,000 steps
Specific: What is the Target Behavior?	
She will average 7,000 steps 4 days a week.	
With what materials or conditions?	
Given a step counter and four 24-hour periods, Kaycee will calculate an average of 7,000 steps across 4 days.	
Measurable: How well must the skill be performed? (Criteria)	**Achievable:** What modifications or accommodations are needed for success? Making the time?
An average of 7,000 steps across 4 days	Step counter (watch) Choreography routines for play In the classroom, dance during brain breaks
How will the skill be measured? And how often?	**Any additional research? People to talk to?**
Kaycee will collect data on her steps 4 days a week. She will chart her steps on a graph to note progress.	Once the play is over, she will need a new plan Join step competitions with family?
Relevance: Why is meeting this goal important?	**Timely:** What is considered mastery for this goal? **Timeline:** When would you like to achieve this goal?
Kaycee misses dancing and wants to add movement to her life. She used to move so much, but her steps seemed limited throughout the day. It's embarrassing to her	3 consistent weeks of an average of 7,000 steps She would like to meet this goal in 6 weeks
What other assessments or data will help assess progress toward the goal?	**What are the next steps in this goal area?**
Reflect with journal Kayce will chart her steps on a graph to have a visual of her progress.	Once she meets this goal, she will focus on another skill.

Jasper Is Jumping into a Workout Routine

Jasper is currently in the off-season for baseball. This schedule works perfectly for his teaching routine, but not for his workouts. Jasper has a "you cannot make me attitude," which proves difficult because Jasper cannot make himself hit the gym either. He does not like relying on going to the gym with his teammates because it conflicts with his teaching schedule.

After researching his current middle school lifting program, he found a way to train with the students and give them tips while looking like a buff college athlete and doing his routine. Jasper loves this structure because it gets him to the gym. Jasper loves to have options and gets bored with structured routines.

Jasper's Chart

Making SMART Goals **Baseline Data** **Tuesday:** 40% of baseball workout. **Thursday:** 80% of baseball workout. **Wednesday:** 60% of baseball workout.	
Specific: What is the Target Behavior?	
Jasper will complete 60% of the baseball workout routine in 4 out of 7 days.	
With what materials or conditions?	
Given 3 weekly workout routines, college gym, and middle school gym	
Measurable: How well must the skill be performed? (Criteria)	**Achievable:** What modifications or accommodations are needed for success? Making the time?
60% of the baseball workout routine 4 out of 7 days	This flexibility also allows him to complete the workout at the middle school or on campus. He will record music to add to his routine. He will also record the routine when he is working with his teammates. This will be motivation when he is lifting alone.
How will the skill be measured? And How often?	**Any additional research? People to talk to?**
Jasper will check off the skills completed at each workout 4 days a week.	Create a workout routine for middle schoolers
Relevance: Why is meeting this goal important?	**Timely:** What is considered mastery for this goal? **Timeline:** When would you like to achieve this goal?
This is my identity, "I am a strong baseball player, and if I want to pitch in the spring, I need to maintain this routine."	3 consistent weeks of 60% of the baseball workout routine 4 out of 7 days Jasper will complete this goal within 6 weeks.
What other assessments or data will help assess progress toward the goal?	**What are the next steps in this goal area?**
Lifting Log	90% of the baseball workout routine 5 out of 7 days

Remember to set your goal around your baseline data. Refer to the Technology Checkpoints for examples to find ways to measure your movement. You can be satisfied with your amount of exercise, so you may want to walk outside during your lunch break. That will work for me! Set an alarm to give yourself extra time to walk outside the building during your prep period or lunch. You can use your watch to set an alarm reminder. Start wearing comfortable but stylish shoes so you do not dread taking steps. Take these efforts to make changes in stride, to become a teacher who is making progress. This is a friendly reminder to check in on your bedtime routines, fuel, and keep progressing.

 Chapter Recap.

Exercise is highly effective at reducing stress
- Lower cortisol, raise serotonin

Find your why—find a reason to get moving

Examples of types of exercise and movement to add to your day
- Running: find a friend and train for a 5k
- Add steps to your day
- Park in a space away from the school
- Take the long way to the copier
- Get your students moving, too

Skiing
- Find an activity you enjoyed growing up and revisit it.
- This could be an activity you can do for free with your school.

Yoga
- A workout, stretch, balance, and mental clarity all in one.
- So many different options for yoga, try a few to find one you like
- Incorporate yoga aspects into your class

Strength training
- Along with stronger muscles and mental benefits, this can be a great way to connect with some students.

"Find good habits to relieve stress"

Accountability—when you find someone or something to hold you accountable, it can help you stick to your goal.
- Workout partners
- Group meet-ups
- Take your dog for walks
- Join a class
- Virtual accountability
- Online workouts
- Battle a friend online
- Challenge family members to a weekly step contest

Convenience
- Make movement convenient, and it will be easier to add it to your routine

Double-check your bedtime and sleep routine, as well as how you are fueling

Prioritize movement in your day

Collaborative Thinking.

Questions to ask your mentors / peers
What various exercise routines have you maintained over the years?
What are some ways you have made movement convenient in your life?
What is your why? Who holds you accountable?

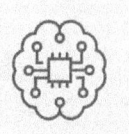
Technology Checkpoints.

Step monitor: These monitors track steps throughout the day so you can hit that magical 10,000 step mark. Step monitors can be very basic or more advanced.
Sticky Notes: Write quick notes on your Windows desktop, but now you can also take your sticky notes with you, allowing you to capture, find, and use your notes across apps and your favorite devices. Make notes for your movement.
Virtual accounts: Peloton, Osmo, Netflix Nike: Workout, Nintendo "Just Dance" With a purchase or account you can exercise anytime or any place.
Youtube: With navigation you can also have free workouts at anytime or any place.
GoNoodle.com: Free videos with nonsensical lyrics which are great brain breaks in the elementary classes.

Teacher Decision-Making.

As mentioned in the previous chapter, please pause here and do a quick evaluation. Do you find that you are in data overload? For example, if you look at your data about sleep (Chapter 2), do you have 3 to 4 weeks where you are meeting your goal for sleep? If so, should you increase your goal, or can you put that aside and stop collecting data on this behavior?

This is your permission. It is okay.

 **Next Steps.**

- What is working? . . .
- What is not working? . . .
- What do I need? . . .
- What am I proud of? . . .
- What do I need to let go of? . . .

 **Weekly Reflection.**

Use the space below to jot down some notes here. Avoid the spiral. Visualize a perfect day. Summarize the main details here. What are your new skills and strategies that made it such a great day? Listen to me telling you that my goal is to help you continue to make progress and, hopefully, with slight changes to your lifestyle, decrease stress and increase joy in and out of the classroom. I believe in you, and you got this!

5

Brain-Centering Practices

Chapter Outline

Hope for Your Brain: Having Spirituality	88
Strength Training Your Brain: Meditation	89
Calming Your Brain: Breathwork	90
Telling Your Story: Positive Visualization	91
Retelling a Story: Meditative Stories	92
Dusting Your Brain: Nature Immersion	93
Nature Connection: Grounding	94
Incorporating Nature in Your Day	94
Organizing Your Brain: Journaling	95
Piecing Together Your Brain: Counseling	96
Brain-Centering Goals	98

Take time with this chapter to think of yourself as an actor, entertainer, athlete, soldier, or speaker who is held to high expectations to perform each day. As your students enter your classroom you step onto a stage where you are expected to perform on an expert level. Your students have purchased pricey front row tickets to watch you perform live each day. This may seem like too much pressure, but start to compare yourself as a performer on the big stage. Next, review these ways that performers like yourself clear their brains to prepare for games, performances, battle, or series. Sample some strategies to find ways to prepare for your best lessons day after day and year after year. Remember, athletes make errors, and actors have to take two. If you need to, take a time out. But promise me you will find something that will help you to center your brain and continue to follow your why. The goal is to find brain-centering practices that help you make good decisions in your day-to-day life. The routines you are about to read can help you to set yourself up for success and handle the problematic situations that come your way. Stress is something that builds over time. Without healthy coping strategies, your brain will continue to take the same approach to handling stress. Those who function in a constant state of stress rewire their brains to always react in stress mode.

Think About It.

What are your physical symptoms of stress? Where do you feel tension in your body? What physical symptoms do you notice when you are overwhelmed?

?

?

Hope for Your Brain: Having Spirituality

Please take this section as it applies to you in any spiritual context. Religious community includes listening to psalms, passages, or verses and having interpretations from experts on how they can use these lessons in their daily lives. I will refer to faith in a general sense of something bigger than yourself. This is a wishy-washy statement for a special educator, so I must add some science. People who believe in a higher power live happier lives than their counterparts (Park & MacKinnon, 2013). What does this look like? Research suggests that when college students are a part of a community, they have a greater sense of purpose and feel less lonely (Pfund & Miller-Perrin, 2019). This is a Christian-based practice with routines such as attending weekly mass. There are many details to the meaning of Christianity across the globe, but to keep this light, for me, it means going to church each week reminds me to pray for peace and mental clarity. It also reminds me that there is something more significant than the problem right before me when times are difficult.

© iStock.com/Pavel Naumov.

Tim Tebow is an example of a professional athlete who is known for publicly sharing his faith as a contribution to his success in football. One example of his practice of incorporating faith into his routine is referring to scriptures. One of his best stories is writing "John 3:16" in eye-black, referring to a Bible passage during a college championship game. The day of that championship, over 90 million people googled the scripture "John 3:16" (Tebow & Gregory, 2022). He goes on to further explain how his statistics, just 3 years later in a professional championship game, were connected to those specific digits in various combinations of 3, 1, and 6. You may be aware of how things around you may be aligning, and you do not even know it. There is actual evidence of a positive energy between two people when you send out positive energy or prayers (Ahsan, Khan, & Siddiqui, 2012). Perhaps Tebow had the energy of the 90 million people who searched that passage. Yes, you must keep church and public school separate, but you can start "Tebowing" in your personal space so that you can include spiritually based energy in your teaching.

Think About It.

What did spirituality look like for you growing up? Were there routines or practices your family followed? Maybe it was more family-based. Did you visit an aunt's house every weekend? How can you build positive energy among a community of people?

?

?

Strength Training Your Brain: Meditation

There are many formats for meditation or mental clarity. The goal is to get your brain out of a beta response (alert decision-making), and into an alpha response (relaxed but alert state). The brain automatically goes throughout the day in a beta decision-making brain response. When teachers spend time transitioning from class to class, they rarely get the mental rest required to make decisions. Whether working with very busy preschoolers, handling awkward middle school conversations, or supporting high schoolers through difficult life choices, your brain must always be in sympathetic mode. A way to help your brain through complex thoughts is through rest in the alpha response (Tang, Holzel, & Posner, 2015). Reflecting on the introduction, you need to reassure yourself that everything is okay so that you can calm your cortisol levels. Deep breathing and brain-centering are one way to tell your brain that fighting, freezing, or fleeing is unnecessary. Katy Perry considers meditation the best nap of her day (Worland, 2016). Because performers like her do not have much free time, meditation is a way to make the most of their day. Think about incorporating meditative stories and breathwork into your classroom. It is a win-win. You are meditating and teaching your students how to control anxious and stressful thoughts. Students can learn to quiet their minds and focus on silence starting at a very young age and can continue to implement these brain-clearing strategies throughout their school career (Brown, 2019).

Inclusive and Culturally Responsive Practices.

Give students opportunities to regulate their emotions. As a teacher, you must acknowledge that everyone needs time to balance their thoughts and feelings. Recognize that many families deal with stress and difficult situations in various ways based on their belief systems. It is essential to help students navigate practices framed around each family's cultural traditions.

Calming Your Brain: Breathwork

There are many ways to do this, one of which is through paced breathing. When you do this, you train your brain to clear and work through stressful situations. The key is to exhale longer than you inhale. You are getting oxygen to your brain, signaling you are okay. You can do this anywhere. You can even practice breathing while driving or waiting in line at lunch. The point is not just to breathe in stressful situations, but to practice your breathwork as a preventative approach before stressful situations. Notice that the Figure 8 pattern could be turned into a steering wheel. Add this to your routine when you are at a red light. Tactical breathing, which is also known as box breathing, is used as a part of military training for soldiers. Box breathing, as shown below, has been proven to help soldiers make superior decisions (Röttger et al., 2021). Given the number of responses and scaffolding teachers need to do in a day, it sounds like teachers can benefit from deep breathing as well. Remember, deep breathing can help you during a stressful situation or be preventative before you get into a difficult meeting or interaction. This takes practice, so make these little exercises a part of your daily routine.

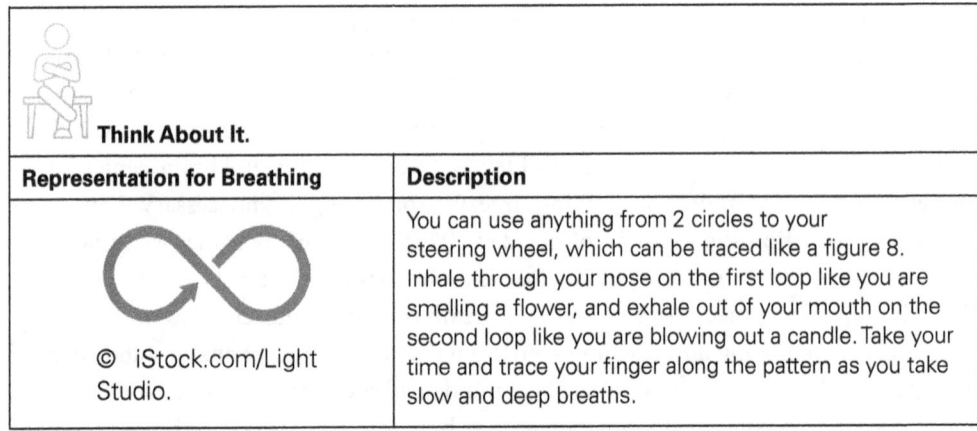

Think About It.

Representation for Breathing	Description
∞ © iStock.com/Light Studio.	You can use anything from 2 circles to your steering wheel, which can be traced like a figure 8. Inhale through your nose on the first loop like you are smelling a flower, and exhale out of your mouth on the second loop like you are blowing out a candle. Take your time and trace your finger along the pattern as you take slow and deep breaths.

Brain-Centering Practices

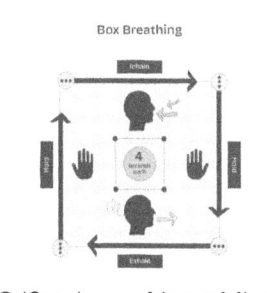 © iStock.com/VectorMine.	(With each line count to 4) Line 1: Breathe in through your nose Line 2: Hold your breath Line 3: Breathe out through your mouth Line 4: Hold the empty lungs [Repeat]
To the beat of "We Are the Champions" There is a distinctive "short, short, long" beat between the chorus. When at a sporting event, people instinctively pound the bleachers and clap.	Use this rhythm for effective and calming breathwork. 2 short breaths in the mouth (each 2 seconds) 1 long exhale out of the mouth (6 seconds)

 **Add Your Ideas.**

Here are some ways you can add just one minute of a silent pause or breathwork with your students.
- During morning routine (homework review or morning meeting)
- Before you leave the classroom
- Before or after a test
- After a disagreement with a peer

-
-

Telling Your Story: Positive Visualization

Try visualizing a positive outcome to your situation. Often your brains catastrophize situations to the point that your brain is retelling a story of events that did not even happen. Yes, I am referring back to the RAS. You need to think to yourself, what if the best possible outcome occurs? Be like Mike, stepping up to the line to shoot a foul shot with your eyes closed. There are videos of Michael Jordan making foul shots with his eyes closed. Visualize it going well before it happens. Michael Jordan had a predisposition for playing basketball, and he is still recognized as one of the greatest players of all time. He contributed his practice and positive visualization to his basketball performance (Lazenby, 2015). Sure, there are factors beyond your control, but with a clear mind, you will make more positive decisions versus being in stress mode, thinking the worst possible scenario. Give it a try. Go to your happy place and visualize your positive story. Narrate the story as though the best case works in your favor.

Retelling a Story: Meditative Stories

Perhaps you are not interested in being the narrator for your situation; another approach to clear your thoughts is through meditative stories. In these stories, a narrator calmly talks you through strolling on the beach or walking through nature. The narrator gives beautiful details about your surroundings. There is a description to awaken all five senses, from the cool breeze on your face to the sand between your toes. You find yourself listening to the waves crash on the shore. Within this setting, the speaker will help you release your worries. You could send them into the clouds or roll them into the ocean.

Oprah Winfrey, a television producer well-known for her spiritual presence and philanthropic deeds, often refers to her daily meditative practice as her way to visualize her success (Scales, 2024). Oprah frequently shares her meditative experience as learned through meditation experts Eckhart Tolle and Deepak Chopra. Through these meditative stories, you can also focus on the present moment and build more self-awareness. In as little as 15 minutes you can center yourself and clear your mind of the distractions around

© iStock.com/colematt.

you. Did you ever notice how you feel better when you return from taking a break? Sometimes the stressful situation feels better than it initially seemed. So, the next time you are anxious or overwhelmed, try meditative stories. It lets you clear your brain to make more informed daily decisions.

Dusting Your Brain: Nature Immersion

There are so many components to being outside that are healthy. You get fresh air and possibly the calming, repetitive sounds of birds when you step outside. Depending on the season, you can have a calming breeze or the sun's warmth shining on your face. My peaceful time is in the spring when the birds start singing at sunrise. I have recently learned that the sounds were more than just my excitement of spring; the sound of birds naturally lowers cortisol levels (Michels & Hamers, 2023). Your outdoor enjoyment may be a walk in the parking lot during lunch or a nature walk during recess. When your students see you getting outdoors, you are modeling this skill of health and well-being by taking your students for a stroll and encouraging them to calm their minds by observing the world around them. Former president Barack Obama launched *Every Kid in a Park* (2015) to support this concept for all kids to access the concept of natural immersion by granting free access for fourth graders to all national parks.

© iStock.com/Nurfatihah Amira Wekoila.

Nature Connection: Grounding

Taking a more profound step into nature and how it can relieve stress is through an approach called grounding. Through this, you place your feet on the earth, whether in the grass or even on the sidewalk, and you ground your feet to recharge your body with the earth's natural waves of energy (Berman et al., 2012). During this time, you recharge your body using the earth's natural negative electric charge to balance your body systems. Some scientists theorize that there is a transfer of free electrons when the human body is in contact with the ground: sand, soil, gravel, or grass (Latino, Cataldi, & Fischetti, 2021). There are benefits to mood, inflammation, autoimmune diseases, and so on, with at least 30 minutes of skin-to-ground connection. Red Sox relief pitcher Adam Ottavino is known for warming up at Fenway Park in his bare feet. This is his way to connect with the energy of the popular Boston Stadium. I think it is relevant to address that he is the relief pitcher, as it is his job to maintain a winning game or get his team out of a slump. For him, grounding is a way to take out the stress of the situation and use the energy from his environment to deal with his problem.

Incorporating Nature in Your Day

Did you ever recognize the sense of relief of putting your feet in the sand? This may be why you enjoy going to the beach. If I am going to spend time outdoors, I try to take my shoes off. I take advantage of downtime by taking off my shoes when camping or attending baseball games. My thoughts immediately go to elementary teachers on the playground for recess. You could take your shoes off during recess for some grounding time. What an excellent opportunity to recharge, just like your students. Think about how you enjoyed

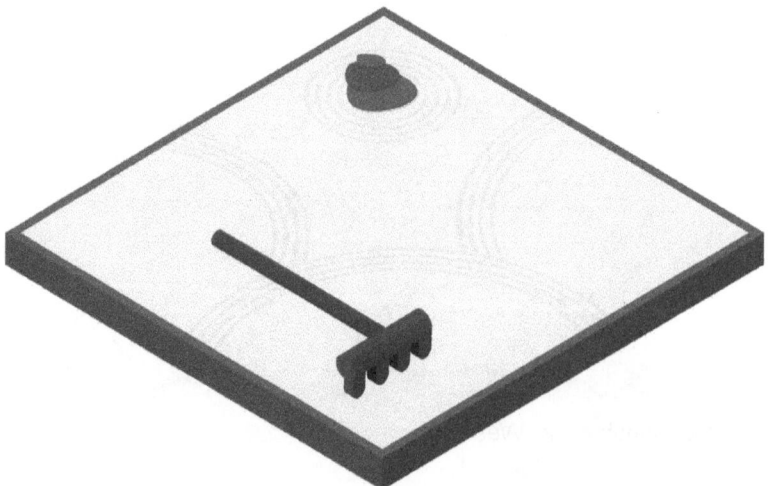

© iStock.com/bor-zebra.

the great outdoors as a kid. Were you always at the beach, or did you love that once-a-year beach trip? Think about incorporating the sound of water into your classroom. Add a sand table with exploration letters and themed items from your unit for younger classrooms. Secondary teachers, do not worry; you could have a Zen garden at your reading corner. Do not be fooled; I met with one of my student teachers just this week, and he got lost making patterns in my homemade Zen garden.

 **Think About It.**

Think back to when you were a kid. What are some of the ways you have enjoyed the great outdoors? Brainstorm some ways that you can incorporate this into your day. Your students may also benefit from your ideas.

?

?

?

Organizing Your Brain: Journaling

Shifting gears into another approach that has proven mind-centering results is journaling. Some people choose to reflect on their day, which has positive effects. When you are having difficulties or continue to think about certain situations, try writing them out instead of rethinking a problem in your brain. You are far better at using paper and a pencil and writing out the situation than letting it fester in your brain. It may not help with a solution, but at least you focus on what you should and should not do. To take your journaling a step further, you can jot down items you are grateful for each day. Writing down a list of things you are thankful for each day helps you rest with a positive mindset (Shintani, 2025). Taylor Swift is a singer and songwriter best known for writing her lyrics through her lived experiences, along with going on tour and selling out stadiums in major cities while spreading her philanthropic deeds. Taylor started journaling as a child, reporting that rewriting positive statements over and over during her times of doubt (Rossman, 2022).

Journaling is a great way to start or end your day. These statements can be simple, from getting your favorite meal in the cafeteria today to being so happy that your mentor teacher returned after a 2-day absence. Pulling out the good in each day helps you flip the script during downtime to have a positive mindset when your brain is at rest. Whether you have a spiritual connection to your gratitude or you simply list positive interactions in your day, acknowledging what you do have can get you through difficult times (Driedger, 2001). Now you try. Add your ideas and bullet your thoughts.

© iStock.com/Natalia Loginova.

 **Add Your Ideas.**

Sentence starter for those who need it.
- A positive from today
- One thing that will go better tomorrow
- I forgive myself for

Keep going with your ideas . . .

-
-

Piecing Together Your Brain: Counseling

You may be at a time when you need more than just mind-centering. You may need to brain dump or get an unbiased opinion from someone who has no impact on your subsequent decisions. Family members and friends are lovely consultants, but sometimes their advice may be motivated by their experiences, and you may not be able to relate. Roommates and friends have gotten you through many difficult times, but perhaps they are motivated by keeping you as a roommate because they do not want to pay more rent. Also, you may have amazing coworkers and mentors, but you could have a work situation or concern and feel uncomfortable sharing your dilemma with another coworker. Simone Biles has taken some of the stigma away from therapy by announcing that she regularly consults with her therapist as a part of her preparation for Olympic-winning performances. Simone always refers to counseling as a tool to help her with the pressures of competition and making the right decision when competing on the world stage (Bissell, Chou, & Dirks, 2024). You may not be competing for a gold medal, but you may carry the stress of previous experiences that prevent you from landing that amazing lesson that you have already prepared. You may also have stressors regarding the decisions of the next chapter after graduation. Therapy or counseling is a great way to piece together these ideas.

Consider a therapist or university counselor as an unbiased source. By going to therapy, you can have someone listen to you without commenting on their lived experiences. They will listen to themes or give you insights into your decisions. As you get closer to graduation, this is probably the first time in your life that you cannot compare yourself to your classmates or family members. There are so many decisions that you will need to make about life as you approach graduation. Discussing these choices and dilemmas with a trained professional can help you through difficult times (Seide, 2024). I remind my students that there is very little you get for free on campus, so take advantage of the free counseling and tutoring. That is why you pay tuition. You can also schedule a chat with your advisor or another trusted professor.

 **Think About It.**

What are some of the dilemmas you keep thinking about, where you would love to get an unbiased opinion? What are some of the conversations you keep discussing with others, but they do not see your point of view?
?
?

© iStock.com/ANDRII SHESHEL.

This chapter discussed many approaches to clear your mind and focus on your goals. Some of these strategies mentioned in this chapter may have been a part of your life before entering college. You may need to get back into a routine or want to try something new. Create a goal to sample these practices. Think about how you spend your week and what is not a good use of time, and replace that time with several scientifically sound practices to help you reach mental clarity. Talk to your peers and colleagues at school; they may have creative ways to spend more time outdoors.

Brain-Centering Goals

Curious about decluttering your brain? Are you visualizing the fog lifting? I am excited that you are making this a priority. Some of these practices may not be a good match for you now. If you are all set with your brain-centering activities, great! In an emergency, revisit if you need some spring or seasonal cleaning. If you get overwhelmed with too many thoughts, get them out of your brain and onto paper. As you think about the Introduction, you will see that natural changes happen to the chemicals and neurotransmitters in your brain when you find ways to step away from a problem. Sample some of these practices and see what resonates—friendly reminder: your brain fog and negative cycle of thinking did not just start last week. Take time to learn skills that will allow the fog to lift. Look at some examples to get your ideas going. If you are ready to make your own goal, go to the end of this chapter to fill in a blank goal chart.

Kaycee's Journey Through Journaling

Remember, Kaycee rarely takes time for herself, let alone allowing time to apply for jobs? She is in a dilemma because her parents want her to apply for jobs near her hometown and live at home to save money. Every conversation with her mom ends with, "Have you applied to Ridgemont Elementary yet?" or "I hear that Mrs. Horne, your first-grade teacher, is retiring; you should get an application in." Deep down inside, Kaycee thinks about how she likes the diverse setting of her student teaching placement. Not to mention, there are so many jobs near her boyfriend's new place of employment. Brainstorming with others where to apply always brings biased opinion. Kaycee has decided that she needs to share her ideas and clarify her next steps in life. She started going to the university counselor once a week. The counselor also encourages Kaycee to journal her thoughts when she gets overwhelmed. Check her journaling chart below.

Kaycee's Goal

Making SMART Goals						
Baseline Data						
Days of the week journaled						
Week 1						
Monday	Tuesday	Wednesday	Thursday	Friday	Saturday	Sunday
✓	✗	✗	✗	✗	✓	✗
Week 2						
Monday	Tuesday	Wednesday	Thursday	Friday	Saturday	Sunday
✓	✗	✗	✗	✗	✗	✓

Week 1 2:7 days
Week 2: 2 out of 7 day

Specific: What is the Target Behavior?	
Kaycee's goal is to journal 3 out of 7 times weekly.	
With what **materials or conditions**?	
Given a daily journal prompt for a 7-day week.	
Measurable: How well must the skill be performed? (Criteria)	**Achievable:** What modifications or accommodations are needed for success? Making the time?
3 out of 7 days	Writing Prompts Attending weekly counseling
How will the skill be measured? And how often?	Any additional research? People to talk to?
I will tally the number of journal entries completed at the end of each week.	Be sure to have a new counselor scheduled when I move
Relevance: Why is meeting this goal important?	**Timely:** What is considered mastery for this goal? **Timeline:** When would you like to achieve this goal?
I need healthy ways to clear my brain. Talking about the future with everyone is just making me more confused.	3 consistent weeks of journaling 3 out of 7 days a week Meet goal within 3 months
What other assessments or data will help assess progress toward the goal?	What are the next steps in this goal area?
Checkoff Journaling on calendar Reflect emotions with habits in journal posts	Journal more 5 out of 7 days a week

Deep Breaths Quentin

Quentin's research expert often finds himself lost in questions, hypotheses, and potential solutions. He is intrigued by the brain-decluttering research on meditation. He loves the idea of falling asleep to meditative stories that include nature. He will use this as his backup plan when he struggles to fall asleep or wakes up trying to solve multiple scientific problems at night. He would like to collect data on his breathing. He found that he needed something to help him clear his mind. Quentin has decided he wants to do a breathing technique in between his classes.

To set up his day for success, he has all the materials ready to complete his breathing routine before greeting students at the beginning of class. He started to collect data on how long it would take him to complete five rounds of box breathing. Quentin did a great job recognizing that he is only at three breathing sessions. He did not reach too far, especially with something new. See that he is using a simple chart and crossing off when he does the box breath.

Quentin's Chart

Making SMART Goals	
Baseline Data	
Number of Times Quentin completed box breathing in between classes	
Days of the Week	Completed 5 Rounds of Box Breathing
Monday	X O O O O X O X
Wednesday	O X X X O O O
Friday	X O O O O O O X
Specific: What is the Target Behavior?	
Quentin will complete 4 out of 7 sessions of box breath routines (5 rounds) 3 out of 5 days in the week.	
With what **materials or conditions**?	
Given 7 breaks between classes throughout the school day,	
Measurable: How well must the skill be performed? (Criteria)	**Achievable:** What modifications or accommodations are needed for success? Making the time?
4 out of 7 sessions of box breath routines each day (5 rounds)	Watch Alarm as a Reminder Box to trace
How will the skill be measured? And How often?	Any additional research? People to talk to?
Quentin will keep the small chart above on his desk and put an X after each session.	NA
Relevance: Why is meeting this goal important?	**Timely:** What is considered mastery for this goal? **Timeline:** When would you like to achieve this goal?
Quentin needs to go into each class with a clear mind	4 consistent weeks of 4 out of 7 sessions, 3 out of 5 days Try to meet goal within 4 weeks
What other assessments or data will help assess progress toward the goal?	**What are the next steps in this goal area?**
Reflect with journal	Add and chart checkmarks at the end of each day 5 out of 7 sessions, 4 out of 5 days/ week

 **Chapter Recap.**

You are a performer, and the classroom is your stage
- How can you prepare your brain for this performance?
- Take a timeout, center your brain, and follow your why

Spirituality
- Having a sense of something bigger than yourself
- People who have a spiritual community live happier lives
- Positive energy is passed on to other people

Meditation
- Strength training for your brain
- Goal is an alpha response, provides a mental rest for your brain
- Helps your brain through complex thoughts
- Examples
- Deep breathing
- Meditative stories
- Incorporate into your classroom

Breathwork
- Pace breathing
- Exhale longer than you inhale
- Takes practice
- Tactical/box breathing

Positive visualization
- What if the best possible outcome happens?
- Visualize the outcome you want

Meditative stories
- The narrator talks you through a calming story
- Helps you focus on the present
- Brings a sense of self-awareness

Nature immersion
- Being outside is beneficial to mental health
- Fresh air
- Calming nature sounds
- Be an example to students
- Take a nature walk during recess
- "Every Kid in a Park"

Grounding
- Put your feet on the earth
- Recharges your body with earth's energy
- Just 30 minutes found benefits to mood, inflammation, and autoimmune disease

Incorporate nature in your day
- Take your shoes off at recess
- Add the sound of water to your class
- Bring in a sand table or a Zen garden
- Walk outside with students if you can

Journaling
- Use as a reflection of your day
- Helps work through difficulties or challenging situations
- Jot down what you are grateful for
- Great way to end your day

Counseling
- When you need more than just some mind-centering exercises
- When you just need to unload your brain
- Offers an unbiased opinion from someone who has no connection to the outcome
- Counseling is often available for free on campuses

Collaborative Thinking.

Questions to ask your mentors /peers
What are various distractions that help you to clear your mind each week?
Are there simple mind-centering tricks that you do, even during the school day? (e.g., Walk outside to get from one side of the building to the other)

Technology Checkpoints.

Calm: Calm is a mental health app offering free or subscription plans to help reduce stress and promote mindfulness. Some of the offerings are guided meditations, soothing music, and movement routines.
Habitica: For the gamer who wants help managing tasks and productivity, Habitica uses rewards and points when a task is completed or a goal is achieved.
Breethe App: Another mental health app offereing guided meditations, hypnotherapy, and calming sounds. Breethe offers a "My Life Kit" to personalize the app to use it in your daily life.
Religious meditations: Meditations can help bring a sense of calmness to your daily routine. By adding in a religious aspect, they can help you reach a sense of spiritual calmness and connection to a higher being.
YouTube Meditative Stories: These meditative stories can help you reach a sense of calmness. Listen to one during a hectic day or add one to your bedtime routine.
Podcast; Body Scan: These podcasts help guide you through body scans in different time lengths. Check in with your body and your breath and reach a sense of calm.
Gonoodle.com: This education-based website has a library of short videos, including dance follow-along, call and repeats, breath work, and focus exercises. These videos are a hit among elementary students and are perfect for brain breaks and transition times.
mindfulschool.net: Mindful Schools helps schools bring mindfulness into their classrooms. On this website, there are videos and articles on how to incorporate mindfulness into your school and at home.

You have made it to the end of Part I. Congratulations. I applaud you for taking the time to learn more about your self-care so that you can maintain these skills to be a teacher who monitors progress in the classroom. Remember to start small; you can always add on when you meet your goal. I am proud of the way you are taking care of your brain. You have so many teacher decisions to make in a day. Take these changes in stride in your efforts to become a teacher who continues to make progress. You have also spent some time in the classroom getting to know your students and other colleagues in the building. As a snapshot into your future, you will continue to work on skills and strategies to help engage your students in the lessons that you take such precious time to plan.

Teacher Decision-Making. Before moving forward with another part, do you feel like you are doing a lot but not getting anywhere? If you look at the collected data, do you need to narrow it down and pick one skill? Or have you mastered your water goals, and is there no need to continue to monitor your progress? Think about what will best serve you and your goals to be a teacher who continues to make progress. This is your permission. It is okay. My goal is to help you continue to make progress and, hopefully, with slight changes to your lifestyle, to decrease stress and increase joy in and out of the classroom. I believe in you and your ability to do great things. Keep going—you got this!

Next Steps.

What is working? . . .
What is not working? . . .
What do I need? . . .
What am I proud of? . . .
What do I need to let go of? . . .

Weekly Reflection.

Jot down some notes. Avoid the spiral. Listen to me telling you that you have this, and I believe in you. I am encouraging these minor changes because you are a quality educator, and students need teachers like you in the field for years to come.

Making SMART Goals **Baseline Data**	
Specific: What is the Target Behavior?	
With what **materials or conditions**?	
Measurable: How well must the skill be performed? (Criteria)	**Achievable:** What modifications or accommodations are needed for success? Making the time?

How will the skill be measured? And how often?	Any additional research? People to talk to?
Relevance: Why is meeting this goal important?	**Timely:** What is considered mastery for this goal? **Timeline:** When would you like to achieve this goal?
What other assessments or data will help assess progress toward the goal?	What are the next steps in this goal area?

Making SMART Goals
Baseline Data

Specific: What is the Target Behavior?	
With what **materials or conditions**?	
Measurable: How well must the skill be performed? (Criteria)	**Achievable:** What modifications or accommodations are needed for success? Making the time?
How will the skill be measured? And how often?	Any additional research? People to talk to?
Relevance: Why is meeting this goal important?	**Timely:** What is considered mastery for this goal? **Timeline:** When would you like to achieve this goal?
What other assessments or data will help assess progress toward the goal?	What are the next steps in this goal area?

Making SMART Goals **Baseline Data**	
Specific: What is the Target Behavior?	
With what **materials or conditions**?	
Measurable: How well must the skill be performed? (Criteria)	**Achievable:** What modifications or accommodations are needed for success? Making the time?
How will the skill be measured? And How often?	Any additional research? People to talk to?
Relevance: Why is meeting this goal important?	**Timely:** What is considered mastery for this goal? **Timeline:** When would you like to achieve this goal?
What other assessments or data will help assess progress toward the goal?	What are the next steps in this goal area?

Making SMART Goals **Baseline Data**	
Specific: What is the Target Behavior?	
With what **materials or conditions**?	
Measurable: How well must the skill be performed? (Criteria)	**Achievable:** What modifications or accommodations are needed for success? Making the time?

How will the skill be measured? And how often?	Any additional research? People to talk to?
Relevance: Why is meeting this goal important?	**Timely:** What is considered mastery for this goal? **Timeline:** When would you like to achieve this goal?
What other assessments or data will help assess progress toward the goal?	What are the next steps in this goal area?

Making SMART Goals **Baseline Data**	
Specific: What is the Target Behavior?	
With what **materials or conditions**?	
Measurable: How well must the skill be performed? (Criteria)	**Achievable:** What modifications or accommodations are needed for success? Making the time?
How will the skill be measured? And how often?	Any additional research? People to talk to?
Relevance: Why is meeting this goal important?	**Timely:** What is considered mastery for this goal? **Timeline:** When would you like to achieve this goal?
What other assessments or data will help assess progress toward the goal?	What are the next steps in this goal area?

Part II

Classroom Management

Now that you have gotten yourself organized, it is time to analyze your school day and see how you spend your time in the classroom. Yes, just as efficient as you are in your personal life, it is just as important to consider your time on task in the classroom. Trust me, I go into classrooms enough to see that there is too much downtime. So, when a student teacher tells me they do not have enough time, I can review their observations to identify ways the teacher can structure their day to make better use of time. Once you have your routine organized, you will look at the instances that are out of your control. Do you still have students who do not follow your classroom routine and your clear expectations? Perhaps they are not motivated to stay on task. When you have an engaging lesson, students will follow. Kids do not want to be bad; you must catch what they are doing well.

6

Assessing Your Classroom Management

Chapter Outline

Connecting with Your Students	112
Rule Reminders and Clear Expectations	114
Opportunities to Respond and Student Engagement	116
Clear Structure for Behavior Challenges	116
Video Self-Reflection	117
Classroom Management Goals	121

As in the last part, you will now measure your progress to identify the skill areas you need to work on within your classroom management. Remember, good teaching happens with time and reflection, which encourages teachers to be lifelong learners. For now, you should focus on setting goals for yourself and making progress. Take the data you collect and focus on the skills that will help you to progress in your teaching. Use the Classroom Management Observation Tool (CMOT) below to assess the following areas of classroom engagement: structure, positive expectations, active engagement, acknowledge appropriate student behavior, and implement a continuum of strategies for inappropriate student behavior (Simonsen, 2020). You can video yourself and complete this assessment, or you can have a mentor or supervisor look for these skills in your teaching.

 **Add Your Ideas.**

Classroom Management Observation Tool (CMOT)

The CMOT includes two components: (a) observation items, which have been validated for informing decisions about relative strengths/needs with positive and proactive classroom management, and (b) a checklist of empirically supported practices to "look for" periodically.
Instructions. Complete observation items routinely to inform decisions about professional development, and complete checklist periodically to check presence/absence of empirically supported practices.

Educator _____ **Observer**_____ **Date**_
_____ **Grade Level** _____ **Content Area:** _____ **Time Start**_____ **Time End** _____ **Instructional Activity:**_____ **Setting notes:** _____

Group size:___ whole class___ small group

CMOT Observation Items
Assess implementation of positive and proactive classroom management practices.
Positive and Proactive Classroom Management Practices. Please complete this portion of the CMA after observing an educator for a minimum of 15 minutes of instruction.

	1 = Disagree strongly	2 = Disagree Somewhat	3 = Agree Somewhat	4 = Agree strongly
1. The educator effectively engaged in active supervision of students in the classroom (i.e., moving, scanning, interacting).	1	2	3	4
2. The educator effectively provided most/all students with opportunities to respond and participate during instruction.	1	2	3	4
3. The educator effectively provided specific praise to acknowledge appropriate student academic and social behavior.	1	2	3	4

4. The educator provided more frequent acknowledgement for appropriate behaviors than inappropriate behaviors (+ to— ratio).	1	2	3	4

Effective active supervision includes systematic scanning, unpredictable movement, and interactions spread across students. Effective OTRs provide opportunities to various numbers of students using various opportunity and response modalities.) Effective specific praise names the behavior and is contingent, genuine, and contextually/culturally appropriate.

CMOT Checklist Periodically, check for evidence of the following effective classroom management practices.

Check for Evidence of Classroom Structure and Expectations		
1. The educator posted a schedule for the day and/or class activity.	Yes	No
2. The educator posted 3–5 positively stated behavioral expectations in the classroom.	Yes	No
3. The physical arrangement of the room was appropriate for the activity.	Yes	No
4. The educator developed routines for the day and/or class activity.	Yes	No
5. The educator taught and prompted 3–5 positively stated behavioral expectations.	Yes	No
6. The educator selected and implemented additional consequence strategies, if appropriate, to support student behavior.	Yes	No

Physical arrangement (seating assignments, furniture arrangement, etc.) is designed to maximize structure and minimize distraction. Students demonstrate fluency with routines, educator provides lesson plans, and/or educator references previously taught routines. Students demonstrate fluency with expectations, educator provides lesson plans, and/or educator references previously taught expectations. Effective prompts are delivered before a behavior is expected and make it more likely for students to engage in appropriate behavior for the given activity/environment. Additional consequence strategies may include classroom systems to acknowledge appropriate behavior or consequences to respond to inappropriate behavior; effective implementation is consistent, systematic, and accompanied by behavior-specific feedback.

Adapted From: Simonsen, B., Freeman, J., Kooken, J., Dooley, K., Gambino, A. J., Wilkinson, S., VanLone, J., Walters, S., Byun, S. G., Xu, X., Lupo, K., & Kern, L. (2020). Classroom Management Observation Tool (CMOT). Storrs, CT: University of Connecticut. Retrieved from: https://nepbis.org/classrooms-data-tools-resources/ Overview.

>  **Think About It.**
>
> After completing this assessment, review your data. Where do you need progress?
> What are your areas of strength?
> What feedback can you apply from your mentor, teacher, or university supervisor?
>
> ?
> ?
> ?

That is okay if you are unsure about the topics in the CMOT. In the following few pages, I will outline and provide examples of each topic area. However, throughout this part, you will uncover why these skills are essential. After reviewing the self-care skills in Part I, I hope that with some modifications, you will notice an improvement in yourself. Just like caring for yourself to avoid burnout, you must have self-awareness to manage your students in your classroom. Classroom management is one of the key skills that new teachers lack when entering their classrooms (Flower, McKenna, & Haring, 2017). You must have opportunities to work on these skills now. If you have not pulled the key elements of classroom management based on the assessment tool, below is a highlight of some research on these key skills, so that you understand the importance of taking the time to work on these skills. You can review your observation with your mentor to identify skills you would like to practice. It is essential to discuss these concepts with the mentor teacher, as it is still their classroom, and you should not incorporate practices that conflict with their classroom procedures. But as a way to implement these evidence-based practices, I always tell students to blame me. So I am passing this hint to you. Try asking your mentor, "I read this book, and the author suggests trying these skills for me to build connections with the students. Could I give this a try?" Remember, as you progress in your career, you will feel more confident and comfortable with these teaching strategies. You have not been in the classroom long enough to experiment with these teacher skills, so the remaining chapters in Part II will provide you with exercises, reflections, and classroom management goal ideas based on the student teachers you met in Chapter 1.

Connecting with Your Students

Though there are no checkboxes for student connections in the CMOT, it is essential to build relationships with your students to get them to connect to the content you are teaching (Larson et al., 2021). As a former history teacher, I often share with my secondary social science majors, "Nobody cares about history as much as you do. Students will not build that love through lecture and video, so find ways for your students to understand the importance of the Social Sciences." The same is true across content areas. Yes, you will have a portion of students who love school and the content you teach. Not all students have positive school memories or favorite teachers. I must remind teachers that they are getting into the profession because of their favorable experiences in school and with their favorite teachers. Therefore, you must find ways for students to see the importance of your content. It is your job to give the content purpose. You can do this by learning more about your students. Investing time in building connections with your students increases student engagement and achievement (Hamre & Pianta, 2017). In the next chapter, there are tools and strategies to help you build relationships with each of your students. From this, you can make more progress with your classroom management as you make a relationship with your students who respect you.

Inclusive and Culturally Responsive Practices.

It is important to reflect on personal life experiences for students within their community. Consider students' culture (as defined below) and consider how their background will have an impact on how they make connections with other individuals and how they learn. Never assume. When you are unsure, ask questions.

Culture

When referring to culture, teachers should consider each category, including but not limited to: race, skin color, ethnicity, gender identity, age, nationality, language, class, economic status, ability, level of education, sexual orientation, and religion. Inclusive and Culturally Responsive Practices have been embedded within each chapter of the book. Teachers must consider providing fair and equitable education to their most vulnerable students (Stansberry Brusnahan et al., 2023). Verbal immediacy is your communication with your students, and the power that each interaction must build a connection. Your words and actions can break that trust. Use friendly and open language and call students by their preferred name. Harkins Monaco and colleagues (2024) explain that effective teachers need to "lean in" to address issues of unfair treatment because when you stand up for students, it shows you can be trusted. If you used a term or phrase that offended a student, you should immediately address the student individually. If the student wishes, you should apologize to the entire group. Building relationships with your students is woven throughout Part II. You need to take time over the next few weeks to learn more about your students and recognize the key elements that make them an individual in your classroom.

© iStock.com/Rudzhan Nagiev.

Inclusive and Culturally Responsive Practices.

Understand that individuals can unintentionally adopt societal biases that can shape the nature of their interactions with groups and individuals. It is your job to engage in critical conversations to be aware of conscious/unconscious biases, stereotypes, and prejudice. Everyone has bias; as a teacher, it is your job to recognize your bias and consciously make efforts to make your classroom equitable for all students and colleagues.

Organization

Most of the time that you have been in the classroom, you have probably followed the teacher's routines. They had their desks aligned and rules posted somewhere in the room. You had no say in the rules unless you started with your teacher at the beginning of their school year. Nor did you see the hours spent building those rules, expectations, routines, and classroom layout. Functional classroom routines are critical for positive student behavior (Ennis et al., 2020). Classroom layout and space for materials are also key elements for students to understand their place and where to go when they need something. Students need a routine to know what you expect of them each day. Chapter 8 outlines tools and materials to help you organize your classroom and your day. There are even considerations for when things do not go as planned.

Rule Reminders and Clear Expectations

Though your mentor teacher taught the rules at the beginning of the year, students still need reminders, especially at the start of the week, after long breaks, and during transitions. You have the advantage of being new to the classroom so that you can play off your reminders as questions. For example, "What should you do when you finish with the questions? Just double-checking. So you should not talk to your peers when you finish your work?" Questioning is a nice way to approach rule reminders, as though the students are reviewing the details for you. Another benefit of being another adult in the classroom is that it is okay to give your expectations when you are in front of the room. Now, you do not want to go against your mentor teacher's rules, but you can enhance or add some rules that suit your needs while you are teaching. In Chapter 8, you will learn ways to have clear expectations and reminders for your students.

Inclusive and Culturally Responsive Practices.

You cannot expect students to come into your classroom knowing the rules and expectations. Some students struggle with focusing, and others may have different structures in their home lives. For example, listening to adults may not be the norm. Be clear and let your students know what you are looking for with each lesson and transition. You can fade these directions as you see students following expectations before you ask.

Provide Behavior-Specific Praise

In Chapter 8, you will learn more about the importance of behavior-specific praise and catching students doing good. Specific praise is especially important for students who have difficulty following the rules. They are used to getting called out and corrected for what they are doing wrong. The longer a student's inappropriate behavior has been effective in the school setting, the more time it will take to build an appropriate replacement behavior (Mace et al., 2010). Students with a history of challenging the rules are twice as likely to get punished as the other students acting out in the same manner. It is a loop. Teachers often get caught in a cycle of correcting the same students but overlooking others. I have a trick for this. Identify students whom the teachers talk about in the faculty room. Catch them doing something good. One or two students have difficulty meeting your classroom behavioral and/or academic expectations. Though there are not many, it makes a difference when you are implementing your lessons. You need to focus on these students and give them specific praise. Call home to these parents and start your relationship with positive communication. Chapter 7 will outline how to build positive relationships with students, and Chapter 10 will highlight what to do when you have students who have difficulty following your expectations.

Opportunities to Respond and Student Engagement

Have you recently planned hours on a lesson, and to put it simply, it flopped? You focused so much on what you would do, how much time everything would take, and what questions you would ask. But you forgot about the most important part—who are your students? What do they already know? How will I keep them engaged? When you plan a lesson and your materials, you must also consider how you will keep all students involved in your lesson during assessment. The following chapters outline multiple ways in which you can keep students engaged during instruction. The great thing about these examples is that you can also check for understanding while the students are answering at the same time. Engaging students during your lesson is one easy way to avoid off-task behavior (Cents-Boonstra, 2020). You can use these approaches to replace calling on one student at a time.

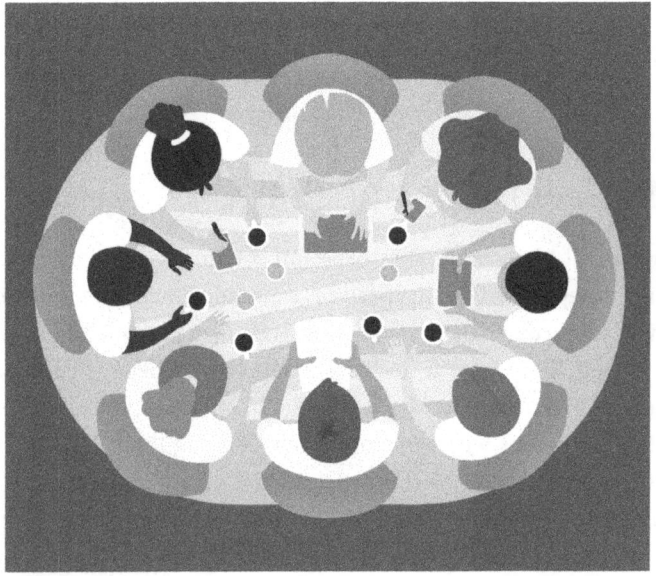

© iStock.com/Semih Akgul.

Clear Structure for Behavior Challenges

Not all students will follow the rules. Some students have learned to challenge the rules. A student may have a skill deficit or have always avoided the desired behavior. The older the student is, the more time they have had to hone their behaviors to work in their favor. Meaning reinforcements shape students' behaviors. For example, if Charlie makes jokes in class to get students to laugh, he will continue to call out to get this attention. If Helena runs out of the classroom during review work and is then sent to the principal's office, she may continue to run out of the school to avoid work. In both examples, we have students who are not going to change. You, the teacher, need to change the response, which will then get the student to change their behavior. This part has more examples of setting up your classroom for success and focusing on shaping skills for students who need to work on following your expectations.

Even if you are starting in the middle of the school year with your students, this does not mean you cannot instill your philosophy of teaching in the classroom. Think about having multiple adult role models in your household. There are instances where you knew when to ask Dad for permission to do something versus defaulting to a grandparent to say it was okay. Despite what many believe, students are resilient and will learn your rules and boundaries quickly. You need to be firm and consistent. Consistency may not sound fun, but failing to enforce the rules confuses students, and they will lose your trust. Say what you mean and mean what you say. This sounds very stern and negative. Do not worry; you will focus on catching students doing what they are supposed to do. Your first step is to give students an abundance of specific praise when they meet your expectations, which prevents you from always making corrections.

Inclusive and Culturally Responsive Practices.
Consider using participation sticks when randomly calling on individual students to answer questions. When you ask questions in the classroom, teachers typically call on students to raise their hands. However, to check the understanding of all students of all abilities, it is important to call on a variety of students, and perhaps students who are not used to speaking up based on their family background.

Video Self-Reflection

You may not know how to improve your results from your CMOT pre-assessment, but that is okay. You may not understand ways to increase student responses or how to present your objectives engagingly. That is okay. This part will highlight and describe these skills and provide examples. In Part II, the chapters will help you learn more about building classroom routines, having clear expectations with your students, and creating an engaging classroom. You can add your ideas and think about ways to incorporate these skills into your practice. Remember, the theme of this book is making progress. Another skill you will work on is self-reflection. Have you ever observed yourself in a video recording? I encourage you to try. Sometimes you are going to be your own best teacher. Video self-reflection is a great tool for teacher candidates to use to build on their professional development (Walker et al, 2023).

As another form of introduction to this part, you are going to learn how to observe yourself and work on finding ways to improve your skills. On the next page is a "Reflection Matrix" to help you observe yourself teaching, and then complete the Matrix to "describe" what you did, "analyze" why you made that choice, "judge" how it went, and "apply" insights for future teaching (Nagro, 2020). This matrix will focus on the skills highlighted in the CMOT. You can also add additional skills that perhaps your mentor or supervisor mentioned in an observation.

Your first step will be to record yourself. Do not include students in your video. You can set up your computer and just record yourself teaching 20 minutes of a lesson. You will get enough data from this amount of time. If you cannot record yourself, then ask your mentor teacher or a peer to record you. Next, just watch the lesson and take some casual notes, "Ugh, why did I wear that?" or "My voice is too soft," and whatever else your brain might be telling you. After that, it is time to complete the matrix below. Use the second observation to focus on the actual data. Perhaps you only want to focus on specific praise and whole group opportunities to respond. You can make tally marks to show how many times you completed each skill to establish a baseline. After you observe the lesson, you will complete the matrix for the skills you observed. Below is a sample of the matrix from Nagro and colleagues (2022). Quentin completed this chart after his observation. Review the brief statements that Quentin uses to describe, analyze, and judge the decisions in his lesson. In the apply column, make note of the changes and connections that he will make for his next lesson based on the skills taught in this book. Additionally, Quentin did get professional development from his mentor teacher and university supervisor. He is learning how to take the feedback and apply it to his next lesson.

© iStock.com/danijelala.

Assessing Your Classroom Management

Think About It.

Name _____ Quentin _____ Sample _____ Date _____ 01/22/2026 _____

Focus Items	**Describe** what happened by detailing the specific teaching choice you made	**Analyze** by explaining the reasons why you made the teaching choice	**Judge** the success of your specific decision by noticing the effect that decision had on a portion of or the lesson overall	**Apply** insight from this review to create a plan for extending effective or changing ineffective practices in future lessons
Taught and followed predictable routines.	Steps for the lab were posted on the board.	I could highlight the steps to tell students what part of the lab they should be on.	This helped students stay on task. All students were finished with 3 minutes to go.	As recommended in Ch. 8, I will use a timer to give students a better sense of timing.
Taught, reviewed, posted, or monitored a few positively stated expectations.	I gave 3 clear expectations of behaviors while in the lab.	I did keep my expectations positive by focusing on what I wanted the students to do.	There was 1 instance where a student needed close proximity and redirection.	Next lab, I will use a precorrection with Jeffe as outlined in Ch. 10.
Provided students with whole group opportunities to respond	I did not check for understanding before we left.	I felt rushed and did not have enough time to complete the exit slips.	I now need to wait until tomorrow to get a sense of students' understanding of the experiment.	I could have had students turn and talk as modeled in Ch. 9.
Provided students with specific academic and behavioral praise.	I focused mostly on behavior praise. I did not acknowledge many appropriate academic responses.	I was nervous about students breaking materials in the lab, so I was more worried about behaviors vs. the students learning from the experiment.	I did a great job of keeping students on task. Again, I do not know what the students learned from the experiment.	As recommended by my mentor, I will highlight 3 key questions to ask students during the lab to check for understanding. I will then follow up with specific praise.
Provided the Least Restrictive Procedure for behavior correction.	I called out Amelia when I thought she was playing with the lab materials.	I chose to leave the lab area to get more papers. I was not in the lab area, and I made an assumption.	Next time, I need to monitor students in closer proximity. My correction led to mistrust of a student.	I will ask another student to get materials so I can stay in the lab. I will address behaviors with a one-on-one approach. [University Supervisor recommendation]

Chart Cited in Nagro, S. A. (2022). Three Phases of Video-Based Reflection Activities to Transition Teacher Candidates from Understanding to Examining Practice. *Journal of Special Education Preparation*, *2*(1), 28–37. The focus items for this reflection matrix were adapted from Archer and Hughes, 2011.

Now it is your turn. You can use this tool to observe the skills you will work on throughout this part. Below is a blank matrix for you to complete independently, with blank spaces for you to complete your focus items. As you observe yourself, it is just as essential to go beyond describing what happened in your lesson, talk more about your teacher's decision-making, judge how you think it went (do you have evidence to support this), and think about the next steps. This is where you can collaborate with your mentor or continue reading the next few chapters to learn how to improve these skills. Please reflect and then continue reading to consider goals you can make for yourself once you complete the classroom management pre-assessment. Remember, you are looking for improvements, and one way to do this is to set target goals and measure progress.

Add Your Points.

Name _____ Date _____

Focus Items	**Describe** what happened by detailing the specific teaching choice you made	**Analyze** by explaining the reasons why you made the teaching choice	**Judge** the success of your specific decision by noticing the effect that decision had on a portion of or the lesson overall	**Apply** insight from this review to create a plan for extending effective or changing ineffective practices in future lessons

Chart Cited in Nagro, S. A. (2022). Three Phases of Video-Based Reflection Activities to Transition Teacher Candidates from Understanding to Examining Practice. *Journal of Special Education Preparation*, 2(1), 28–37. The focus items for this reflection matrix were adapted from Archer and Hughes, 2011.

Classroom Management Goals

How is your classroom management? Did you make any instant changes after you reflected on your assessment? If so, lovely. If this is good enough for you, move on to the next topic, and know that you can always jump back here and set clear goals. However, you could also look at completing the assessment again after you have completed it to improve your classroom management score. This is up to you to decide.

Are you interested in setting a goal for classroom management? What is working for you, and what needs to change? Remember that you are working on classroom management strategies to help build connections with your students and make a more engaging classroom. Only you can convince yourself that it is worth doing. Furthermore, it takes time. What is a realistic goal of improvement that you are looking for when you complete this part and complete another observation? Below is Simone's sample goal. This is up to you. Would you like to target one small area to focus on as you read through the following four chapters? Or you can just read through the chapters and make goals as you go along. View Simone's goal to see a sample of how you can turn your CMOT into a goal for progress.

Simone Can See Clear Expectations

After reading section 2 of her CMOT, Simone learned that she has difficulty giving clear expectations within her lessons. She can focus on the positive aspects of monitoring her students when they are working, but this approach is not the most efficient use of time because she states her expectations as she goes around the room. After reviewing her pre-assessment data, she determined that she would like to improve from two out of six yes marks to four out of six yes marks in section 2. Simone is confident that after reviewing evidence-based strategies to be more explicit, she will meet her goal when assessed again. You can write your goals using the blank SMART goal charts at the end of Part II.

© iStock.com/AnnaSivak.

Simone's Chart

Making SMART Goals Baseline Data	
CMOT Checklist Periodically, check for evidence of the following effective classroom management practices.	
Check for Evidence of Classroom Structure and Expectations	
1. The educator posted a schedule for the day and/or class activity.	Yes / <u>No</u>
2. The educator posted 3–5 positively stated behavioral expectations in the classroom.	Yes / <u>No</u>
3. The physical arrangement of the room was appropriate for the activity.	<u>Yes</u> / No
4. The educator developed routines for the day and/or class activity.	<u>Yes</u> / No
5. The educator taught and prompted 3–5 positively stated behavioral expectations.	Yes / <u>No</u>
6. The educator selected and implemented additional consequence strategies, if appropriate, to support student behavior.	Yes / <u>No</u>

Specific: What is the **Target Behavior**?	
Simone will increase the number of positively stated expectations.	
With what **materials or conditions**?	
Given a 30-minute observation, Simone will have 4 "yes" components as assessed by the same observer (mentor teacher).	
Measurable: How well must the skill be performed? (Criteria)	**Achievable:** What modifications or accommodations are needed for success? Making the time?
Simone must have 4 areas of defining, teaching, and posting the expectations.	Complete Chapters in Part. Observe 2 other teachers with these strengths Make a list of common positive expectations and outline consequences to review at Simone's desk
How will the skill be **measured**? And **how often**?	Any **additional research**? People to talk to?
Mentor teacher will complete the observation form once a month.	Continue reading the chapter.
Relevance: Why is meeting this goal important?	**Timely:** What is considered mastery for this goal? **Timeline:** When would you like to achieve this goal?
Simone needs to state her expectations for her students and give rule reminders to improve classroom management.	2 mentor observations with 4 out of 6 "yes" statements.
What other assessments or data will help assess progress toward the goal?	**What are the next steps in this goal area?**
Observe 20-minute video with chart every other week Tally clear expectations 1/week	Simone will focus on increasing her scores on the positive and proactive section of the observation tool.

 **Chapter Recap.**

Connecting with your students
- Be creative and prioritize their interests

Culture
- Understand what makes each student unique
- Learn their backgrounds

Organization
- Know the rules
- Have clear procedures and routines

Rule reminders and clear expectations
- Be consistent
- Give reminders during transitions

Provide specific behavior praise
- Tell your students what they are doing right

Opportunities to respond and student engagement
- Make sure you check for students' understanding
- Give them extra opportunities to share

Clear structure for behavior challenges
- Follow school procedures
- Make communication with family members

Video self-reflection
- Record and review your lesson
- Describe, Analyze, Judge, Apply

 **Collaborative Thinking.**

Questions to ask your mentors / peers
What are some strengths in your classroom management?
What areas are in progress? and how did you improve them?
What are some ways you get to know your students? Their cultures? Their abilities and needs?

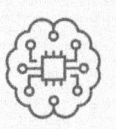

Technology Checkpoints.

Class Dojo: In the classroom, Class Dojo is a classroom management tool that allows the teacher to award points for positive behaviors. Outside of the classroom, Class Dojo allows for parent communication and involvement.

Pickerwheel.com: You can use the Pickerwheel website to assign partners, call on students, give classroom jobs, or review topics. Enter whatever information you need and let the wheel randomly pick!

Curipod.com: tool to develop slideshows, quizzes, and polls for interactive lessons. AI can generate a draft of the lesson.

Dreambox.com: helps teachers to differentiate Math and ELA instruction K-12.

EdWeek.org: Here you will find unbiased news articles and recent happenings in the world of education.

Larryferlazzo.edublogs.org: Larry Ferlazzo offers his "Best of" lists to help you in your education journey. This blog includes a wide range of topics from classroom practices to art and music and ELL.

Ahaprocess.com: This website offers training, tools, and other resources to help you reach all of the students in your classroom, with a focus on those in poverty.

Teacher Decision-Making.

How do you feel about shifting your focus to creating goals for the classroom? Take a minute to reflect on your self-care, are you able to keep up with your goals from Part I? You do not have to make a goal for this chapter. This is only a sample to show how Simone set a goal for her post observation. You can review/analyze the goals from Part I. Identify where you see enough progress so that you can make space for classroom management in the following chapters.

Next Steps.

What is working? . . .

What is not working? . . .

What do I need? . . .

What am I proud of? . . .

What do I need to let go of? . . .

 **Weekly Reflection.**

Use the space below to jot down some notes here to brainstorm some good ideas you have in your free time. Listen to me remind you that you have this, and I believe in you. I am encouraging these minor changes because you are a quality educator, and students need teachers like you in the field for years to come. You got this!

7
Responsibility = Respect

Chapter Outline

Survey Your Students	128
Family Survey	131
Check Your Biases	133
Finding Individuality in Elementary Students	133
Finding Individuality with Middle Level and Secondary Students	135
What do Your Students Value	136
Adding Cultural Considerations to Your Classroom	138
Making Considerations for What Is Happening Outside of Your Classroom	140
Give Students Community	141
Take Opportunities to Participate in Out-of-School Events	142
Responsibility and Respect Goals	143

The CMOT pre-assessment does not focus on building connections with your students. Still, building relationships is the first step to getting your students to appreciate and understand your expectations. Think about your favorite teacher. What made that teacher so special? It was not the rules posted on the wall, but perhaps you recall him correcting a student who made fun of one of your answers in math class. Think about how they made you feel, how they gave feedback, and how they challenged you. The teacher sets the expectations in your classroom that everyone will respect each other. To do this, you need to learn about each student's interests. Building these connections can seem overwhelming if you are in a secondary classroom and see over 100 students each day. Still, there are evidence-based tools for connecting with students that you will read about in this chapter to help speed this process along.

 **Add Your Ideas.**

Think about the class you enjoyed because you remembered the engaging activity you completed. Outline your favorite classes and what made you want to get up and go to class each day.

-
-

Survey Your Students

The first step is to have your students complete one of the following surveys below, based on content or age-appropriate. ChatGPT generated both surveys. I edited them to get to the questions I was most interested in. Feel free to make your survey or add questions relevant to your classroom. It is essential to review any Artificial Intelligence (AI) generated work to make sure all questions and statements are accurate and appropriate. After the students complete the survey, you then apply what you have learned. Did several students share a personal experience that you can connect with one-on-one? A student may play an instrument that you are unfamiliar with. Take the information from these surveys to build your relationships with your students. Some students will naturally gravitate to you because you are new and cool. The younger the students are, the more this is true. But what is most important for you is to dive deeper into the surveys of the students you have not connected with yet. Maybe she is absent each week, and you miss the mark when you call on her in class.

© iStock.com/Iconic Prototype.

Inclusive and Culturally Responsive Practices

The first stage in Cultural Awareness is reflecting on your own cultural lens. Connect your own life experiences in relationships within your school community. Next, understand that you may have unintentionally adopted societal biases that can shape your interactions with others. As you review students' responses, are there any comments that you instinctively cannot connect with or relate to? These are the areas you may need to "lean in" and learn more.

Add Your Ideas

Questions for Elementary Students

1. Preferred name or nickname
2. What's your favorite subject in school, and why?
3. What do you enjoy doing during recess or break time?
4. Do you have a favorite book or story? What is it about?
5. What's something new you've learned recently that you think is really cool?
6. If you could invent something, what would it be and why?

Hobbies and Interests

7. What do you like to do when you're not in school?
8. Do you play any sports or musical instruments?
9. Do you have a favorite game, either a video game or a board game?
10. What's your favorite movie or TV show?
11. Do you like drawing or making crafts? What's the best thing you've made?

Aspirations and Dreams

12. What do you want to be when you grow up?
13. Where would you go if you could visit any place in the world?
14. If you could have any superpower, what would it be and why?

Fun and Imaginative

15. If you were an animal for a day, which one would you be?
16. If you could meet any character from a story or movie, who would it be?
17. If you could eat only one food for a whole week, what would it be?

Reflection and Growth

18. What's something you've worked really hard on and are proud of?
19. What's one thing you think adults could learn from kids?
20. How do you help your friends when they're feeling sad or upset?

 **Add Your Ideas**

Questions for Middle Level and High School Students

Preferred Name_____

Academic Life

1. What's your favorite subject, and what do you like about it?
2. Are there any subjects or topics you find particularly challenging? How can I help you with them?
3. What's one thing you enjoy most about school?
4. What's your preferred way of learning new things (lectures, hands-on activities, group work, etc.)?
5. Do you have any specific academic goals this year?

Personal Interests and Hobbies

6. What do you like to do in your free time?
7. Are you involved in any clubs, sports, or extracurricular activities? What do you enjoy about them?
8. Do you have a favorite book, movie, or TV show? Why is it your favorite?
9. What's a new skill or hobby you've picked up recently?
10. Do you have a role model or someone you look up to? Who is it, and why?

Relationships and School Environment

11. What makes a teacher or class stand out as your favorite?
12. Do you feel comfortable asking questions or seeking help in class? Why or why not?
13. What's the best way for a teacher to support you when you're struggling?
14. Do you feel connected to your peers? What's something teachers could do to help build a positive classroom community?
15. What's something a teacher has done that significantly impacted you?

Aspirations and Goals

16. What are your plans or dreams for the future?
17. What's a career or field you're curious about exploring?
18. If you could learn any topic from this class, what would it be?
19. What motivates you to work hard or try your best?
20. Where do you see yourself in 5 or 10 years?

Fun and Imaginative

21. If you could design your dream school, what would it look like?
22. If you could have any superpower, what would it be and why?
23. What's one thing you wish adults understood better about being a teenager today?
24. If you could instantly master any skill or subject, what would it be?
25. If you could go back in time or visit the future, which would you choose and why?

Reflection

26. What's something you've achieved recently that you're proud of?
27. What's one thing you think you could improve on, and how can I support you?
28. How do you handle stress or challenging situations?
29. What's a lesson you've learned from a past mistake?
30. What's one piece of advice you would give to younger students?

Inclusive and Culturally Responsive Practices.

Reflect on how to meet the needs of your students. Integrate various perspectives into your lessons and classroom environment that capitalize on learners' experiences, identities, and heritage.

Family Survey

I require my students in "Introduction to Special Education" to interview the parent of a child with a disability using the survey questions below. The following questions come from the "McGill Action Planning System" MAPS (O'Rourke & Beaudoin, 1998). These are personalized questions for teachers and staff to learn more about a student and the family's goals for their child. Suppose you have a "hard-to-reach" student or students going through the transition process with their Individualized Education Plan (IEP). In that case, you can ask these questions to get to know your students better and learn more about the family's vision for the student. The student does not have to be in special education for you to ask these valuable questions to the family.

MAPS Interview For Families

Understanding the Student

1. Can you tell me about your child? What are some of their strengths and talents?
2. What are your child's favorite activities or interests? What excites them most?
3. How does your child typically approach challenges or new experiences?

Family's Perspective on School and Learning

4. What does your child enjoy most about school?
5. Are there any specific subjects or activities where your child excels?
6. What areas of learning or school life do you think are most challenging for your child?
7. How does your child feel about their teachers and peers? Do they share positive experiences?

Hopes and Aspirations

8. What are your hopes and dreams for your child's future?
9. What skills or qualities do you want your child to develop as they grow?
10. What would it be if you could change one thing about your child's school experience?

Home and School Partnership

11. What role do you see yourself playing in your child's education?
12. How do you currently support your child's learning at home?
13. Are there any specific ways the school could work better with your family to support your child?

Challenges and Support Needs

14. What are some barriers your child has faced at school or in learning?
15. Are there any resources, tools, or strategies that have worked well in supporting your child?
16. What support do you feel your family needs to help your child succeed?

Social and Emotional Well-Being

17. How does your child typically interact with their peers? Do they have close friends?
18. Are there any social situations your child finds particularly difficult?
19. What strategies work best to help your child manage stress or emotions?

Vision for the Future

20. What kind of person do you envision your child becoming as they grow?
21. If you could imagine your child thriving five years from now, what would that look like?
22. What do you think are the most important steps to help your child achieve their potential?

Feedback and Recommendations

23. How do you feel about the school's current approach to supporting your child?
24. What do you think the school should focus on to help your child thrive?
25. Is there anything else you'd like to share about your child or their education that we haven't discussed?

Inclusive and Culturally Responsive Practices.

Recognize that every family/caregiver, regardless of their differences, wants the best for their children, and oftentimes they are doing the best they can with the resources they have. Be sensitive to this balance of helping students and knowing the difference if you are overstepping. Make sure that you learn the local resources and community members who can provide support to students and their families. View engagement and family insight as a priority.

Think About It.

What did you learn more about in the survey with your students? Focus on the students who may not stand out or participate as much. Are there similarities you can associate with? Are there new topics you can learn based on their background?

?

?

?

Check Your Biases

Biases are preconceived notions that you have about a person or group based on their culture, beliefs, body type, and so on. You unconsciously have blind spots based on your background and experiences. You need to check those biases. Yes, we all have them, and as teachers, you are going to pay the most attention to the students who come to class, participate, and do well academically. You could also connect with the students in your Reading Competition Team or share a similar interest in music. These are easy connections because you already have similar interests. You need to dig deeper with the students who have hobbies or cultural practices that are unfamiliar to you. It is easy to gravitate to people with similar interests. You need to reflect on your natural predisposition toward your students. Biases are a part of the natural human experience. You may have a certain bias toward a person or particular culture. You may also respond differently to a student based on your lack of exposure to their cultural norms. It is your job to check your biases.

In the next few weeks, I am encouraging you to get outside of your comfort zone and get to know the quieter students in your class. Start up a conversation with the student who intimidates you. Perhaps he calls out and wants to talk about his obsession with "Magic Cards." When students shed light on their interests, you must find common ground and build on their familiar background. You can do this through examples in class, pictures, or books that you have represented in your room. The following chapters will highlight ways you can use these surveys to learn more about your students and incorporate their interests into your lessons.

Think About It.

What are your biases? Do you have students you do not connect with easily? What are some ways you can learn more about their interests?
?
?
?

Finding Individuality in Elementary Students

Surveying your students will look different based on their age and ability. One way to learn more about your students is to focus on learning more about one or two of your students each week. You can have them share pictures or talk about items that are important to them. In elementary school, you could have a "Star Student." It may be a good idea to ask a family member to help complete the form. If you have a hard-to-reach family, you

© iStock.com/Kudryavtsev Pavel.

could always ask a school-aged family member to fill in some survey questions at the end of the school day. In my career as a high school teacher, cousins and siblings across grade levels often could have a positive impact on each other. Have your students complete this questionnaire, and then you can call students throughout each week to present their survey details. You can even give the student special privileges that day. Some students may want to perform their unique talents or share a special artifact from home.

 **Add Your Ideas**
Star Student Questionnaire

Basic Information

1. What is your name?
2. How old are you, and what grade are you in?
3. What is your favorite color?
4. Do you have any siblings or pets? If so, what are their names?

Hobbies and Interests

5. What do you like to do for fun?
6. Do you like to draw, write, or make crafts? If yes, what's your favorite thing to create?
7. What kind of music do you like to listen to?

School Life

8. What do you enjoy most about being in school?
9. What's something you've learned recently that you think is really cool?

Fun Favorites

10. If you could eat only one food for the rest of your life, what would it be?
11. Do you have a favorite superhero, cartoon character, or fictional character?

Imagination and Aspirations

12. If you could have any superpower, what would it be? Why?
13. If you could visit any place in the world, where would you go?

Personal Reflection

14. What's something you're really good at?
15. What makes you feel happy or proud of yourself?

Fun and Random

16. If you were an animal, which one would you be? Why?
17. What's one secret talent or fun fact about you?

Responsibility = Respect   135

© iStock.com/Rudzhan Nagiev.

Finding Individuality with Middle Level and Secondary Students

With older students, you can change the name of this activity to Very Important Person or Classroom Executive Officer. Make this a fun theme for you to get to know your students. You can have all students fill out your forms at the beginning of your class. You can model an example by sharing details about yourself. With older students, it is essential to recognize that they may not want to share all of these questions or details with the class. But they may feel comfortable opening up to you. Prepare with your students and ask them to share a few of these topics with the class.

 **Add Your Ideas**

Older Student Questionnaire

I like to use this questionnaire to get to know my students better; however, this survey is confidential. Though I love to share your interests in my lessons I can only share these facts as they only relate to you with your permission.

Personal Information

1. What is your name, age, and grade?
2. What are three words that best describe you?
3. What's something about you that makes you unique?

School Achievements

4. What is your favorite subject or class in school? Why?
5. Have you received any awards, honors, or recognition for your academics or extracurricular activities? If so, what are they?
6. What is a school project or assignment you're most proud of? Why?
7. How do you contribute to your school's culture or community? (e.g., leadership roles, clubs, mentoring, volunteering)

Extracurricular Activities

8. Are you involved in any sports, clubs, or activities outside of school? What do you enjoy about them?
9. Do you have a leadership role in any of these activities? If so, what is it?

Personal Growth

11. What motivates you to work hard or give your best effort?
12. What's a challenge you've overcome, and what did you learn from it?
13. What's a personal quality or skill you've worked on improving recently?
14. How do you handle stress or balance your responsibilities?

Community and Service

15. Have you volunteered or contributed to your community in any way? If so, what did you do?
16. Why do you think giving back to your community is important?

Aspirations and Goals

17. What are your goals for the next year, both academically and personally?
18. What are your long-term dreams or career aspirations?
19. If you could make one change in the world, what would it be?

Recognition of Strengths

20. What do you think is your greatest strength?
21. What are three achievements you're most proud of?
22. If your teachers or friends were to describe you, what would they say?

Fun and Personality

23. What's your favorite hobby or way to relax?
24. What's a fun fact about you that most people don't know?
25. What's your favorite inspirational quote or piece of advice you've received?

What Do Your Students Value

After completing your interview, it is time to apply these details to your lessons. Scan through all the information, but focus primarily on the students you do not know. You could start by highlighting the students you do not know as well. Make key notes about the students and their interests. Do they have a part of school that they enjoy? If the students are involved in extracurricular activities, take some time to attend these events. This notion will go a long way for some students who may not typically have an audience for their interests. You can use the additional responses to build a relationship with your students. For example, you can research more about their hobbies or include examples of their interests with the topics you discuss in class. If you have journaling in your class, you can use this as a channel to communicate more with your students. Below are some examples of methods in which you can allow students to express their likes and interests. Add some of your ideas below.

© iStock.com/forest_strider.

 **Add your Ideas.**
Connecting with students in your class

Artwork
Books from different backgrounds (refer to tech resources)
Journaling
Sports
Music
Storytelling
Math problems with cultural names and experiences

-
-

Find ways to include their interests in your class time. Remember to plug your students' interests into your lesson plans to incorporate their favorite animal into word problems. You could add a place a student used to live to your geography lesson. Use the pictures students share in your presentations. When you have downtime, play a student's favorite genre of music. Include their hobbies or interests in your class rewards. If a student has a hidden talent, use some downtime to have him teach you the skill. Take time to learn more about your students and build connections with them when they do not connect with other teachers in the school. This is a great way to make connections so that your students can then invest more time in your lessons. When you give respect, you get respect. You need to remember that not all students have had a positive school experience. Though you are not to blame, you may have to undo the students' natural reactions they have to adult figures in the school.

Inclusive and Culturally Responsive Practices.

Recognize and reflect on diversity as an asset to the entire learning community. Assist learners in valuing their own and others' cultures and help them develop a sense of responsibility for recognizing, responding to, and addressing bias, discrimination, injustice, and bullying.

Adding Cultural Considerations to Your Classroom

Developing cultural competence involves reflecting on your routines and beliefs while building an understanding of others around you. You may have noticed that culturally relevant and inclusive practices have been interwoven into each chapter because you need to be thinking about all students and how new skills apply to students with different backgrounds and beliefs. Equal education is a vehicle of community survival and cultural revitalization, particularly for historically marginalized populations (Paris & Alim, 2017). In this section, take some time to develop your cultural competencies. Learn more about the traditions of your students and pronounce their names correctly, and call on them by their preferred names. Build a classroom of rich storytelling to enhance other cultural beliefs beyond your own. By learning more about your students' lives outside of the school, you can build more connections inside the classroom. Learn the skills and qualities that students and their families value beyond the classroom. Learn more about what each student brings to your classroom (Boveda & Aronson, 2019). Banks (2021) highlights his four levels of ethnic content integration that may be useful in integrating multicultural content into the school curriculum. Outline the four levels of integrating other cultural themes into your curriculum. To help your students build a deeper understanding of the world around them, provide students with opportunities for level 4 social action experiences to help them relate to situations from other perspectives.

 **Add your Ideas.**

Four Levels of Ethnic Content Integration

	Elementary Examples	Middle/High School Examples
Level 1 Contributions characterized by a focus on heroes, holidays, and discrete cultural elements	Celebrating Lunar New Year by reading a book about Chinese traditions and making paper lanterns. Teaching about Martin Luther King Jr. during Black History Month.	Poster project on Hispanic Heritage Month featuring biographies of Latinx leaders.
Level 2 Additive accomplished by the addition of a book, a unit, or a course to the curriculum without altering its overall structure	During a unit on pioneers, include the story of Harriet Tubman and the Underground Railroad. Reading a Native American folktale during a traditional fairy tale unit.	While studying American westward expansion, add lessons about the impact on Indigenous peoples.
Level 3 Transformative enables students to view concepts, issues, events, and themes from the perspectives of diverse ethnic and cultural groups by altering the curriculum's structure; and, ensuring that multiple voices and experiences are included	In a unit on communities, include different cultural definitions of family and roles (e.g., extended family structures in African, Latinx, or Indigenous cultures).	In a history unit on colonization, analyze events from both European settlers' and Indigenous peoples' perspectives. Students read diverse authors and discuss themes of identity and belonging.
Level 4 Social Action encourages students to make decisions based on important social issues and to take action to discover solutions by themselves	Kindness campaigns Student-led advocacy project	Students design a campaign to address inequities for food access in their community. Partnering with local organizations to support refugee or immigrant families.
Adapted from: Banks, J. A. (2021). Transforming Multicultural Education Policy and Practice: Expanding Educational Opportunity. Multicultural Education Series. Teachers College Press.		

Inclusive and Culturally Responsive Practices

Identify literature and professional learning opportunities to understand the biases that can result in disadvantaged learners, educators, educational leaders, and families. Identify and make efforts to remove bias in teaching materials, assignments, curriculum, and other educational services.

Making Considerations for What Is Happening Outside of Your Classroom

Another concept that you need to consider is that you may have students with more significant priorities than school. I was surprised to learn the expectations of my high school students. I had a student who was often absent because he had to watch his baby sister when she was unable to attend daycare. Another student missed because she had to take her mother to cancer treatment. Learning about a student's family responsibilities outside of school is essential. Some students work a job in the evenings to help pay the bills. By learning more about what your students' lives look like outside of school, you can learn how to meet your students' needs in your classroom (Ryan & Deci, 2020). If your students work after school, find opportunities to limit homework and help them complete their work during the school day. Make sure they are making good use of their downtime during school. If you have families with food insecurities, be sure to help them with the resources found in your community.

Because of added pressures outside of school and with extracurricular activities, remember that any student's behavior is not about you (Butler & Monda-Amaya, 2016). Undesired student behavior is challenging not to take personally, but students often come to school with an invisible backpack of responsibilities and expectations highlighted above. So if you question why a student did not complete her homework, her frustration may not be with you; it could be about the lousy basketball practice she had last night, where nobody passed her the ball, and she turned her ankle doing a lay-up, so she may not be able to play in the big game on Friday. Be sure to greet your students at the door with a positive and ready-to-go energy. Your first interaction with your students should be positive. Positive engagement should start in the hallway by meeting students with a high five or a fist bump. Make time for this meaningful interaction.

Responsibility = Respect 141

© iStock.com/Nataliia Nesterenko.

Inclusive and Culturally Responsive Practices

When addressing student behavior or private topics, be sure to address students one-on-one. Even when talking about behavior or consequences, it is vital to give the student individual attention and not draw additional peer attention. For example, Sam, I need your help. I have a special lesson today, and I really need you to raise your hand when you have a question. This is a good example of a conversation that should be held one-on-one.

Give Students Community

When you build a sense of community and ownership in your classroom, students will benefit from a sense of belonging and be less likely to exhibit disruptive behavior and disrespect their peers (Dumbaugh & Haunsperger, 2022). For example, when students have classroom responsibilities, they will put more care into representing the classroom. So, if Maelyn must clean the floor at the end of the day, she will be less likely to throw trash on the floor, and she may encourage her peers to keep the floors clean during lab work too. Some students build emotional connections to animals. By having a class pet, students are more likely to meet your expectations, so that they can spend time with the pet. Students may also be motivated to keep a quieter classroom environment to have a calm setting for the pet.

Some more active students may need more movement around the room. By learning about their gifts and talents, you can find ways to use their skills to help you in the classroom. People are inclined to help. Explain to your students that you need their help. Even when you are going to teach a lesson, you can explain one-on-one with your talkative students, sharing, "I need to give several ideas during this short amount of time, so I need

© iStock.com/Rudzhan Nagiev.

your help by raising your hand when you have a question." Students who may need breaks can pass out materials or deliver materials to another teacher down the hall. Give clear expectations: "I need you to take these handouts to Mr. Baran, then grab a drink and come right back to class." You are giving the student a break without calling out that they need a break.

Inclusive and Culturally Responsive Practices

Create learning communities and spaces that are inclusive and free of negative comments or actions that subtly and often unconsciously or unintentionally express a prejudiced attitude. Engage in affirming and reflexive practices that validate others

Take Opportunities to Participate in Out-of-School Events

Observe students participating in their extracurricular activities. An everyday activity can be going to their sporting event because they talk about the practice during class, or always wearing a jersey. But you may have to do a little investigative work if they are artists. They could have their artwork in the local craft showcase. You can use the inventories and surveys to get ideas, but you will also need to give students time to talk about these events. Announce to your students that you would love to see their activities, and to please share if there is something you can attend. It means so much when you make additional connections to your students, especially to those who may not get as much academic praise or support from their family members at home. Try to prioritize the students who may not have observers in their activities.

Think About It

What are some after-school or community events you can participate in after school? You have a busy schedule, so prioritize and pencil in the dates for these events. Which events would allow you to see several students in one activity?
?
?
?

Responsibility and Respect Goals

How are you making connections with your students? Did you make any instant changes that have improved the relationships you have with your students? If this is your case, beautiful. Schedule yourself for the next chapter (Routines and Time on Task), and know that you can always return to this section and set clear goals for yourself. That is fine if you are not ready to commit to writing and collecting data on that goal. Remember, when you have a new student who has joined your class or another student has gone silent, please revisit Chapter 7 for some ways to connect with your students.

Does this topic spark your interest? What do you like about your relationships with your students, and what needs to improve? Remember, you decrease undesired behaviors in your classroom when students feel connected to you and have responsibilities. The relationships you build with your students may not change in a week. So, do not get frustrated if things do not change immediately. Relationships take time, especially when students have a history of negative relationships with adults in the school. Prepare yourself to be consistent and think about manageable adjustments you can make for the next 3 months. After you review the student teachers' goals for inspiration, outline your own classroom management goals in the blank SMART charts at the end of Chapter 10.

Inclusive and Culturally Responsive Practices.

In some familial formats, there is a multigenerational hierarchy of authority. Consider how students refer to family members beyond their parents. In some family structures, children are encouraged to question authority figures, whereas in other cultures, educators are highly revered and students will not question adults. It is essential to understand this dynamic with your students. This will play a significant role in how classroom management practices and family communications are handled.

Kaycee Is Adding After-School Activities

After completing the classroom survey, Kaycee has a range of students involved in after-school activities beyond her spectrum of theater and reading competitions. Several of these students are shy and withdrawn and dislike participating in class activities. Kaycee is going to review the surveys and interviews to learn more about the activities the students participate in after-school hours. Kaycee will then attend more of these after-school and weekend activities. She recognizes that some of her 20 students are in the same activities, so there will be some overlap.

Kaycee's Chart

Making SMART Goals	
Baseline Data After 4 weeks in the classroom, Kaycee has never attended an after-school activity beyond the school play and reading competition.	
Specific: What is the Target Behavior?	
Kaycee will average attending the events of 3 students each week.	
With what **materials or conditions**?	
Given a 7-day schedule, Kaycee will attend the events of between 2 and 4 students.	
Measurable: How well must the skill be performed? (Criteria)	**Achievable:** What modifications or accommodations are needed for success? Making the time?
2–4 student events within 7 days.	Kaycee will make a calendar of students' schedules. She will focus on the "hard-to-reach" students first. She will also go to events that have multiple students participating.
How will the skill be **measured**? And **how often**?	Any **additional research**? People to talk to?
Kaycee will calculate her events on her calendar at the end of each week.	Check with parents and coaches/teachers regarding the schedules.
Relevance: Why is meeting this goal important?	**Timely:** What is considered mastery for this goal? **Timeline:** When would you like to achieve this goal?
Kaycee needs to make more connections with my students and their families outside of school.	When Kaycee attended 1 event for each of the 15 students, who were not affiliated with the play or reading competition. Kaycee would like to finish this goal by the end of her placement.
What other assessments or data will help assess progress toward the goal?	What are the next steps in this goal area?
Kaycee will print off a roster and cross off each time she attends an event.	Kaycee will incorporate the students' interests into the lessons.

Quentin's Principal Investigators (PI)

To work on classroom management and build relationships with his students, Quentin has students present more about themselves through a Student Questionnaire Sheet he adapted from this chapter. Quentin has an average of 25 students in his classes and will have PI presentations every other day. First, he will start by having all students in his classes complete PI Sheets. The student teacher will review the sheets and have students discuss the topics they wish to discuss with the class. As recommended, he is focusing on the students he does not know well at first and would like to learn more about them in the early weeks. He will have this goal completed in 10 weeks.

Quentin's Chart

Making SMART Goals	
Baseline Data Currently, Quentin has 2 to 3 students in each class who naturally get his attention and offer to help out and participate in class.	
Specific: What is the Target Behavior?	
Every 2 days, Quentin will rotate a new PI student who will present several facts from their "Principal Investigator Sheet" and be the class helper as needed.	
With what **materials or conditions**?	
Every 2 school days, a new student will be assigned as the student PI.	
Measurable: How well must the skill be performed? (Criteria)	**Achievable:** What modifications or accommodations are needed for success? Making the time?
Students will present 3 points about themselves at the end of the first day. Students will be given at least 1 task to help the teacher.	Display the student PI for each class. Provide time at the end of the class. Have 1 task prepared each day for the student to help
How will the skill be **measured?** And **How often**?	Any additional **research**? People to talk to?
Quentin will have a calendar and a chart to check off the student presentation and the tasks to complete each day.	Quentin will take some notes so that he can incorporate students' interests into his lessons.
Relevance: Why is meeting this goal important?	**Timely:** What is considered mastery for this goal? **Timeline:** When would you like to achieve this goal?
Quentin needs to get to know my students better, and he wants students to learn more about each other.	By keeping a 2-day rotation, this task will be completed after 10 weeks of student teaching. Quentin would like to complete this goal by the end of student teaching.
What other assessments or data will help assess progress toward the goal?	What are the next steps in this goal area?
Quentin will print off a roster and cross off each time he has students present in the classroom.	Quentin will incorporate the students' interests into the lessons.

Chapter Recap.

Survey your students
- Use surveys to get your students' interests
- Learn more about cultural backgrounds

Family survey
- Ask your parents big-picture questions about their students
- Learn more about family values, traditions, and strengths
- MAPs—dreams and nightmares

Check your bias
- Identify your natural interests and areas that you question

Finding individuality in your students at every level

Adding cultural considerations to your classroom
- This should be an expectation in all classrooms
- Use AI to incorporate traditions into lessons

Making considerations for what is happening outside of your classroom
- Go to school events
- Recognize the responsibilities your students have at home

Give students community
- Take ownership in the classroom, and responsibility among their peers

 **Collaborative Thinking.**

Questions to ask your mentors/peers
What are some ways you learn more about your students?
How have you checked your biases to grow in relationships with your students?
How do you connect with students who have difficulty in your classes?
What resources and materials do you use to connect with students from different cultural backgrounds?
What resources do you use for students with more responsibilities outside of school?

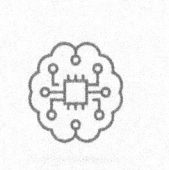

Technology Checkpoints.

AI Surveys: Using AI, you can generate surveys for students on any topic. The results can help you connect and build relationships with your students.

Timetoast.com: Students can use this site to create a timeline of their history. Teachers can learn more about key moments in students' lives.

Nationalequityproject.org: This nonprofit provides training and professional development, along with other resources, to help educators and districts better serve students with multicultural backgrounds.

Understood.org: A nonprofit website that has free resources and information on ADHD, dyslexia, dyscalculia, language disorders, and written expression disorder. There are topics ranging from school support, parenting children with these learning needs, and signs to watch for.

Panoramaed.com: SEL lessons to improve school climate. Includes check-ins, assessments, interventions, and feedback surveys.

BlackonBlackEducation.com: This website focuses on the involvement of students in leading their education. One item offered on this website is a journal for the student and teacher that has guided prompts and exercises to help build classroom community.

Nea.org NEA is an organization fighting for public education excellence. You can find topics for public school teachers and students as well as fair workplace rights.

courageousconvesation.com: Practical tools and protocols to forge a path for equity. There are professional development opportunities.

FacingHistory.org: Focuses on using history lessons to teach students to identify bigotry and hate, you can find lesson plans and topics as well as professional development to help broaden student's thinking.

Learnningforjustice.org: Helping educators teach the hard lessons of history, in an age-appropriate way. Resources include podcasts, read-alongs, lessons, and other strategies.

Teacher Decision-Making.

Getting to know your students is the foundation of classroom management. Review these interviews and surveys and find ways to learn more about them. Remember that connecting with your students can take an emotional toll, so stay observant with managing your own self-care. Consider the areas where you see enough progress to make space for classroom management in the following chapters.

✎ Next Steps.

What is working? . . .

What is not working? . . .

What do I need? . . .

What am I proud of? . . .

What do I need to let go of? . . .

Weekly Reflection.

In the space below take a minute to jot down some of your glowing moments so far. You are making progress. I am reminding you that you have this, and I believe in you. I am encouraging you to highlight new connections you have made with your students because you are a quality educator, and students need teachers like you in the field for years to come. You got this!

8

Routines and Time on Task

Chapter Outline

Give Clear Rules and Expectations	149
Have Clear Consequences	151
First-Then Statements	153
Give Behavior Specific and Varied Praise	153
Scheduling Each Day	155
Have Engaging and Inclusive Seasonal Activities	159
Prepare for the Unexpected	161
On-Task Goals	161

Give Clear Rules and Expectations

Be sure that you follow your school-wide rules and expectations. Highlight these rules in your classroom, and do not contradict them. For example, if there is a "no chewing gum policy," stick to it. Then it will be essential for you to post your rules and routines specific to your classroom. Have clear and positively stated rules. Some rules may need to be more deeply defined. For example, being prepared can mean having a pencil and calculator ready. Being prepared can also mean sitting quietly in your seat, but your students need to know these expectations as soon as they walk into the room. Below is a sample of classroom rules. Note that these rules have a positive tone, telling the students what to do. What are some rules that are relevant to your classroom? Add questions to your students' surveys to assess what rules they value in safe classrooms. Add to the bullet points below.

 **Add your Ideas.**

Some classroom rules are listed below. Add additional rules that work for you and your mentor.
Be prepared with completed Materials/ Homework

Be on Time.

Listen when your peers or the teacher are talking.

Keep your hands and feet to yourself.

Cell phones away

-
-

When you see several students following the expectations, "catch them doing good," or following the rules (Steele & Whitaker, 2019). "Neha, I like seeing how you put your review work away and pull out your homework notebook." You will often see more students following suit. You can also generalize: "I love how many students have their books open and started reading." This can cue your chatty students to follow along versus calling out other students or asking them to "stop talking." Praise students for doing what they should be doing.

When students have started their work, let them know how long it should take. Make clear statements like, "I would like everyone to spend 6 minutes reading before they start reviewing the question section." They should also know your expectations when they leave your classroom. Be sure to make announcements like, "When we are in the hallway, we should be at level 0." Level 0 is often a school-wide code for no talking. If you are trying to correct an issue, be sure to give those reminders. Some students need reminders, and some students who like to test boundaries will hear your cues that you are looking for students to follow expectations. For example, "I saw some running in the hallway before lunch. I need to see your walking feet when you leave this classroom." This statement is an example of precorrection. You give opportunities for clear expectations before students have a chance to fall short of your expectations. Chapter 10 summarizes the seven specific steps for precorrection when several students have difficulty meeting expectations.

© iStock.com/bagira22.

Think About It.
What school-wide rules and routines are difficult for you to enforce? List some rule reminders you need to add to your lesson plans. List some students that you need to "catch doing good?"
?
?
?

Have Clear Consequences

A common practice that I have observed over the years is the immediate reaction to take things away. Especially recess. Please, never take away unstructured social time or recess. Never threaten to take away field trips. Yes, I still hear these threats in the classroom. Remember that students do not choose to be bad. In many cases, they are still learning how to follow the rules. So, in many instances, they need rule reminders and boundaries. You can do this by informing students what the consequences are if they do not follow the rules. Hopefully, there will be a school-wide structure so you can be consistent with other teachers and follow the school-wide plan. Talk with your team, and make sure the teachers who work with the same groups of students stay consistent as well. It may sound simple, but be clear about your rules and the consequences for noncompliance.

When a teacher provides consequences, he should be clear, consistent, immediate, and match the misbehavior. Students should know what the punishment means. The teacher should be fair and consistent. If the teacher gives a warning, he needs to follow through. The consequence should happen right away. There should not be an extended time between the action and the consequence. The consequence needs to match the misbehavior. Thinking of an appropriate consequence on the spot can be difficult. However, as you get to know your students and learn about their common misbehaviors, you will learn about the appropriate consequences. Below are some examples and non-examples of clear consequences.

 **Think About It.**

Do you follow clear and consistent rules? What non-examples do you need to improve?

	Grade Level	Example of a warning	Non-example
Clear	Elementary	Please sit in your seat, or you will need to move your desk to my desk.	You are not going to like what happens if you don't stop.
	Middle Level/Secondary	Please talk at a level 1 or you will need to work independently.	Lori, I am sick and tired of what you are doing.
Consistent	Elementary	Boys, please stop talking, or I will have you call your parents during lunch.	Boys, stop talking out. Gerald, I am calling home. Nelson, talk with me and tell me what you two are doing.
	Middle Level/Secondary	You need to move on to the essay questions now or you will have to do this for homework.	Raj you get detention for your behavior. Sasha since you have practice just come to see me tomorrow morning.
Immediate	Elementary	Parents are called within 1 hour.	The following week the students have to stay inside for recess.
	Middle Level/Secondary	Everyone move back to your seats and work independently.	The next time we have a lab everyone will be working independently.
Match the misbehavior	Elementary	The teacher discusses the behavior with the student. They create a contract about callouts, and the parents will see the communication log each day.	You are not going on the field trip if your homework is not done.
	Middle Level/Secondary	Students who do not finish the lab must finish during activity period.	Since several of you did not complete the presentation you are not going to the assembly next week.

First-Then Statements

Using first-then statements can help you be clear and concise with your expectations and help your students understand the expectations and the consequences. This precise phrase can be used to let students understand: *first*, you do this, *then* you get that. It can also help students understand that *first*, you continue to do this, *then* this will be the consequence. Sometimes you may highlight natural consequences. For example, if you do not tie your shoe, then you could trip and fall. Below are some examples of first-then statements you can use in your classroom. It is also a good idea to start charts of your own once you identify the target issues in your room and then create motivating statements for your students. Add some of your statements in the bullets below.

⊕ **Add Your Ideas.**

First	Then
Finish your homework, Everyone stays on task for 5 minutes, You keep the volume to a level 1,	you can read with a partner. I will add 5 more minutes of free time. I will play background music.
You continue to talk, You do not have your work finished before the bell, • •	then I will have new seating arrangements. then you will have homework • •

Give Behavior Specific and Varied Praise

When students are paying attention and following directions, it is essential to let them know that you notice their efforts to follow your expectations. Let your students know that you recognize that they are doing what they should be doing. It is also essential to use different forms of praise so that students can see you are authentic. Too often, teachers get caught in the repetition of saying, "Good job." You can also add gestures to signal that your students are doing nice work. Hand signals like high fives, thumbs-up, smiles, and fist bumps, matched with identifying the accurate behavior, are all positive ways to indicate positive praise.

Using specific praise for a few students for following expectations is also a way to redirect students who are not following the rules (Ennis et al., 2018). For example, if you have a few

154 Skills and Behaviors for Student Teaching

© iStock.com/Natalia Smuriakova.

students working quietly, you can acknowledge that group or a few students with specific praise. Specific praise can often remind the other students who are being loud to start working quietly. Reminders can be a positive way to get students to follow directions without calling them out. If you ever do need to redirect students, do this individually. It may take more time, but you are saving your relationship with this student by avoiding their embarrassment. Below are some samples of specific and varied praise. Be sure to use age-appropriate language when you deliver praise. Add some of your favorites in the bullet points below.

 **Add Your Ideas.**

Examples of specific and varied praise.
Have this list accessible until it becomes a part of your daily responses.

I love that answer, way to add detail.
Great remembering of that spelling rule.
Nice example here, you are paying attention.
Thank you for following the hallway rules.
Good answer, Thank you for recalling the steps.
Way to add details in your response.
Wonderful insight here, you explained your thought process.
I appreciate the groups who are staying on topic.
Lovely manners, way to be kind.
Way to show responsibility.
I am glad the volume is low, it shows you are sharing ideas.
Give feedback immediately, and feel free to mix and match.

-
-

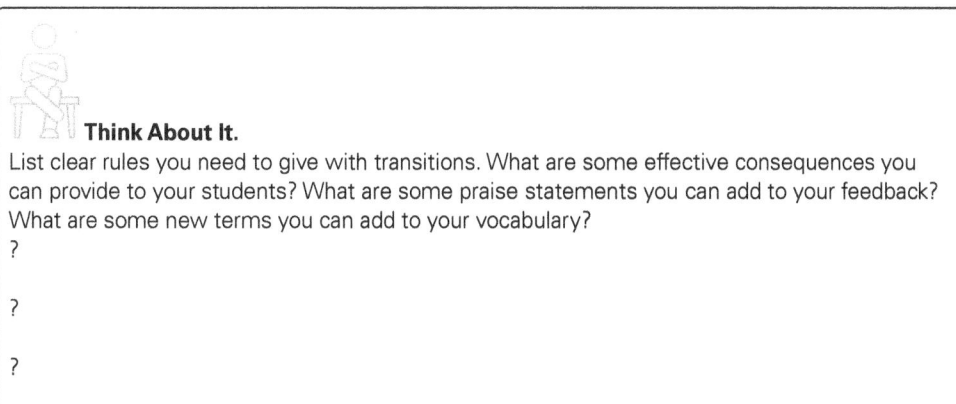

Think About It.
List clear rules you need to give with transitions. What are some effective consequences you can provide to your students? What are some praise statements you can add to your feedback? What are some new terms you can add to your vocabulary?

?

?

?

Scheduling Each Day

Everything starts with a good routine. You may have some flexibility within your day if you are an elementary teacher. Even in special education, you may get to choose when you pull students for your classes. But if you are in middle or secondary classrooms, your day may be planned bell to bell. Regardless of your situation, you are responsible for building predictability in your classroom each day. Students enjoy predictability. Adults and animals alike love predictability. Everyone wants to know when it is time for lunch, so put your schedule on display. If you have students who are nonreaders, make your schedule more visual. When your schedule and timers are visible, you can stay on task. If you start your class with a bell ringer, put a visible timer in the room. The visual helps students understand the concept of time and helps you, the teacher, pace your lessons and identify what you have time for and when you need to transition. I will talk about this more in relation to the pacing of your lessons. Do you need accountability? Have students help you with staying on schedule.

Introducing Your Lessons

Each lesson will start with a review and background of content knowledge. You may be reviewing from yesterday or making connections from the previous chapter. Another way of doing this is reviewing homework or morning seatwork to help you see what students remember, and this also allows students to make connections for today's lesson. Talk about your objectives for the day. Be clear. Read some of the samples below with connections to make the lesson relevant for your students. Think about a lesson you are teaching this week, create a lesson objective, and add your ideas to make it applicable to your students.

156 Skills and Behaviors for Student Teaching

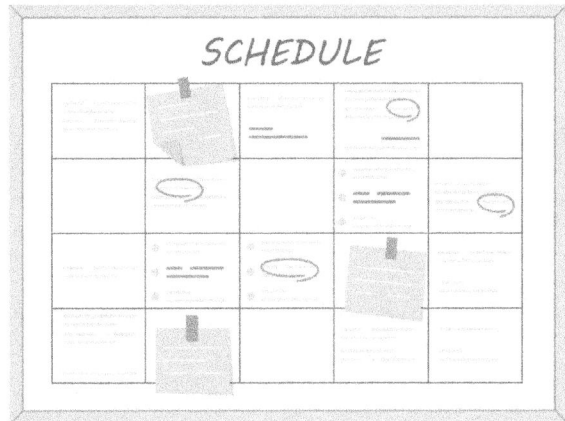

© iStock.com/Rudzhan Nagiev.

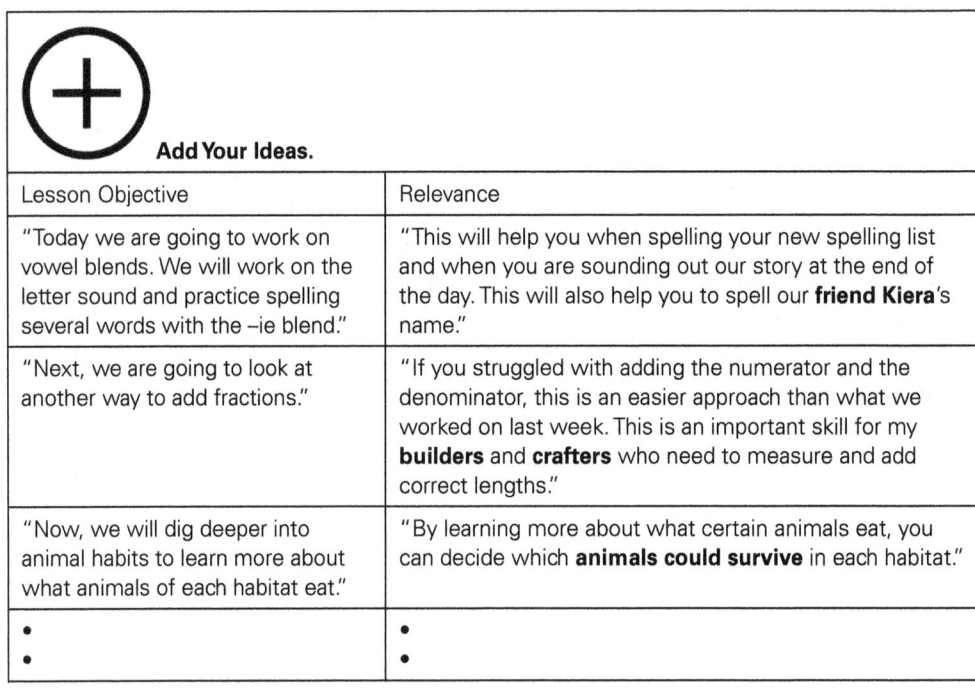

Add Your Ideas.

Lesson Objective	Relevance
"Today we are going to work on vowel blends. We will work on the letter sound and practice spelling several words with the –ie blend."	"This will help you when spelling your new spelling list and when you are sounding out our story at the end of the day. This will also help you to spell our **friend Kiera**'s name."
"Next, we are going to look at another way to add fractions."	"If you struggled with adding the numerator and the denominator, this is an easier approach than what we worked on last week. This is an important skill for my **builders** and **crafters** who need to measure and add correct lengths."
"Now, we will dig deeper into animal habits to learn more about what animals of each habitat eat."	"By learning more about what certain animals eat, you can decide which **animals could survive** in each habitat."
<ul><li></li><li></li></ul>	<ul><li></li><li></li></ul>

Attention Getters

Attention getters are great for starting lessons and indicating transitions. Once cues are learned, cues take minimal effort, and they help students to identify what is next. When students are in the middle of a task, you let them know a transition is coming. You give students your timeline. Visual timers are good practice to gain a sense of time for younger students and help with time management for older students. Call responses are a good way to get students' immediate attention. For younger students, you could yell, "class, class," and all students respond with "yes, yes." For older students, you ask for their attention and you announce, "I will wait for everyone to be listening." Student teachers often report that waiting feels awkward, but it frequently works. Do not forget about using close proximity if there are one or two students talking. Remember, this only works if you hold your expectations. So once you give a call, you must make sure that everyone responds. Do not be afraid to say, "Let's try that again. I need to hear everyone." It is more age-appropriate to use timers and alarms as cues at the middle level and secondary levels.

© iStock.com/pijama61.

Efficient Transitions

It is crucial to give rule reminders when transitioning from the classroom to the hallway. Remind students how to get in line and identify the expectations in the hallway. There are school-wide rules that you can use as cues for what the rules are in each setting. You will also need to provide transition cues in the classroom. When you complete an activity, remind students where to put their materials and give them a timeframe for finishing their current task and moving on to the following subject. Keep reading for examples of rule reminder scripts. Please note the specific expectations the teachers provide. They also provide visual and auditory reminders with clear directions for materials.

Think About It.
Elementary Going into Library Class

Teacher: In 2 minutes, I need you to put away your materials in the red take-home folder and get out your library books.
(teacher sets the timer)
(90 seconds later)
Teacher: If you haven't done so already, please put your materials away and get your library books before you walk into line.
Please meet me in a single-file line at the door.
Teacher: "Jamie, thank you for walking. Dalton, I like how you pushed in your neighbor's chair."
[insert specific praise to catch students doing good]
Teacher: Everyone remind me, what volume level are we at when we walk in the hallways?
[teacher signals for a response]
Students: Zero
Teacher: I did not hear everyone respond, "What volume level are we at when we walk in the hallways?"
ALL Students: Zero
Teacher: Thank you, everyone show me where your hands should be when you are walking in the hallway.
[Students put their hands at their sides.]
Teacher: I appreciate that response everyone. Now please remember you are going to be at the library. Can someone raise their hand and tell me the volume expectations when you are at the library? Justina?
Justina: We need to whisper when we are looking for books and raise our hands when we have a question for the librarian.
Teacher: Yes, I love both of those responses. I expect a positive report from Librarian Alvarez when I pick you up.

Think About It.
High School Transition Example

Teacher: Okay, ladies and gentlemen, we have 6 minutes before the bell rings. I need you to wrap up the problem you are working on with your group and return to your seats in 3 minutes to pack up. Please raise your hand if you have any last-minute questions about the problem you are working on. [Teacher sets a 5-minute timer.]
[3 minutes later]
Teacher: Please return to your seats and write down the homework in your planner. Everyone, please tell me what problems you have with for homework.
Students: 16–30 even problems.
Teacher: Thank you for your response. If you have any questions, I will be on Google Meet from 7 to 8. I need to see everyone writing down the homework in their planners.

Think About It.

Restate your directions with clear expectations. How can you provide visual and auditory reminders for your students? Where can you insert time into your lessons so that students have enough time to stay organized?

?
?
?

Prepare for Downtime

Whether you are completing group work or students finish a test early, have something for students to do when they finish their work. Some teachers prepare an "all done" packet with review and enrichment. Have themed activities for students to complete so they can expand on the content you are teaching. No cell phones or technology, please. Let this be for extremely special occasions. Technology should not be your go-to for downtime (Dontre, 2021). Work on building social skills. You will also find that there is downtime throughout the school year. Perhaps your parent organization is doing a fundraiser day, or there is a positive reward assembly. These things happen; show your flexibility by having engaging and straightforward activities prepared so that students are still learning. I have mixed responses when I hear, "I do not have time for this" in one week. But the following week, I heard, "I will not be teaching this week because of the themed events."

Inclusive and Culturally Responsive Practices.

Remember, not all students have the same level of hype for picture day. Whether the family cannot afford the latest clothing trends or a student cannot be in the school photo. Consider having your students complete special tasks or have something for them to do if they are not included in a school-wide activity. Perhaps they can help another teacher.

Have Engaging and Inclusive Seasonal Activities

Sometimes, teachers in school buildings take on the holiday spirit with themed costumes for Halloween and Christmas-themed events. For example, some parent organizations

© iStock.com/BRO Vector.

fundraise through Santa's Workshop, where students can buy gifts for family members. Teachers must consider that not all students celebrate the same holiday traditions, and when students follow uncommon traditions as compared to their peers, they can feel left out. As the student teacher, you need to know what traditions students celebrate and what traditions the students do not recognize. Sending home a list of practices you plan on celebrating in your classroom is a good way for family members to identify events that they do not want their child to participate in. This should be your indication to adjust your plans to be more inclusive for all students.

Inclusive and Culturally Responsive Practices.

Some experiences that many of your students may be counting on may not be the same celebration for all. Remember to keep some structure before and after holiday breaks.

If you decide to have holiday parties, be sure to have structure and educational value throughout your day. Nothing makes me cringe more when I hear a student teacher say, "I am not teaching today because we are having a holiday party," or "It is the last day before a holiday break." Be sure to make the best use of your time. Warning, I recognize this goes against popular beliefs, but I am speaking from my experience as a special education teacher. I go into schools and hear, "Let's just get through the week." In my experience, students have more success when they are engaged in fun activities and have clear expectations throughout their day. For example, if you have a Valentine's party in elementary classrooms, have the students write out their Valentine's cards and add a sentence. They can play vocabulary or word games with conversation hearts. If you have shorter days before your winter break, show students how to make snow in your science class by going outside with hot water (use a freezer in warmer climates). Again, my motivation comes from watching students who need structure and predictability in their day and who struggle with several hours of watching a movie or running around the classroom eating candy. Often, this is where you will see most of your behavior problems, and organizing engaging stations or games is more beneficial. As mentioned previously, not all families focus on major holidays, so spending large amounts of time celebrating more commonly practiced traditions can exclude students who do not practice accordingly.

Prepare for the Unexpected

Have routines for your known unknowns. Let's say there an early dismissal, and you do not want your one section of class to get further ahead than the other sections. Have enrichment activities planned for the students who meet that day. You may not always use these activities, but if you teach the content again or need a review for assessments, you will already have these activities prepared. If half of your class is involved in a school-wide activity and the other students are in your classroom, use this time to work on social skills games with your students. Have packets readily available, with clear directions, so all students can complete the tasks efficiently and independently.

Another unknown is an unexpected absence. It happens. Whether you wake up sick or you have a family emergency, life happens. Be sure to work with your mentor teacher to have a plan for someone else to step in and teach your lessons. Ask your mentor how they handle this. Have an "emergency folder" that another teacher can quickly locate in your room. This folder should have the essentials: class list, allergy information, daily schedule, and routine. With this, you should include extra activities along with your regular plans to help the substitute teacher with downtime. Despite your ability to shape your classroom expectations, a few students will attempt to take advantage of another teacher in the room. Having a colleague as your point person who can give your students reminders and check in to help the substitute teacher is a good strategy.

On-Task Goals

Now that we are getting to the priorities of classroom management, there is so much you could work on. I am here to remind you to take small steps toward progress. The two upcoming goals are prevalent skill areas that most of my student teachers need to work on at some point during their student teaching. If unsure where to start, pick a skill from Simone or Quentin. Remember to start with your baseline data. If you are comfortable with what you have started, feel free to engage in the next chapter (Participation and Student Engagement). If at any point you need to refresh your routines and expectations, be sure to return here.

Simone Gives Clear Expectations

Simone has learned that she will save time with her classroom management if she takes a minute during transitions to explain the steps. She also noticed that when she sends students to complete activities, she finds herself walking around the room just to repeat expectations rather than checking for understanding. After reviewing her video recording of a 20-minute lesson, she saw three opportunities where she could have added clear expectations for her students. Currently, she does not present any expectations for academic skills. After reviewing the sample goals in this chapter, use the blank charts at the end of the Part II to make your own SMART Goal.

Making SMART Goals	
Baseline Data Simone does not give clear expectations during transitions or before starting an activity.	
Specific: What is the Target Behavior?	
Simone will give 3 reminders or expectations	
With what materials or conditions?	
During a 30-minute lesson, Simone will give 3 reminders or expectations.	
Measurable: How well must the skill be performed? (Criteria)	**Achievable:** What modifications or accommodations are needed for success? Making the time?
3 reminders or expectations in a 30-minute period.	Simone will place an outline on her desk, that includes key reminders: starting class and transition expectations. She will review this before her lessons. Plug 3 reminders or expectations into each lesson plan.
How will the skill be measured? And how often?	**Any additional research? People to talk to?**
Simone will collect the data with tally marks once each expectation has been completed. She will measure 3 times a week across 3 different class periods.	NA
Relevance: Why is meeting this goal important?	**Timely:** What is considered mastery for this goal? **Timeline:** When would you like to achieve this goal?
By giving clear expectations and reminders, Simone can focus on checking for understanding when circulating around to talk to students.	This goal will be mastered once she has 2 straight weeks of 3 class periods of meeting the goal. Simone wants to meet this goal in 1 month.
What other assessments or data will help assess progress toward the goal?	**What are the next steps in this goal area?**
Observe areas where students are confused and would benefit from reminders and expectations.	Once she meets this goal, she will focus on specific praise.

Quentin Will Give Relevance to His Lesson

Quentin has had two observations now where he has not given relevance or connected to real-world experiences. He recognizes that it is essential to outline lesson goals and build real-world applications in his lessons. Quentin currently does not give relevance or discuss lesson objectives before any lessons. Each day, he would like to incorporate lesson objectives and/or real-world connections to what he is teaching (three times) throughout the day.

Quentin's Chart

Making SMART Goals	
Baseline Data Quentin does not give relevance or connect to real-world experiences before starting an activity.	
Specific: What is the Target Behavior?	
Quentin will start each lesson by presenting relevance or connecting to real-world experiences	
With what materials or conditions?	
Across 5 lessons in a day, Quentin will give relevance or connect to real-world experiences within 3 of those lessons.	
Measurable: How well must the skill be performed? (Criteria)	**Achievable:** What modifications or accommodations are needed for success? Making the time?
3 statements of relevance or connection to the real world out of 5 class periods.	Plug relevance or connection to real-world experiences into each lesson plan.
How will the skill be measured? And how often?	**Any additional research? People to talk to?**
Quentin will collect the data with tally marks once relevance or real-world connections have been completed. Each week, he will measure for one whole day (all 5 class periods).	Survey background information and prior knowledge of students. Investigate more real-world connections to the topics presented.
Relevance: Why is meeting this goal important?	**Timely:** What is considered mastery for this goal? **Timeline:** When would you like to achieve this goal?
Making connections to the skill we are learning will help students find relevance to the skill and be more likely to be motivated to learn.	This goal will be mastered once he has two consecutive weeks of three class periods of meeting the goal. He will meet this goal in 1 month.
What other assessments or data will help assess progress toward the goal?	**What are the next steps in this goal area?**
Observe areas in which students are confused and would benefit from relevance or connection to real-world experiences. Tally 1 class period every other day.	Once Quentin meets this goal, he will increase his goal to 8 out of 10 lessons within a week.

Chapter Recap.

Give clear rules and expectations
- State rules so that students know what they should be doing
- Have clear consequences
- Follow school-wide management plans
- First-Then Statements help students understand if they do one task, then they can move to the next step.

Give behavior specific and varied praise
- Let students know exactly what they are doing right
- Give a range of compliments beyond—good
- Redirect students who are not following the rules by complimenting those who are meeting expectations

Scheduling each day
- Have a predictable routine
- Give meaningful objectives at the beginning of your lesson
- Use Attention Getters so that students know what is next
- Give warming and have smooth transitions to the next activity
- Prepare for downtime with extra activities
- Always overplan

Have engaging and inclusive seasonal activities
- Know the holidays that your students celebrate and do not celebrate

Prepare for the unexpected
- Organize makeup work so that it is easy for absent students
- Have plans for fire drills
- Substitute teachers

 **Collaborative Thinking.**

Questions to ask your mentors/peers

Ask your teachers about some of the practical consequences for misbehavior.

What are the ways you have built specific praise into your lessons?

What activities do you use for downtime and known unknowns?

What are some strategies you have to stay on schedule in your lesson and throughout the day?

What are some engaging activities you implement leading up to the holidays?

Technology Checkpoints

Canva: Free educational tool for teachers to design presentations, graphic organizers, and certificates.

Flowcabulary.com: Standards-aligned video-based lessons that engage students with hip-hop and storytelling.

Smartclassroommanagement.com: This website by Michael Linsin has classroom management advice for every grade level. He also offers coaching on classroom management techniques.

Class Dojo: In the classroom, Class Dojo is a classroom management tool that allows the teacher to award points for positive behaviors. Outside of the classroom, Class Dojo allows for parent communication and involvement.

Teachervision.com: Teachervision offers a rich variety of resources for educators in grades K-12. Among the numerous items available, some examples are worksheets, graphic organizers, classroom activities, lesson plans, teaching tips and advice.

Responsiveclassroom.org: The Responsive Classroom is an approach to classroom management centering on building positive and safe learning environments. There are professional developments available and on-site consultations.

Positivediscipline.com: Available for parents at home and educators in the schools, Positive Discipline offers books and tool kits to help with both parenting and classroom management.

Teacher Decision-Making. Yes, there are many moving parts are happening in this part of the book, and your semester. You have taken on more responsibilities in the classroom. I hope you can embed some of these skills from each chapter into your daily routines. As former habits creep back into your schedule. Focus on what really matters. It is what you do on most days that counts.

Next Steps.

What is working? . . .
What is not working? . . .
What do I need? . . .
What am I proud of? . . .
What do I need to let go of? . . .

Weekly Reflection.

Use the space below to jot down some notes. Write down some of your classroom management success stories. You are making a difference. Listen to me telling you that you have this, and I believe in you. I am encouraging these minor changes in the classroom because you are a quality educator, and students need teachers like you in the field for years to come.

9

Student Participation

Chapter Outline

Verbal Opportunities to Respond	167
Quiet Opportunities for Everyone to Respond	171
Student Participation Goals	175

Verbal Opportunities to Respond

Once you have a classroom routine and well-thought-out lessons with data to drive your instruction, you must ensure students are engaged. One easy way to do this is to set up routines where all students can provide more responses throughout your lessons. Increased opportunities to respond is a great way to check for understanding and limit disruptive classroom behaviors (MacSuga-Gage & Simonsen, 2015). As you go through your lesson, you can understand what students are thinking. During student response, you can correct errors and identify students who need to review the material.

Another benefit of providing all students with opportunities to respond is that all students will be able to engage in the class activities. Instead of calling on one student at random, you require all students to give responses, whether they are all choral responding with short answers, writing answers on whiteboards, or sharing ideas with a partner. By having various formats for responding, you will include the students who do not always participate in class discussions (Common et al., 2020). These students may be shy or less confident in their responses and will likely share their ideas in writing, with a partner, or in small groups. Getting feedback from a peer or teacher providing specific feedback might encourage some students to participate in front of the whole class.

Think-Pair-Share

In Think-Pair-Share, the teacher allows students to think about what they are asking. You can share in a small group and then share with the whole group. This approach gives students time to think about their ideas, so you do not put students on the spot. Then they can brainstorm with their peers and get feedback on their ideas. The teacher can circulate and listen to students share their ideas. The teacher can also give specific praise to students who are staying on topic. Sharing ideas is an easy way for all students to share their ideas without taking up time, while the teacher calls on one or two students who consistently participate. This approach also saves time because you can assess more students as you circulate the room. You will know before class is even over who has learned the content and who needs review, rather than waiting to review tomorrow's homework. Below are two examples of how a teacher uses think, pair, and share in an elementary and middle-level classroom. Think about a lesson you are teaching this week, add a few bullet points of questions that you could ask your students to think, pair, and share their ideas.

© iStock.com/YoGinta.

 **Add your Ideas.**

Elementary—Teacher Reading a story

Think about why the main character is upset with her sister. How would you feel if your sibling broke your favorite toy?
[after 1 minute]
Now pair with a partner and share your idea. You have 2 minutes to share. After this, the teacher can call on students to share their answers or their partner's answers.

"I like how Jonelle already came up with a solution to what she would do if she were the main character in the story. This tells me she is already thinking ahead as to what might happen next."

-
-

 **Add your Ideas.**
Secondary Science Class
Teacher: What is your hypothesis when you mix these 2 ingredients together.   First, for 2 minutes, write down your idea.   [after 2 minutes]   Now pair your idea with your partner. Do you have similar or different answers? Could both of you be correct? You have 3 minutes to discuss your answers.   "Everyone is doing a nice job at this table." I hear students discussing real-life substances that they have combined with the same properties. That's a great real-world example. Now, I need you to decide what you would like to share. I need one hand up from every group.   •   •

Choral Responding

Choral responding is a way for students to give the same short answer at the same time. For example, there can only be one possible brief answer in choral response. Whole group response is appropriate across subject areas and grade levels. The teacher uses a signal to cue the students to respond in unison. Cues can be moving a hand from overhead to the class audience. All students must respond at the same time. If you do not hear all students, do not be afraid to say, "Let's try that again." Below are some examples that can work effectively with choral responses. Think about a lesson you teach this week and add choral response questioning techniques following the bullets below. Be sure to practice with your students if this is a new concept for them. Start with simple questions that you are sure they will all know the answer to before you expand to assessing student learning. Including choral responses helps you, as the teacher, to be consistent with your language so that students can respond with one possible answer.

© iStock.com/Visual Generation.

 **Add your Ideas.**

Topics Where Teachers can include the Choral Responding Technique

Vocabulary Terms
Spelling Words
Letter sounds
"Where do we put our homework"
"What is the answer to #3?"
What level are we at when we are silent reading?
Who in the story didn't show up for the play on time?
What is today's date
What is the capital of our state?
Who was the last president?
Name the National Park in our city.

-
-

Turn and Talk

Turn and talk with a partner is a way to get conversations started about a new topic or a way you can have students brainstorm the concept you are discussing. If you find you have a chatty group of students who always like to talk, this is a solution—let them talk. Just make sure your students are on topic. You can assess students and assign them to a long-term partner. Teachers call these "peanut butter and jelly partners" in elementary classrooms or "brainstorming partners" with older students. You could simply call this a turn-and-talk partner. By making consistent partners, you have many choices when organizing your students. You can put students who work well together, need to challenge each other, or model students with students who struggle working with others. If you are completing a lesson where you plan on having several turns and talks, but several students are absent, it may be beneficial for students to move to another seat.

Again, if this is a new skill, start simple. Make sure you ask questions so all students can share ideas based on their experiences. Circulate while students are talking and give specific feedback on their discussions. You can also give students specific praise for staying on topic. Be sure to provide specific objectives of what they should be talking about, and make sure that both students have an opportunity to share. Give a timeline for the conversation and a transition reminder before you call all students' attention to the whole group. You can then call on students to share what each group member shared or ask a student to share what their partner talked about. Below are some samples of effective turn-and-talk samples across the content area. Think about a lesson you are going to teach this week and add some examples of good turn-and-talk conversations your students can share.

 **Add your Ideas**.
Turn-and-Talk Responses
Talk about your hypothesis of what is going to happen next in the experiment. Talk about the foreshadowing in the story and give one detail of what could happen next. Explain the definition of the vocabulary word and use it in a sentence. What were some of the contributions to the new law that is currently in place. How did the homework go? What did you struggle with? Share your favorite part of the story. Explain how you got your answer. • •

Quiet Opportunities for Everyone to Respond

An alternative way to get the whole group's response and check for understanding is through various typed or written responses. You can implement this for multiple reasons. Your question requires that students share different opinions or more than one answer. You can have students type or handwrite responses so that you can walk around and see the answers. You can display answers so that you can see all responses at once.

Whiteboard Responses

Whiteboards are nice to have students solve problems or write answers and then show them to the class. You can even have students come up to the front of the room and show their answers to the whole class. After students write a response, they can share their answers with a partner. If your teacher does not have whiteboards, maybe there is another teacher whom you could borrow from if you would like to use this approach a few times during your teaching.

 **Think About It.**

Some things to consider with whiteboards:
Remember to have clear rules to keep markers closed while you are talking.
Answers should be the only items written on the whiteboards.
Have students wipe their boards or tables clean at the end.
Have an efficient way for students to use and return these materials.
Inexpensive considerations:
You can write on some school desks with the correct markers.
Start collecting unmatched socks and old T-shirts to use as erasers.

?
?

Hand Signaling

Thumbs-up or down is a great way to check in with your students. You can get students' opinions through a survey on whether they would like to do something or not. You can also get an individual answer from a student, and you can ask the entire group if they agree or disagree with the answer given. When you are doing this, you want to scan the crowd to see who is immediately answering and who is looking around to see how their peers respond. Below is a list of questions you can ask your students to answer with a thumbs-up or down. Just like in choral responding, you will want students to give their answers at the same time, so you will want to have a signal for when it is appropriate for students to answer. Add other ways to incorporate thumbs-up or down in your classroom to check for understanding. This is also a good opportunity to teach basic sign language. You can teach

© iStock.com/Victor_Brave.

signs for colors, shapes, and letters. By having the students sign their responses, it will promote a quieter classroom environment.

Add your Ideas.

Ways to use thumbs-up and thumbs-down
- Alicia said the answer is $11.25. Do you agree with thumbs-up or disagree with thumbs-down?
- Would you like to work with a partner thumbs-up or work by yourself thumbs-down?
- Orca whales are on the endangered species list, true thumbs-up, or false thumbs-down?
-
-

Finger representation is another way to get students to show their answers. You can give students multiple-choice questions and have them answer one for A, two for B, and so on. If you are teaching a math class in the young grades, you could have students answer numerical problems with 10 or fewer digits using their hands. In these examples, the students can also turn in a check with their peers to check their answers.

Cue Cards

Cue cards are another great way to keep students engaged when you are asking questions. You can have "yes" and "no" cards or letters A-D for multiple-choice questions. You can also create cue cards that match the part you are teaching. Students can even make these cards with visual representations. For example, you give all of your students four cards with each angle. You can ask students questions that require them to put up the correct angle. In science, you can have cards for categories of animals: mammals, amphibians, reptiles, birds, and fish. You could show various animals or habitats, and your students can all provide answers by showing their flashcards. As you scan the room to assess your students, you can quickly use a checklist to indicate which students are missing these answers.

© iStock.com/OksanaTkachova.

 **Think About It.**

What formative assessments do you use to conclude your lessons? What whole group assessment practices can you start adding to your lessons?

?

?

Poll Everywhere/Clickers

I like to use polleverywhere.com with older students and adult learners. Students can respond to questions using their cell phones. These formats can be used with any platform: Google Forms, Microsoft. Then, the students' answers will be displayed on the screen. You can let the responses be anonymous to gather students' experiences or preferences. You can also survey students' interests. Surveys help when you are giving examples in your lessons.

You can also have students respond with various short answers. I can call on students who may not typically raise their hands to respond. But I can say, "I like this response. Who can talk more about this?" It will give the student who wrote the answer an opportunity to share their thoughts. Still, often, other students feel more confident in sharing their thoughts because the example has already been recognized as a good idea.

© iStock.com/gmast3r.

Student Participation Goals

How is your student participation? Did you make any instant changes as you read this chapter that increased the number of students' opportunities to respond? If so, awesome. If this is good enough for you, move on to the next topic, and know that you can always return here and set goals for student participation. If you are not ready to commit to writing a goal, remember where to come when you need to check more for students' understanding.

Are you looking for ways to add more classroom engagement? Then what do you like, and what needs to change? Remember that you are taking more time to increase students' responses to engage them in your lessons and check for understanding. If you have students talking out or you are unsure what your students know at the end of a lesson, this might be the area to focus on. Just remember that adding to your lessons takes time. There is a classroom routine, and maybe students are not used to sharing much in class. Do not get frustrated if things do not change within one week. What is realistic for you to work on for the next month? After examining the goals provided by the student teachers, please navigate to the end of Chapter 10 to formulate your own student participation goals.

Kacyee's Chatter Boxes

Kaycee has a lot of students who like to talk out during her lessons. She has difficulty completing a lesson because she finds herself redirecting her students. She has allowed students to turn and talk more during her lessons. The students love that they can talk during class, and Kaycee better understands what students know by the end of class. Listening to students' conversations helps her assign homework and put students into groups daily. After reviewing her baseline data, she determined that she needed to add four turn-and-talks during a 40-minute lesson.

Kaycee's Chart

Making SMART Goals
Baseline Data Tuesday—0 turn-and-talks Thursday—2 turn-and-talks Friday—1 turn-and-talk
Specific: What is the Target Behavior?
Kaycee will complete 4 turn-and-talks where each partner gets an opportunity to share the answer to the teacher's question.
With what materials or conditions?
During a 40-minute lesson, Kaycee will complete 4 turn-and-talks.

Measurable: How well must the skill be performed? (Criteria)	**Achievable:** What modifications or accommodations are needed for success? Making the time?
4 turn-and-talks with both partners sharing.	Plug 4 to 6 turn-and-talks within each lesson. Use attention getters when students are chatty.
How will the skill be measured? And how often?	**Any additional research? People to talk to?**
Kaycee will collect the data with tally marks once each turn and talk has been completed. Her mentor will observe 1x a week across 3 different class periods.	Use AI to list good turn-and-talk questions with the lessons.
Relevance: Why is meeting this goal important?	**Timely:** What is considered mastery for this goal? **Timeline:** When would you like to achieve this goal?
Using turn-and-talks gives students more opportunities to talk during class. This can limit unnecessary talking.	This goal will be mastered once Kaycee has 2 straight weeks of 3 class periods of meeting the goal. Kaycee would like to meet this goal in 1 month.
What other assessments or data will help assess progress toward the goal?	**What are the next steps in this goal area?**
Reflect on the amount of additional talking that occurs during instruction. Kaycee will tally number of turn-and-talks 2x per week.	Once she meets this goal, she will focus on written forms of whole group response.

Quentin's Questioning

Quentin loves to question others, and he gets so excited about his lessons that he forgets to ask his students for their understanding. By the time he gets to the review before test day, he sees that some students are missing the mark. His mentor teacher reminds him that formative assessments throughout the lesson will help him understand what materials he needs to review the next day. After reviewing baseline data, Quentin only asks three questions with his exit cards for each class. His goal is to ask 10 questions with whole group responses or check-ins during his class.

Quentin's Chart

Making SMART Goals	
Baseline Data Tuesday—3 exit questions Wednesday—8 questions with individual responses Friday—1 turn-and-talk	
Specific: What is the Target Behavior?	
Quentin will complete a series of 10 questions (whole group response, individual questioning, turn and talk)	
With what materials or conditions?	
During a 45-minute lesson, Quentin will ask 10 questions with varied responses.	
Measurable: How well must the skill be performed? (Criteria)	**Achievable:** What modifications or accommodations are needed for success? Making the time?
10 questions with varied students' responses in a 45-minute period.	Plug 10 varied questions into each lesson plan.
How will the skill be measured? And how often?	**Any additional research? People to talk to?**
Quentin will collect the data with tally marks once each question has been completed. He will measure 2 times a week across different class periods.	Use AI to get a varied list of questions with my lessons.
Relevance: Why is meeting this goal important?	**Timely:** What is considered mastery for this goal? **Timeline:** When would you like to achieve this goal?
By asking more questions during class, Quentin can check for students' understanding before we get to the tests. The discussions will help him to build reviews for their tests.	This goal will be mastered once he has 2 straight weeks of 3 class periods of meeting the goal. Quentin wants to meet this goal within 1 month.
What other assessments or data will help assess progress toward the goal?	**What are the next steps in this goal area?**
Quentin will tally questions 2x week His mentor teacher/ University Supervisor will observe this behavior 1/ month.	Once he met this goal, Quentin will focus on different opportunities for written whole group response.

These are just examples. Remember to frame your goal around your baseline data. Refer to the "Technology Checkpoint" examples to find ways to measure your goal. Maybe you do not want to measure student participation. Perhaps you just want to ensure you are asking more open-ended questions during class. That is great. You could set an alarm and ask "turn-and-talk questions" each time it goes off. Whatever your efforts, I applaud you for becoming a teacher who makes progress. Please continue to the next topic for classroom management: Targeting Appropriate Examples for Classroom Success, but remember to keep your students engaged and collect data to measure your progress. Keep going. I believe in you and your ability to do great things, and you got this!

Chapter Recap.
Make sure students are given many opportunities to talk about their understanding
- Think—about your answer, Pair—with a partner to discuss Share—with the whole group
- Short one-word answers can be checked with choral response
- When all students want to share their examples, you can have them turn and talk with a peer

Students can also have group responses that are quiet through hand gestures or writing/typing
- Whiteboards can be inexpensive for math responses or short answers
- Students can use their hands with: sign language, show me a number, thumbs-up/ down
- Students can use the same color-coded notecards for multiple-choice questions
- For classrooms with technology, students can submit answers (Poll Everywhere/ Clickers) then you can call on ideas

Collaborative Thinking.

Questions to ask your mentors/peers.
How do you ensure you provide all students with opportunities to respond?
What are the different ways that you check for understanding with your students?

Technology Checkpoints.

Poll Everywhere: You can create different interactive polls that involve your audience. Poll Everywhere allows you to create word clouds, introduce new lessons, quiz your class with multiple-choice and open-ended questions.
Kahoot!: Kahoot! is more than a competition quiz game. It can also be used to introduce new lessons, engage students, and assess key points.
Blinkist: Blinkist summarizes podcasts, books, and articles on a full library of topics in manageable 15 minute sound bites.
smartclassroommanagement.com: Find helpful articles as resources for classroom management.
BrainPop.com: BrainPOP offers resources for grades 3–8 in subjects like Science, ELL, and History. There are also freebie printables to use in your classroom.
Padlet.com: Padlet helps you create engaging presentations and materials while allowing you to upload and share with colleagues and students.
NearPod.com: Lessons on NearPod are organized by grade-level standards and provide interactive delivery. You can use NearPod to check for student understanding, as exit tickets, or a fun competition review.

Teacher Decision-Making.

Are these steps working? Are you seeing the benefits? Make sure that you are making modifications and adaptations to make more improvements in the classroom, not more difficult. Take a minute to reflect on your classroom management. Add some deep breaths to your day and recognize the changes worth making for your overall health.

Next Steps.

What is working? . . .
What is not working? . . .
What do I need? . . .
What am I proud of? . . .
What do I need to let go of? . . .

180 Skills and Behaviors for Student Teaching

 **Weekly Reflection.**

Use the space below to jot down some notes here, or write a picture of something that is going well. Highlight something that is helping your day go well. Picture a great day. Hopefully, with slight changes to your classroom management, you will decrease stress and increase joy in your classroom experience. I believe in you, and you got this!

10
Identifying Appropriate Behaviors for Classroom Success

Chapter Outline

Classroom Umbrella	182
Positive Behavior Interventions and Supports	184
Teaching a Behavior	186
Precorrections	188
Class-Wide Motivation	190
Classroom Reinforcements	193
Appropriate Behavior Goals	194

Okay, so you have connected with your students, made clear rules and guidelines, and implemented engaging lessons, but there are still a few students in your classroom who are not meeting your expectations. These are the students who are "dancing in the rain." The "Classroom Umbrella Approach" will be discussed in this chapter. Remember not to take a student's undesired behavior personally. It is not about you. To add comic relief to this stressful situation, please keep singing "It's Not About You" to the melody of "It Had to Be You," by Frank Sinatra. However, remember students who repeatedly do not meet expectations because their approach is to meet their needs to get or avoid something (Deci & Ryan, 2000). The student may need to learn the skill explicitly. Yes, teach student behavior just like you would any academic skill.

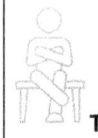 **Think About It.**

Are you taking a student's behavior personally? Review their survey from Chapter 7. List some details you could use to connect with the student(s). What are some skills the student(s) need to learn?

?
?
?

Classroom Umbrella

A helpful way to assess your classroom climate is to fill out your classroom umbrella (Stevens & Lingo, 2013). A classroom umbrella is a teacher's way to observe and reflect on students' behaviors and performance in the classroom. The umbrella represents the groundwork in Chapters 6 through 9. You are making connections with students and preparing engaging lessons. Despite this, some students will not meet your expectations despite your efforts. You will observe your students to get a closer look at how they react in the classroom based on typical classroom routines. By observing your students, you can categorize which students are your regular rule followers and which students typically challenge the rules. With this observation, you can identify students who need an intervention beyond the classroom techniques that have been outlined thus far in this part. After the directions for the "Umbrella Approach" observation, several specific interventions will be highlighted.

 **Think About It.**
Sample Classroom Umbrella

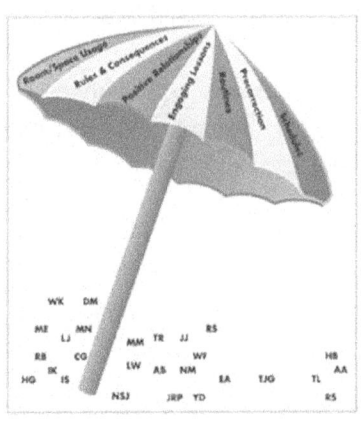

Sample classroom umbrella. Stevens, K. B., & Lingo, A. S. (2013). Assessing Classroom Management: The Umbrella Approach. *Beyond Behavior*, 22(2), 19–26. https://doi.org/10.1177/107429561302200205

Once you have identified your students, you can put them into these four categories. I adjusted the names of two labels to put a positive spin on their identity. Stevens and Lingo refer to the third group as "Damp and Doubtful" and this last group of students as "Drenched and Disruptive." But I want to remind you that these students get reinforcement from their actions and the teacher and/or student responses that follow. Do not take this personally, and do not let their behavior negatively affect you. Adjusting your reference can help you prepare for their behaviors with a positive mindset (and maybe even a smile). Once you have your students classified, it is time to investigate what motivates them to be inconsistent or to "puddle jump" and "dance in the rain." Below is a description of the four categories you can put your students into.

Think About It.
What do these behaviors look like at the:

Students with the Umbrella	Elementary Level	Middle/ High School Level
Handle huggers: Huggers are teacher pleasers. With little direction, they will go out of their way to follow adult expectations. They will also be responsible for encouraging their peers to follow directions.	They will be the first to give rule reminders to their peers.	These students take accelerated courses and make great peer mentors.
Dry and Dependable: These students typically follow rules and directions provided there are clear expectations and routines.	Easily redirected when other students are praised for their behaviors. If there is a rule for taking turns they will follow it.	These may need reminders to meet expectations.
Damp Puddle Jumpers: These students exhibit inconsistent behaviors. They can be rule followers but can easily manipulate to avoid following expectations.	They can follow the class expectations but they can be easily manipulated. This inconsistency can be frustrating for the teacher.	These are your class clowns. They draw attention to themselves in the lunch room.
Dancing in the Rain: These are your students who do not follow the rules despite extra rule reminders and preventative classroom management techniques. Despite all of their efforts, they consistently break their teachers' expectations.	When these students start on a bad day, they continue to have a bad day. They often need one-on-one attention to be redirected.	These students avoid the rules despite warnings and threats. They easily get into fights and it is difficult to find what motivates them.

Continue with this chapter to learn a few skills that could encourage more students to come under the class umbrella. Here is a blank umbrella for you to complete for your own students. If you have multiple classrooms, there is another blank copy at the end of this chapter.

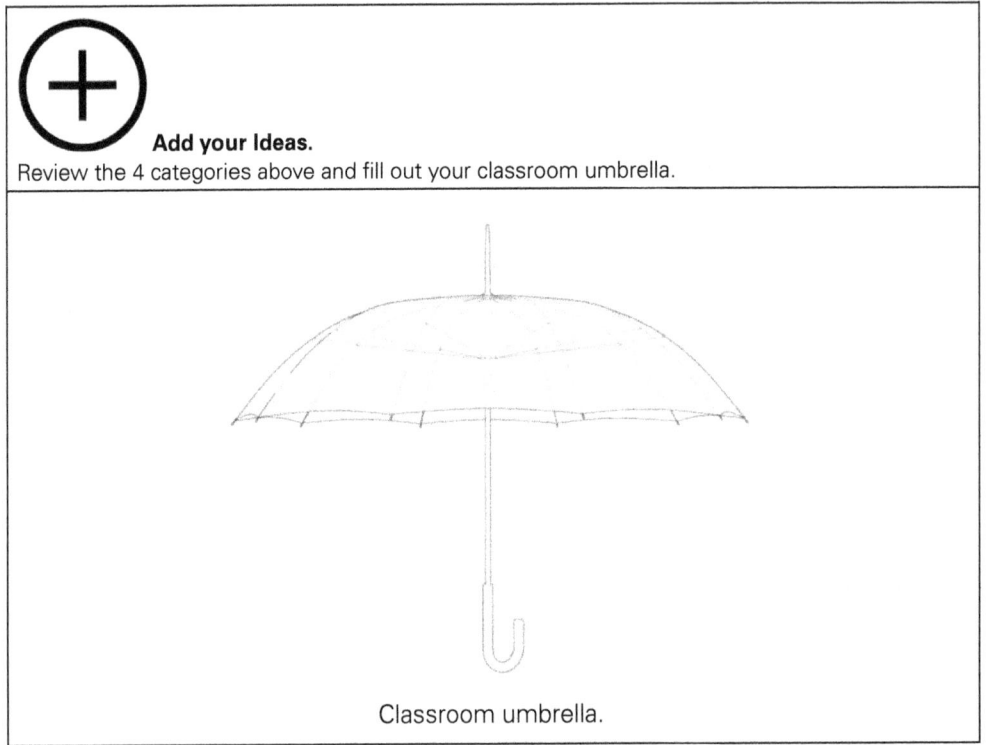

Add your Ideas.
Review the 4 categories above and fill out your classroom umbrella.

Classroom umbrella.

Positive Behavior Interventions and Supports

Now that you have your students identified as ultimately rule followers through easily coerced students and those who challenge the rules, it is time to go through the triage of supports that schools implement to get most students under the umbrella. The approach to all classroom management is a tiered system of support for students in the schools (Sugai & Horner, 2009). This will look different across grade levels and school buildings. Please view the chart below to see the tiered system of supports you should be looking for in your school. In this chapter, most skills outlined are in tiers 1 and 2 as Universal Supports that work for most students. Please note that if you are a specialist, you may have more responsibilities than what is highlighted in this chapter. Add your ideas to document the interventions and supports you see or would recommend in your school.

⊕ **Add your Ideas.** Tiered System of Supports.		
• Prevention of problem situations • Teach replacement behaviors • Acknowledge desired behavior • Systematic procedures • Safety routines • Accurate and sustained implementation • Data collection procedures • Include family and other systems of care	Tier 3	
• Self-management • Check-In, Check-Out • Small group social skill instruction • Targeted academic supports	Tier 2	
For teachers • Mentoring and coaching • Team planning for fidelity • Shared vision • Target goals • Data analysis For students • Teaching Behaviors • Clear Expectations • Consistency • Routine • Time on Task • Engaging Evidence-Based Instruction	Tier 1	
Modified from: Sugai, G., & Horner, R. (2009). Responsiveness-to-Intervention and School-Wide Positive Behavior Supports: Integration of Multi-Tiered System Approaches. *Exceptionality*, *17*(4), 223–237. doi: 10.1080/09362830903235375		

Teaching a Behavior

Sometimes students do not follow the expectations because they lack practice in applying the skills, and they may have negative influences who are not modeling the rules and routines you are expecting. It is time to break down the behavior and the skills and explain why it is essential. Sometimes, video footage can be helpful for students to see what following the rules should look like. Explain the importance of implementing the skill. Provide specific praise along the way. Examples are a great way to show students many ways to apply the skill in various settings. Non-examples are another way to show students what could happen if they do not follow the steps appropriately. Below are several examples across age-appropriate events to help you understand how to break down the teaching of a skill.

© iStock.com/exxorian.

 **Think About It.**

Taking Turns
This is clearer than sharing. It shows that both participants get an opportunity to use the object.
Importance: So that everyone gets an opportunity to use the materials. Consider if your friend was working with something you wanted to use. Turn-taking is an opportunity for you to get a chance too.
Step 1: Explain that you would like a turn with the book.
Step 2: Example: Agree on a clear timeline of when it is your turn to get the book. Can I see the book in 2 minutes? Ask the teacher to set a timer.
Step 3: Non-example: Can I see the book when you finish it? This does not provide a clear timeline for when you will get the book.
Step 4: You can provide a video or have 2 students model this skill with the students who are having trouble taking turns.
Step 5: Specific praise: Joy, you did a great job using your words to ask for a turn. Carlos, you did a great job getting the teacher to set the timer and following through when the timer went off.

 **Think About It.**

Cleaning up a Lab/ Putting away Materials
Importance: It is crucial to put away lab materials when you are finished with the experiment so that the next class will know where to find the materials. It is also essential to properly clean and put away materials safely and avoid contamination.
Step 1: Wash and dry all glass (Beakers and test tubes)
Step 2: Put away all chemicals where you got them.
Step 3: Put away all equipment
Step 4: Return all lab gear (goggles and apron).
Non-example: do not put lab gear away first because you could spill something while cleaning.
Step 5: Watch a video of the steps. Accommodation: provide a checklist of all the steps.
Step 6: Specific praise: Edward did a great job of safely communicating while walking around with breakable items. Dion, I appreciate you completing the checklist as he and his group members cleaned their space.

One group can model a skill, and the other students watch each step. Fill out the chart below with a skill that your students need to work on. Find the importance of teaching and learning the skill. Be sure to include the steps and examples or non-examples. Will you have a few students model the skills for the group? Have some specific praise statements ready when the students complete the skill.

Skills and Behaviors for Student Teaching

⊕ **Add your Ideas.**

Teaching A Skill

Skill:
Importance:
Steps:
Example: Non-example:
Specific Praise Statements;

Precorrections

Precorrection outlines the expected behavior before any behavior of concern occurs (Sherod et al., 2023). Using precorrection requires far less energy than redirecting students. Precorrection also sets students up for success by giving the teacher more opportunities to praise students for the expected behavior. By leading a situation with precorrections, you are giving students the momentum to continue with positive behaviors. There are seven steps to the precorrection model. The first chart contains a model of two different age groups, in which you can see how precorrection works. In the following chart, consider a skill your students need preventive expectations for. Complete the chart with a script on what you can say to your students.

Identifying Behaviors for Success

⊕ **Add Your Ideas**

Seven Steps of Precorrection	Younger Student Sample	Older Student Sample
1. Identify the context and the predictable behavior of concern;	Problem Context: Transitioning from morning meeting to seat work.	Problem Context: Staying on topic when working in groups
2. Specify expected behaviors;	"Once I tell a group to return to their seats, each student needs to walk, at level 0, with your hands to yourself."	"When you are working with a partner or in groups, you will need to talk about the assignment in front of you."
3. Modify the context;	Play transition music with a timer.	The three topics I should hear in the discussion include: Importing, exporting, tariffs
4. Conduct behavior rehearsals;	Everyone showed me how to walk to your seat. I did not see everyone in group 1 walking, come back and try again.	"I hear some talking about a dance, group leader point to the question you are on" OR "If you hear someone off-topic, reread the question to your group."
5. Provide strong reinforcement for expected behaviors;	Great walking everyone. "Ali, thank you for giving the level 0 cue. Yes we all should be at level 0."	"I love Chen's example of how taxes have an impact on imports." "Nice work, group 3, I hear you discussing the last problem. Way to get the work done"
6. Prompt expected behaviors before performance; and	"Remember, when you get back to your seats you should get out your reading workbook." "Everyone, show me what level you should be when you get back to your desks."	"Be sure to take turns sharing your thoughts that are on topic." "Remember to ask 3, then me. If you have a question, ask someone in your group; and then ask 2 people from another group"
7. Monitor the plan.	"You had 2 great transitions getting into our seats, and you need to get better at coming into the room after lunch time."	"For the first 10 minutes I heard everyone on topic. In these past 5-minutes I have had to redirect 2 groups. Stay on track to finish the task."

Class-Wide Motivation

In your classroom, you need to analyze when and how students meet the expectations and when they do not. You could set a class goal of 5 consecutive days of turn-taking. You need to clearly define that, which means there are no incidents of students unwilling to agree on turn-taking. You could set a similar goal of safety in the science lab. You can post a sign with 10 Days Safe and Clean on Lab Days with no accidents, and then you give students an appropriate amount of time to clean up after completing a lab. Sticking to your expectations can be difficult. Perhaps your goal is more about participation in group work. Explain that you would like each person in the group to provide an answer to the questions on the handout. Clear expectations help to increase individual accountability for the whole group's success.

Inclusive and Culturally Responsive Practices.

Give students opportunities to regulate their emotions. As a teacher, you must acknowledge that everyone needs time to balance their thoughts and feelings. Recognize that many families deal with stress and difficult situations in various ways based on their belief systems. It is essential to help students navigate practices framed around each family's cultural traditions.

Teacher Versus Student

Another way to add motivation for the students in your class is to incorporate a behavior competition between you and your students. First, be clear about what specific behaviors you are looking for with your students. Then, set a clear timeline for when you and the

© iStock.com/gmast3r.

students will play the game. Through playing the game, you will give specific praise to students and the whole group. You will also be able to identify which students may need more one-on-one interventions at the end of the chapter. Below is a description of how to play the teacher versus student game (McKenna & Flower, 2014).

 **Think About It.**
Teacher versus Student

STEPS
1. Pick a class, routine, or time of day when you want to improve behavior. Within that time, choose whether you want to improve behavior: a) Across all school-wide expectations OR b) For one positive behavior you want to see more often
2. Teach (or reteach) and practice expectations for that setting or routine. (1) Provide a brief rationale (2) Demonstrate examples and non-examples (3) Provide practice and performance feedback
3. Introduce and teach the rules of the Game. (1) Explain how students (and the teacher) will earn points (i.e., for positive behavior) (2) Share a point goal (e.g., 5 points, double the teacher points) (3) Define the time period (e.g., 30 minutes) (4) Share the rewards for winning (e.g., class dance party, extra recess time)
4. Start the Game. Tell students (a) the Game is starting, (b) when it will end, (c) the point goal, and (d) the reward. Note: Provide precorrection (reminders) before challenging transitions or routines
5. Run the Game. Tally student and teacher points on the board throughout the game. • When students follow expectations: ➢ Give the students a point and state the behavior that earned it (e.g., "I love the way everyone is sitting quietly waiting for my instructions. You just earned the class a student point.") • When students show unwanted behaviors: ➢ Do not remove points ➢ Consider giving a teacher point instead (e.g., "Almost everyone is quiet and waiting for my instructions, but I hear chatting, so I earn a teacher point.") ➢ Give reminders and reteach the expected behavior • Try to provide at least 4 student points for each teacher point
6. End the Game. At the end of the time period, announce the end of the Game and final score ➢ If the students win, provide the reward! ➢ If the students do not win, reteach and provide encouragement
7. Play regularly and monitor progress. • As students experience regular success, increase the point goal and/or time period • If students are not regularly winning the game, try to figure out what skills are needed

Group Versus Group

Another way to set up this game is to have students compete in groups against each other. Class-wide contingencies require more multitasking on the teacher's part because you need to observe which groups earn the points. As mentioned at the beginning of Part II, it is easier to implement classroom management strategies when you are fluent with your lesson plan. It is vital to have an efficient way to calculate these tally points during teaching. Then, after a group has earned the predetermined set of *points*, the members of that group will get to choose the reinforcement.

Self-Monitoring

So, you have taught the classroom rules and implemented class-wide motivation, but you still have a student who is struggling with a specific behavior. It is now time to get help. But you will have to collect data. Some of the best information you can obtain is through interviews and observations. It is time to work with the student to self-monitor her behaviors. When students can identify, chart, and reflect on their undesired behaviors, teachers have seen an increase in replacement behaviors (Justus, 2023). Ask the student if she understands the expectations to see what is holding her back. Work on data collection to monitor student baseline. Remember, where are they at now, and with intervention, are we seeing progress? Just because you are seeing progress does not mean that it is still appropriate for the classroom.

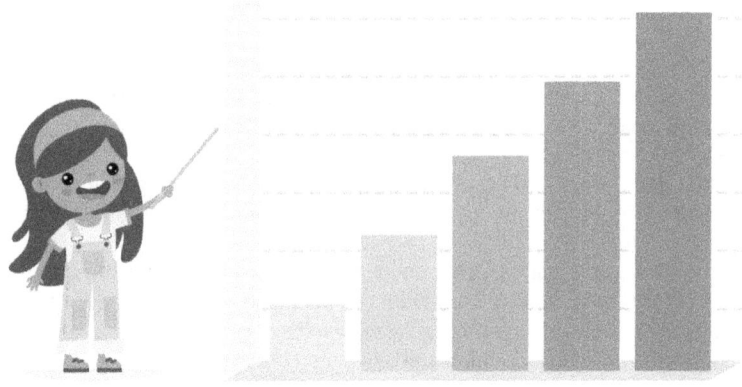

© iStock.com/eliflamra.

You can apply most interventions with little preparation, and most students can benefit from these reminders and reinforcements. Suppose you have one or two students who are still not meeting expectations. In that case, you should increase the intensity of explicitly teaching the student the expectations for your rules, followed by student self-monitoring. Remember, if a student has an undesired behavior, they must replace it with a desired behavior. You can work closely with the student to practice the skill, have the student sit by a model student, and even have the student watch a video of expected behaviors. "Technology Checkpoints" has video modeling through Edutopia. Keep reading for some undesired behaviors parallel with some ideas for replacement behaviors. Add some examples of behaviors you are observing in your classroom. After identifying a replacement behavior, you can have the student monitor their behavior. They can create their own goal and use tally marks to keep track of undesired and replacement behaviors.

⊕ Add your Ideas.	
Undesired Classroom Behaviors	Replacement Behaviors
Talk outs	Raise your hand
Touching other students	Hold a fidget or a small object
Running the hallways	Walk in the hallways on the appropriate side
Leaving the seat without permission	Raise your hand to get permission
Playing with a cell phone	Use your cell phone when you have permission
Teasing your peers • •	Treating your peers with kind words •

Classroom Reinforcements

Just like the discussion with specific praise, reinforcements should be decided on and distributed as soon as possible. It is a good idea to build a reinforcement menu so students can look at the options available to earn enough points through any of the activities listed above. You should show the menu at the beginning of the year and also brainstorm with your students. Oftentimes, they can generate great ideas for activities they are eager to earn. Some of these reinforcements can be low-cost, but it is ideal to find free activities. Like every skill, there is balance. It is essential to fade these reinforcements as you build intrinsic motivation. Continue for a list of ideas across the age groups. Consider additional reinforcements you have observed in the past and add your ideas.

⊕ Add your Ideas.	
Younger Student reinforcements	Older Students reinforcements
Dance Party Lunch with the Teacher Lunch with an older Peer mentor Get your nails painted at Vo-tech Use the teacher's seat for a day Be a teacher helper for the day Access an educational game Be the line leader Choose a book for reading time Get a sticker or stamp Extra time with class pet • •	Watch a video Play a game Snack Pick the music during work time Extended Break No-homework pass Class celebration School-wide tokens/ tickets Choose your seat Bonus points Use an educational App • •

Appropriate Behavior Goals

Do you have some students who need to work on appropriate behaviors? Are you thinking about the skills you need to teach? I am excited that you are making this a priority. Some of this chapter may not be a focus for you now. If you are all set with your classroom routine, great! In an emergency, revisit if you need seasonal reminders to target appropriate classroom behaviors. After you review the student teachers' goals, proceed to the end of this chapter to develop your own goals.

© iStock.com/Fahmi Ramdani.

Jasper Is Dancing in the Rain to Make Connections with His Students

After completing the classroom umbrella, Jasper has four students across different classes who enjoy the attention as class clowns or deliberately do not follow classroom rules. They are the students who are out in the rain. Jasper is going to focus on one student each day and take time to get to know each of them better through surveys and interviews. After learning about these skills, Jasper will spend the next week implementing one activity or skill that each student can connect to based on their interests.

Jasper's Chart

Making SMART Goals **Baseline Data** Currently, Jasper has 2–4 students in each class who naturally get his attention by not following the rules or getting peer attention as class clowns.	
Specific: What is the Target Behavior?	
In each class daily, Jasper will incorporate an interest-area topic or activity that connects with a student's interests.	
With what **materials or conditions**?	
In each class, a student who is "dancing in the rain" or "jumping in puddles" will have one activity or topic of interest embedded within the lesson.	
Measurable: How well must the skill be performed? (Criteria)	**Achievable:** What modifications or accommodations are needed for success? Making the time?
In each class, Jasper will incorporate 1 interest area of one student.	Jasper will use AI to develop some examples of areas of interest.
How will the skill be **measured**? And **how often**?	Any **additional research**? People to talk to?
Jasper will mark off a checklist when he incorporates a student's interest in the lesson at the end of each day.	This may include research on topics Jasper is unfamiliar with.
Relevance: Why is meeting this goal important?	**Timely:** What is considered mastery for this goal? **Timeline:** When would you like to achieve this goal?
Jasper needs to get to know his students better, and he wants their peers to also learn about each other's interests.	By keeping this rotation, this goal will be met by the end of the semester.
What other assessments or data will help assess progress toward the goal?	What are the next steps in this goal area?
Jasper will check off when he incorporates interests into his lessons. He will also make note of students' behavior when interests are incorporated.	Once Jasper meets this goal, he will then incorporate these areas of interest into his assessments.

Students Versus Simone

Simone would like to play the teacher versus student game to highlight desired student behaviors as she continues to work on her explicit teaching of skills. She was hesitant to try this activity with high school students. Still, she has found that teenagers enjoy the competitive nature of the game and that it builds camaraderie among students. It is a win-win! Simone has given rule reminders before starting class, but now she is looking to target two different student skills, including participation and varied classroom management skills. Simone will begin the week by assessing what skills each class needs to work on and creating a reinforcement menu that motivates the students to complete their work.

Simone's Chart

Making SMART Goals **Baseline Data** Currently, Simone gives rule reminders and corrections before transitions. So, she would like to play teacher vs. student with 2 skills once a day, rotating through her classes, starting with her busiest class first.	
Specific: What is the Target Behavior?	
Implement teacher versus student with 2 predetermined target students' behaviors based on the needs of each class.	
With what **materials or conditions**?	
During 30-minute class period, each day of the week, 2 predetermined target students' behaviors	
Measurable: How well must the skill be performed? (Criteria)	**Achievable:** What modifications or accommodations are needed for success? Making the time?
In each class Simone will incorporate 2 behaviors to measure.	She will use AI to come up with some examples of areas of interest.
How will the skill be **measured**? And **How often**?	Any **additional research**? People to talk to?
Simone will create a calendar with target behaviors and mark off with one teacher versus student has been completed.	Observe students to identify target behaviors for each class. Distribute a reinforcement menu for each class to generate ideas.
Relevance: Why is meeting this goal important?	**Timely:** What is considered mastery for this goal? **Timeline:** When would you like to achieve this goal?
Playing this game will help her to "catch students doing good," give specific praise, and encourage students in each class to work together.	She would like to consistently play the game once a day for 2 weeks
What other assessments or data will help assess progress toward the goal?	What are the next steps in this goal area?
Simone will calculate tally marks at the end of each class. She will also list the target behaviors she has measured.	She will increase the game to twice a day.

You have made it to the end of Part II. Kudos! I applaud you for taking the time to learn more about classroom management. You have learned how having clear routines and engaging your students helps minimize classroom disruptions. Remember to start small; you can always add on when you meet your goal. I am proud of how you care for the students in your classroom. Take time this week to complete another observation using the CMOT. Revisit your first assessment. Are there improvements? Did you make a goal for yourself? Did you meet that goal? Continue to think about the areas of classroom management highlighted in this part. What do you need to continue to focus on?

You have so many teacher decisions to make in a day. Take these changes in stride with your efforts to become a teacher who continues to make progress. Take a minute to congratulate yourself. You have taken the time to work on yourself, so you can be a better teacher who is ready for class each day. Next, you worked on ways to build connections with your students and enhanced strategies for your classroom management. As a sneak peek into the book's last section, you will now work on skills and techniques to effectively plan and communicate among members of your school community. You have already spent time in your school community by meeting administrators, colleagues, staff members, and parents. Having effective relationships with the people in your school community is an essential tool for preventing burnout. Fortunately, Part III is all about working well with others.

 Chapter Recap.

Break down your students under the classroom umbrella
- Rule followers
- Rule followers who need rule reminders
- Easily manipulated to break rules for attention
- Not motivated by typical reminders and consequences, needs individual attention to identify appropriate goals

Positive behavior interventions and supports
- Tier 1—Collect data, have consistent rules and routines, have a shared vision, and time for team planning
- Tier 2—Self-management, teach check-in/ check-out, small group targeted instruction
- Tier 3—Have safety routines, teach replacement behaviors, include family in care plan, acknowledge replacement behaviors

Explicitly teach classroom behaviors
- Show videos or model what this looks like
- Provide non-examples and consequences

Precorrections
- State what is expected before students have an opportunity to do the opposite
- Teach students replacement behaviors

Class-wide Motivational Games
- Complete against students by giving them points when you see specific rules being followed
- Reward students when they meet these goals

Group versus Group Behavior Competitions
- Have student groups compete against each other for following the rules
- Identify what the students are doing right when they earn points
- Students can regularly earn rewards

Once students learn the skill, they can self-monitor
- Have the students tally and reflect on their progress
- Set goals based on the current baseline

Classroom Reinforcements
- Get donations from local businesses
- Have teachers and older students donate their time and talents

Collaborative Thinking.

Questions to ask your mentors/peers
What skills have you had to teach/ reteach during the school year? How did you teach the skill to the students?
What are some low/no-cost reinforcements that your students find rewarding? Are there businesses in the community that provide low-cost treats for teachers?

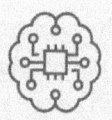

Technology Checkpoints.

donorschoose.org: Teachers from across the country can request needed materials for their students. Provide a small description of the cost and materials for your project.
Freecycle.org: Free membership for individuals to reuse and keep good stuff out of landfills. Find gently used furniture and supplies in your local area.
Coupon Book: Coupon books can be used as a reward system to promote favorable behaviors. Use coupons like "Lunch with the Teacher," "Get out of Homework Free," or "Pajama Day" for the students to choose.
Edutopia: This website is full of articles on many different educational topics like assessment, project-based learning, and social-emotional learning. Be sure to check out their 60 second video library for classroom management.

Teacher Decision-Making.

Before moving forward with another part, are you doing many things but not getting anywhere? If you look at the collected data, do you need to narrow it down and pick one skill? Or have you mastered your specific praise, and there is no need to continue to monitor your progress? Think about what will best serve you and your goals to be a teacher who continues to make progress. This is your permission. It is okay. My goal is to help you continue to make progress and, hopefully, with slight changes to your classroom management, decrease problem behaviors and increase clear expectations and praise in the classroom. I believe in you and your ability to do great things, and you got this!

Next Steps.

What is working? . . .

What is not working? . . .

What do I need? . . .

What am I proud of? . . .

What do I need to let go of? . . .

Weekly Reflection.

Use the space below to jot down some things you are grateful for in the classroom. Remember, it is about progress. Review your data to highlight where you are making progress. Listen to me tell you, "Keep going, you have got this." I am encouraging these minor changes because you are a quality educator, and students need teachers like you in the field for years to come.

Making SMART Goals

Baseline Data	
Specific: What is the Target Behavior?	
With what materials or conditions?	
Measurable: How well must the skill be performed? (Criteria)	**Achievable:** What modifications or accommodations are needed for success? Making the time?
How will the skill be measured? And How often?	Any additional research? People to talk to?

Relevance: Why is meeting this goal important?	Timely: What is considered mastery for this goal? Timeline: When would you like to achieve this goal?
What other assessments or data will help assess progress toward the goal?	What are the next steps in this goal area?

Making SMART Goals

Baseline Data

Specific: What is the Target Behavior?

With what **materials or conditions**?

Measurable: How well must the skill be performed? (Criteria)	Achievable: What modifications or accommodations are needed for success? Making the time?
How will the skill be measured? And How often?	Any additional research? People to talk to?
Relevance: Why is meeting this goal important?	Timely: What is considered mastery for this goal? Timeline: When would you like to achieve this goal?
What other assessments or data will help assess progress toward the goal?	What are the next steps in this goal area?

Making SMART Goals

Baseline Data

Specific: What is the Target Behavior?

Identifying Behaviors for Success

With what **materials or conditions**?	
Measurable: How well must the skill be performed? (Criteria)	**Achievable:** What modifications or accommodations are needed for success? Making the time?
How will the skill be measured? And How often?	Any additional research? People to talk to?
Relevance: Why is meeting this goal important?	**Timely:** What is considered mastery for this goal? **Timeline:** When would you like to achieve this goal?
What other assessments or data will help assess progress toward the goal?	What are the next steps in this goal area?

Making SMART Goals

Baseline Data	
Specific: What is the Target Behavior?	
With what **materials or conditions**?	
Measurable: How well must the skill be performed? (Criteria)	**Achievable:** What modifications or accommodations are needed for success? Making the time?
How will the skill be measured? And How often?	Any additional research? People to talk to?
Relevance: Why is meeting this goal important?	**Timely:** What is considered mastery for this goal? **Timeline:** When would you like to achieve this goal?
What other assessments or data will help assess progress toward the goal?	What are the next steps in this goal area?

Making SMART Goals

Baseline Data	
Specific: What is the Target Behavior?	
With what **materials or conditions**?	
Measurable: How well must the skill be performed? (Criteria)	**Achievable:** What modifications or accommodations are needed for success? Making the time?
How will the skill be measured? And How often?	Any additional research? People to talk to?
Relevance: Why is meeting this goal important?	**Timely:** What is considered mastery for this goal? **Timeline:** When would you like to achieve this goal?
What other assessments or data will help assess progress toward the goal?	What are the next steps in this goal area?

Part III

Relationships and Collaboration

You have put yourself first with self-care in Part I and built relationships with your students in your engaging classroom in Part II. Now it is time to step outside your classroom to work with your colleagues, administrators, families, and community members. Part III will focus on strategies and routines you can build within your school community to build effective relationships to help you succeed and enjoy your job. Granted, you may change school districts, and other educators will move into your school community as well. However, just like any other behavior you have reviewed so far, it takes practice to implement effective strategies to build collaborative skills to work with other people. You spend more time each week with your coworkers than with family and friends. Therefore, within your control, you will want this to be a positive experience. Focusing more on your role as a teacher and your relationships with your administrators and associates will likely determine your career as a teacher (Billingsley & Bettini, 2019). Like self-care and classroom management, you may have been handling situations with others out of habit. Additionally, the only behavior you can change is your own, but there are actions that you can take to help you have a positive experience when working with others. Through these chapters, I will highlight evidence-based practices that will help you to work effectively with the people in your school and community.

11

Works Well with Others

Chapter Outline

Learning Your Tendency Is Based on How You Meet Expectations	206
How Do the Four Tendencies Relate to Teacher Collaboration?	208
After Your Tendency Quiz	219

As in the previous chapters, you will continue to measure your progress to identify the skill areas you need to work on. Remember, effective relationships happen over time. Additionally, you cannot control how people will react or respond. You do have control over your actions, which can affect the reactions and responses of others. So, no, I do not have the answer for how to work with Mr. Grumpy Guerrero or Ms. Lazy LeFlur, but I will highlight effective ways in which you can respond. For now, you should focus on setting goals and making progress.

Learning more about yourself will help you to work with others. In the following chapters, I will outline and provide examples of ways to work effectively with those in your school. You may even find helpful tips for your personal relationships. Throughout this part, you will uncover why these skills are essential in collaborating with colleagues. Just like caring for yourself to avoid burnout, you must manage the relationships with the adults in your workplace. Building positive relationships is one skill that new teachers feel uncomfortable addressing (Shirrell, 2021). You must have opportunities to work on these skills now. If you are not yet sold on the importance of working on your relationships, I have included some research on these key skills so that you understand why working on these skills is so important. Remember, as you progress in your career, you will feel more confident and comfortable experimenting with these collaborative strategies during student teaching. You have not been in the classroom long enough to experiment with these teaching strategies, so the remaining chapters in Part III will provide you with exercises, reflections, and goal ideas with the same student teachers you met in Chapter 1.

© iStock.com/Vera Cheredova.

Learning Your Tendency Is Based on How You Meet Expectations

The only way to learn to work well with others is to reflect on your characteristics and behaviors. Please go online to take the Gretchen Rubin *Four Tendencies Quiz*. From this assessment, you will learn more about yourself, and then as you continue to work through these chapters, you will learn more about ways to work with other people. The Gretchen Rubin Four Tendencies Framework is shaped around two automatic tendencies of how you complete tasks with: internal and external accountability (Rubin, 2017). Please take this quiz before you jump to the next page. It is important not to conclude from the charts. The questions are deliberate so that you learn more about what motivates you to complete tasks. Now, if you are comfortable, you could take this opportunity to go a step further and ask your mentor, co-teacher, partner, roommate, or anyone you regularly have interactions with to take the test. This can help you learn what motivates the people you work with so that you can effectively collaborate with others toward common goals.

External Accountability

Though some expectations are easily identified, how we meet many of our outer expectations is automatic and with little decision-making. Social pressure is just one example of how expectations may influence our automatic interactions with others. As a teacher, it is essential to acknowledge that there are numerous individuals who can hold your external accountability, such as superintendents, teachers, colleagues, other staff,

© iStock.com/VectorMine.

parents, and students (Leo et al., 2020). Some individuals do not concern themselves with external accountability, whereas others rely on external accountability with rewards or others' expectations to complete tasks. We will break down how this works for you and the people you work with, depending on your response or indifference to external accountability.

Internal Accountability

The next step in decision-making is how you hold yourself accountable when you make decisions or complete tasks. Intrinsic motivation is the term commonly used for individuals who are motivated to complete tasks without external rewards or accountability. These individuals focus on their individual needs and uphold their expectations. Having strong internal accountability, as its entity, has neither good nor bad outcomes (Cochran-Smith, 2021). What matters in the Four Tendencies Framework is how the internal accountability pairs with external accountability when individuals are making decisions. Are individuals focused solely on their own goals? Or does a teacher not have any motivation to hold themselves accountable? When examining yourself, it is important to consider the goals, values, and purposes your actions serve. Fullan and colleagues (2015) believe that, in terms of academic success in the classroom, a student's internal accountability must mean more than external accountability if one is looking for maintenance of any skill. Below is a chart that breaks down the focus on internal and external accountability. This includes a breakdown of specific actions of those who meet or resist expectations of themselves or others. Add your ideas as you connect to this concept.

© iStock.com/Naveed Anjum.

Add your Ideas.

Breakdown of Meeting and Resisting Internal and External Accountability

	Meets	Resists
Internal (Self)	Follows a calendar Does not cancel appointments Has clear goals for themselves Does not make exceptions for the rules ●	Does not care about making arbitrary goals Cannot make themselves complete a task ●
External (Others)	People pleaser Focuses on the needs of others Goes out of ones way to help others ●	Does not like to follow arbitrary rules Other people cannot make them complete a task. ●

How Do the Four Tendencies Relate to Teacher Collaboration?

In 2016, the Four Tendencies Quiz was administered to 1,564 participants, including many demographic characteristics such as geographical locations in the United States, household income, age, and a mix of genders. The breakdown of tendencies was: "Obliger" (41%), "Questioner" (24%), "Upholder" (19%), and "Rebel" (17%) (Kirk et al., 2017). I have had cohorts of student teachers complete this Four Tendencies Framework for the past 10 years. I am going to make a guess based on the 2017 study and my 10 years of student teacher data that you are an Obliger. Not only is the Obliger the most common tendency, but with my 10 years of student-teacher data, 80% of my student teachers were Obligers (McConnell, 2020). At first, I thought it was a coincidence. Still, within the third year of having student teachers complete the quiz, I found it very logical that people who like to help people, put others before themselves, would naturally find themselves in teaching. That does not mean that if you are not an Obliger, you do not like to help others; it just means that your approach to completing tasks and starting new habits may look a little different.

Additionally, after Obligers continue to put others first, they then find themselves in Obliger Rebellion. I have learned from this with firsthand experience. Studying the work of Gretchen Rubin has taught me so much about myself. By having my students and colleagues complete this quiz, I have learned more about how to collaborate with them too. By learning more about the Obliger Rebellion, it has also helped me to theorize that this could be a link as to why there is such a high rate of burnout in education. I also encourage you to read "The Four Tendencies Framework" or, for those who spend more time in the car, listen to the podcast "The Happiness Project." The examples below will help you to understand more about your tendency with the teacher samples.

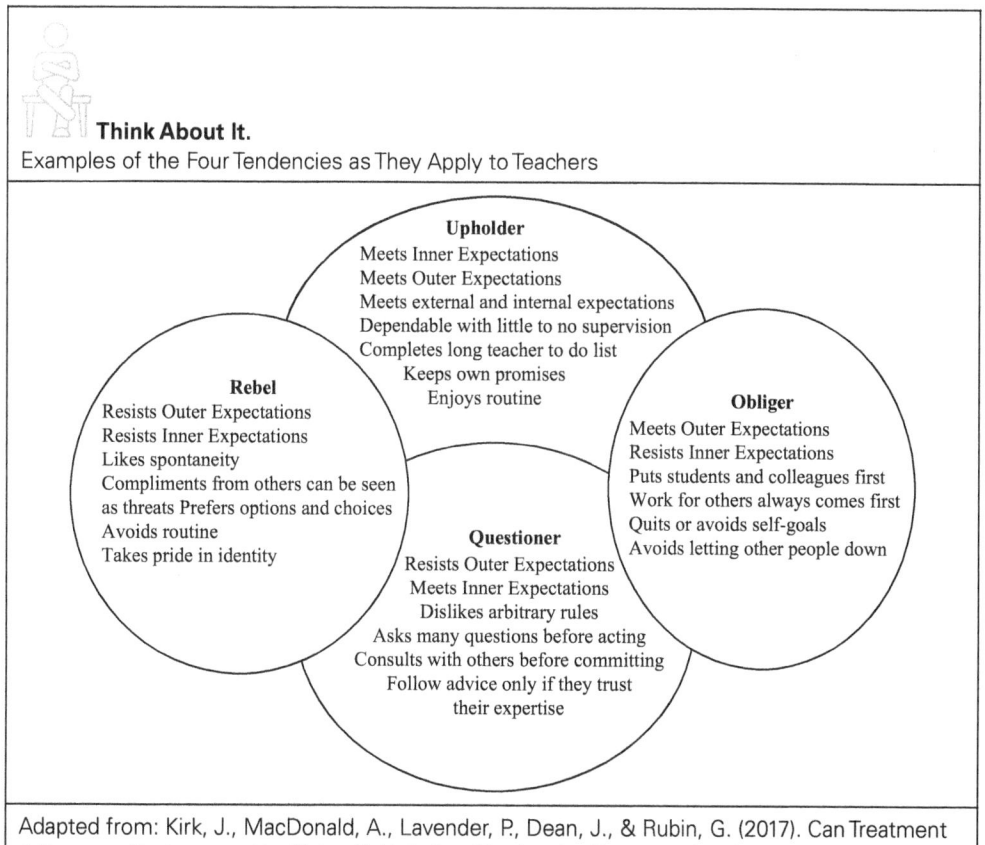

Think About It.
Examples of the Four Tendencies as They Apply to Teachers

Upholder
Meets Inner Expectations
Meets Outer Expectations
Meets external and internal expectations
Dependable with little to no supervision
Completes long teacher to do list
Keeps own promises
Enjoys routine

Rebel
Resists Outer Expectations
Resists Inner Expectations
Likes spontaneity
Compliments from others can be seen as threats Prefers options and choices
Avoids routine
Takes pride in identity

Obliger
Meets Outer Expectations
Resists Inner Expectations
Puts students and colleagues first
Work for others always comes first
Quits or avoids self-goals
Avoids letting other people down

Questioner
Resists Outer Expectations
Meets Inner Expectations
Dislikes arbitrary rules
Asks many questions before acting
Consults with others before committing
Follow advice only if they trust their expertise

Adapted from: Kirk, J., MacDonald, A., Lavender, P., Dean, J., & Rubin, G. (2017). Can Treatment Adherence Be Improved by Using Rubin's Four Tendencies Framework to Understand a Patient's Response to Expectations. *Biomedicine Hub*, 2(Suppl 1), 1–12. https://doi.org/10.1159/000484261

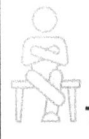 **Think About It.**

After completing this quiz, reflect on some patterns you notice.
Explore "The Four Tendencies" websites and podcasts and jot down some more details about your tendency.
What feedback can you apply to working with others?

?
?
?

No need to double-check, this part is about working with others, but similar to cultural awareness, you need to know and understand how you work and process routines to work with others. Within the introduction, there are more details to help you learn how to be a motivated and productive colleague in the workplace. A good working relationship with your colleagues is another key predictor of your success in education. Once you figure out the ways to be your best self, you will then be able to practice from a range of evidence-based approaches to work with colleagues, administrators, families, and community members.

How Do People's Tendencies Impact Collaboration?

As you read about these behaviors and tendencies, you may observe some patterns in others. As you transition into the following chapters, you will learn more about the effective practices and key considerations for administrators and the people you work with. Encourage your colleagues and peers to take the Gretchen Rubin "Four Tendencies Quiz." By learning more about the people you work with, you can help build your collaborative efforts by designing the responsibilities in ways that highlight both of your tendencies for productivity. Below are some considerations for individuals from each of the Four Tendencies. Add your ideas as you learn more about these concepts as they relate to you.

 **Add your Ideas.**
Considerations for the Four Tendencies

Obliger Considerations
Always putting others first leads to burnout. Obligers then go into Rebellion.
Obligers have difficulties holding other Obligers accountable
Obligers benefits from working in groups and attending scheduled classes

-

Upholder Considerations Trouble adjusting to scheduling changes Avoids risks or mistakes Defensive when corrected Expects others to follow through too Difficulty delegating responsibilities •
Questioner Considerations Meets an expectation only if they believe it is justified Does not like to be questioned Needs to put a limit on research Persistent questioning may make them seem uncooperative or defiant •
Rebel Considerations Will not be forced to do anything, and cannot make themselves do anything Competition can be motivating Choices and consequences are helpful Deadlines are mandatory Consequences help follow through with "first then" statements •

How Do the Four Tendencies Impact the Success of Student Teachers?

It is time to talk more about the four student teachers mentioned throughout the book, but now they will be addressed through their tendencies. You can probably already identify which student teacher has what tendency, and the student teacher with similar issues and ways of addressing problems has the same tendency as you. Even with the examples that started from the very beginning of this book, the goals they set and the behaviors they were working on were based on the natural motivation of their tendency. You may have even made a connection with the actions of a student teacher based on their experiences. Here is a breakdown of a few more examples that have occurred with these student teachers and builds based on how they view working for themselves and with others. I have also included how their tendency has impacted their relationships in the schools where they teach. At the end of each proceeding chapter, I will highlight how these student teachers have built goals based on their experiences and the research they have learned from Part III.

Kaycee the People Pleasing Obliger

Ever since the beginning of teaching, Kaycee has overcommitted herself by saying "yes" to her colleagues and overextending herself with her students. I always must remind my

© iStock.com/mrPliskin.

Obligers that I love their care and energy, but always putting others first will not last. As I mentioned previously, Obligers say "yes" for so long, and then they go through an Obliger Rebellion. This is called teacher burnout in the field of education. Have you experienced this? For example, Kaycee has shared that she overworks herself with her students, family, and friends, and by the time the weekend rolls around, she says "no" and checks out of everything and everyone.

Kaycee has learned to build her health goals by having students keep her accountable. She is getting more movement and exercise throughout the day by coaching the dance team. She has also added journaling/drawing during brain breaks. Several of her students have connected with journaling, so they are asking Kaycee for more time to write. This has been an excellent way for Kaycee to add reflection and gratitude to her day. Kaycee has learned that accountability from others has helped her to stick to her goals. But Kaycee needs to balance and only say "yes" to the opportunities that will help her to meet her goals.

Obligers are often recognized as people pleasers. This part is so essential for Kaycee and all Obligers alike because Obligers need to learn how to work effectively to create boundaries to avoid burnout by constantly feeling the need to say "yes" (Kollerová et al., 2023). In teaching, there are so many external pressures and people to account for; these lines are especially complicated for new teachers. It is vital to address self-care for teachers. There is more evidence to support improved well-being and increased commitment to the field of education (Carroll et al., 2021). Kaycee has learned that many of her fellow grade teachers are Obligers, and therefore they are not good at holding each other accountable. Distractibility is often present among teachers in their weekly meetings. Because the teachers do not get much accomplished, Kaycee ends up saying "yes" to her mentor to get the work done because she is a novice teacher. If this happens to you, you will learn more about how Kaycee holds productive meetings in Chapter 13. In Chapter 14, you can learn more about an active listening strategy that Kaycee is practicing when working with parents instead of trying to scramble and solve problems. Similarly, by listening to others first, Kaycee got caught up working with an older male teacher, whom she looked up to as a male mentor. Her university supervisor had heard that there were pictures of them together on social media. They began discussing the importance of setting boundaries with others at work. Continue reading Chapter 15 to learn more about how Kaycee learned the importance of healthy relationships in and out of school.

Simone Upholds Herself and Others

Simone may come across as rigid and inflexible. This is just how Simone meets all of her expectations. This is great for healthy routines and emphasizing her role as an educator in the building. As mentioned previously, individuals who uphold their expectations are well suited to be successful in the classroom (Fullan et al., 2015). The only piece upholders need to consider is that there are many people to work with in the schools. So, for Simone, she has built some goals working with others' expectations. For example, when it comes to working with teenagers, she has learned to give clear expectations in the classroom. This has drastically changed her classroom management. She has also built on the classroom management strategy, "Teacher versus Student." This forces her to give her students reminders of the rules and specific praise. Though she does not need praise to complete tasks, she sees how her students are motivated when she notices their efforts. She also values reflecting on her own needs and making goals for herself. One issue for Simone is sleep. When she wakes up in the morning, she feels exhausted; she thinks she needs to hit snooze to get more sleep. But what she has learned is that a longer night's sleep is more important, so she can prioritize her bedtime. Throughout the year, when working with Simone, she has easily shaped routines to keep her expectations to herself. However, to her peers and colleagues, she sometimes appears inflexible. As we know, with teaching, flexibility is key.

As Simone learned more about the underpinnings of the four tendencies, she gained a better understanding of how she can effectively collaborate with her colleagues. She used to assume that everyone made to-do lists and met deadlines, but this skill is unique to her personality. Working with her colleagues taught her the importance of building some flexibility when working with others. In talking more with her colleagues and learning more about the "Four Tendencies Framework," she has learned that not everyone follows clear expectations. In contrast, others need a rationale before making decisions, so Simone has learned the importance of check-ins with her co-teacher. In Chapter 13, you will also learn how to effectively have meetings and check-ins with the many people you work with regularly so that you are meeting each other's expectations.

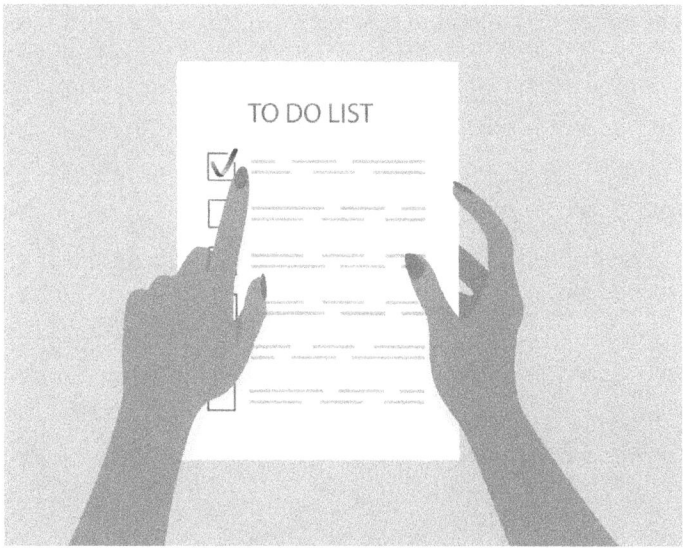

© iStock.com/Olga Ubirailo.

Jasper the Resisting Rules Rebel

Though I have only had a few student teachers identify as rebels, it is a tendency I can relate to most because Amelia, my daughter, is a rebel. You may think a rebel who resists both outer and inner expectations could never make it as a teacher. This job requires too many routines and expectations for a rebellious person. But I can tell you as an eyewitness, my rebel student teachers have turned into some of the best teachers I know. This includes my daughter Amelia. She has taught me more about working with people than any class I have taken. As I think about Jasper, he has shared some of his success stories, and they may seem very random to anyone else. He became a successful athlete because his cousin told him he could never pitch a no-hitter during the regular season. He identifies as an athlete and relatable teacher, so he is motivated to complete tasks that help him to keep that persona. As in the previous chapters, Jasper built goals that helped shape the identity he values as a relatable teacher. But sometimes, when there are outside expectations from peers and colleagues, it is almost like Jasper revolts. Jasper was able to recognize that most athletes eat healthy and work out. Jasper has also worked on incorporating his students' interests into his lessons. He has witnessed that this personal attention to his students helps them to cooperate in class and understand the material.

Though Jasper has a great relationship with students, this has posed some difficulty with the teachers he works with. Because Jasper does not hold himself accountable, he sometimes presents himself as careless. He is not thoughtless; he is carefree. The difference in these two statements is that Jasper does care about other people and meeting specific goals, but he does not stress about these situations. One benefit for Jasper, because he does not get stressed, and he is less likely to burn out from teaching. His mentor teacher and I just had a follow-up meeting to discuss several professional issues, which are highlighted in the following few chapters. Jasper is learning to understand the value of time and the importance of taking other teachers' time seriously. In learning more about the roles of administrators in Chapter 12, by noting his patterns of resisting expectations, I knew it was best to present

© iStock.com/Rudzhan Nagiev.

Jasper with the problem and the consequence. This was a similar successful approach in a medical study applying the Four Tendencies. Once the doctor recognized the patterns of resistance, he focused more on the patient's choice along with the potential consequences (Kirk et al., 2017). Jasper is very interested in working at this school, so he is invested in making goals to be more collaborative with his colleagues.

Jasper learns more about the best use of time and focus during meetings. In Chapter 15, the topic of healthy relationships is discussed. It is crucial to understand boundaries with your students. Though Jasper presents himself as the cool teacher, he thought nothing of sharing his social media pages with his students as a form of communication. Other teachers voiced their concerns when student teachers share their personal information with other students.

Disclaimer: Obligers must review the Rebel tendency too, as when an Obliger burns out, he or she will go into Obliger Rebellion. From my own experience, getting out of Obliger Rebellion can be very challenging.

Quentin Questions Your Questions

It is logical to connect mathematicians and scientists as Questioners. This is the case for Quentin. Quentin is learning to balance his natural curiosity and is constantly questioning others. Reflecting on Quentin's behaviors and patterns, you will notice that most of his decision-making is framed around investigating the best option. To help him make decisions, he has to consult with others to limit decision fatigue. Once he has the evidence to prove something is worth doing, he can easily change his personal and professional life. For example, once Quentin learned the science behind deep sleep, he could shift priorities for that REM sleep cycle. Adding deep breaths throughout the day helped Quentin recognize the cognitive benefits of brain clearing. One setback is when Quentin overanalyzes and troubleshoots his options. As you may recall, he stayed up so late because he was stuck in analysis paralysis. By finishing his decision-making with his mentor teacher, Quentin could move on to his daily lesson planning. Therefore, he was able to get more sleep. He also learned that he needed more time connecting with his students. He failed to realize that not all students love science as much as he does. By treating his students like principal investigators in his classrooms, he has learned more about his students. He also saw the relationships his students were building as they learned more about each other. Quentin knows the importance of fostering a favorable classroom climate where students can respect each other's talents and differences.

In Quentin's questioning, he has always felt that his questioning makes him look interested in the topic, and his investigative style shows off his knowledge. But in reading the details about the "Four Tendencies" (though he questioned it 😊), he is now more observant of his interactions with others. He has noticed that people get uncomfortable when he continues to question ideas and arbitrary rules during meetings. Continue to Chapter 12 to learn more about how Quentin is learning to prioritize his questioning in interviews and meeting situations.

© iStock.com/VectorBird.

Use the chart below for a summary of tips with examples for each tendency. Remember, the only way for this to be accurate is if you have this person take the quiz. Their motivation for each action is based on internal decision-making. There is no way for you to identify this just by observation. Add some of the ideas that you have found to work for you.

Add your Ideas.
What are some things that help you complete tasks? Add some tips that work for you.

Tendency	Example
The Upholder • Make new rules when there is a schedule change • Explain your boundaries with others • Pair your desired tasks with less desirable activities • Make goals you can measure • •	• Have a backup plan for after fire drills • "I need to babysit on weekends, so I will need to complete this assignment during the week. Let me know what you need me to do" • Grade papers while listening to fun music • Study 30 minutes each night for the teacher certification tests. • •
The Obliger • Put it on the calendar • Say "I will thank myself later." • Talk to others about your goals they can become your accountability partners • Say "yes" to the things that you value • •	• Write down now "planning meeting every Tuesday" • "If I grade now, I will appreciate later" • Tell your mentor, "I will text you once I finish the presentation." • Say "Yes to study night, and no to karaoke on a school night" • •

The Questioner • Balance the amount of research you do • Find go to research experts for your decisions • Recognize decision fatigue • Find your own purpose for arbitrary deadlines and rules	• "If I finish my part of the project first, I will not have to check in over the weekend." • Consult with your lab partner about the materials you are using for Bio lesson tomorrow. • You have done so much research for the schools you are thinking of applying to, but you never applied to any of them. • "I have time to grab a coffee if I sign in before 7:00 a.m." • •
The Rebel • Shape goals around your identity • Make "all done" lists • Break up tasks into choices and consequences • Shape your decisions with possible consequences	• Completing the bulletin board will make me look well prepared to my colleagues • Make a list once you have finished your daily tasks versus following a to-do list • "I can grade papers or plan for tomorrow" • "If I grade papers tonight, I can give out candy for students who made progress" • •

Through these final chapters, you will uncover ways to collaborate within your work community. Every school has a building culture. I will help you navigate the various groups of people you work with by sharing evidence-based approaches on working with others. Your relationships with administrators, colleagues, and families determine your job satisfaction. It does not matter how successful you are in the classroom; you must work well with others.

 **Think About It.**

What does collaboration look like for you? List your glow and grow in giving feedback? List your glow and grow in receiving feedback?

?
?

What are the skills you need when working with others? In this last part, I will highlight strategies for successful co-teaching. Actual team teaching is where you prepare, present, and assess students as a team. You may say, "Nobody has time for that." However, there are ways that you can delegate and plan effective lessons individually, then come together as a team to work with students. Clear communication is also essential when working with

© iStock.com/TopVectors.

individuals and groups. You have probably taken a course in public speaking, but have you ever learned how to listen? Working with colleagues means asking effective questions and listening to what they have to say.

Not only will you work with colleagues as your equals, but you will have administrators in your school building and across your school system. Learning more about their roles in the workplace is vital. Getting along with your administrators can determine how much you enjoy coming to work. I will outline their responsibilities and the skills they seek in quality teachers.

You will also get to work with families. This is not just parents; you may find yourself connecting with older siblings or cousins who are primary caregivers of your students. Working with family members and building positive connections from the beginning is essential. It is helpful for you to understand the family background so that you can build relationships that students will make at school. Beyond working with families, you will be a connection to the school community. Not only is it valuable for you to understand the resources available to families, but you will also find that it is helpful to know how community members can work with you in your classroom. From guest speakers to service providers, community members can be very supportive in assisting you with various materials, funds, and services. Reading Chapter 14, you can learn more about accessing your school community.

Inclusive and Culturally Responsive Practices.

As you review the tendencies of others and learn how to work with people. Respect their practices and do not look to change the person and their approach to success. When you self-reflect, do not wish you were someone else. Figure out how to work with your natural behaviors to meet expectations for yourself and others to be a successful collaborator.

To wrap up this book, I will summarize considerations for building healthy relationships outside school. You need to decide: do you want to live where you work? Many teachers would not have it any other way; they want to live and teach where they grew up. I have found that school administrators often hire alums because these teachers are familiar with the community and the school district, and they are more likely to stay. Hiring and training teachers is a multi-million-dollar investment. Administrators want to hire teachers who wish to remain in the district. But this does not apply to everyone. Some teachers prefer to move based on their partner's job or relocate to a high-needs area. This may seem overwhelming, but a balance in your social life is another priority for achieving career happiness. So, just like every other skill reviewed thus far, I will wrap up the book with evidence-based ideas so you can have a healthy life outside the classroom, too. I am invested, and if you have made it this far, you are too. Keep going.

After Your Tendency Quiz

How is your collaboration with others? Did you make any instant changes after you reflected on your assessment? If so, fabulous. If this is good enough for you, move on to the next topic, and know that you can always jump back here and set clear goals. This is up to you to decide.

Are you interested in making goals to suit your tendency? Then what do you like, and what needs to change? Remember that you are working on collaborative skills to help build connections with your colleagues and make productive use of your time. Only you can convince yourself that it is worth doing. Furthermore, it takes time. What realistic improvement goal are you looking for upon completing this part? Below is Jasper's sample goal. Would you like to target one small area to focus on as you read through the following four chapters? After you review Jasper's goal, you can use the blank charts at the end of Chapter 15 to create your own SMART goal that matches your tendency. Or you can read through the chapters and make goals as you go along. Remember that Jasper is a Rebel, so this goal may only work for you as a Rebel or if you are in an Obliger Rebellion. As an obliger, you kept saying "yes" to every opportunity to help others at the school, and now you do not have the energy to complete tasks that you need to graduate and get that dream job.

Jasper Is Becoming a Reliable Rebel

As Jasper approaches the end of his student teaching placement, he continues to rebel against the final projects he must complete. He has doubled down on using his identity to motivate himself to get things done. Since he wants to be viewed as a reliable teacher and athlete, he has used this image to help him make better decisions on how to spend his day. He has worked with his mentor teacher and coach to develop a list of tasks to complete that will help Jasper remain reliable at the end of his student teaching placement and toward the end of his athletic career. Notice how Jasper is working with others to build this goal. Throughout this part, you will notice a theme of shaping goals with the support of others. As you continue through these chapters, you will see the importance of effective collaboration in your teaching.

Jasper's Chart

Making SMART Goals **Baseline Data** Jasper currently has a list of 15 tasks that he needs to work on and complete during his final weeks of student teaching.	
Specific: What is the **Target Behavior**?	
Jasper will select 5 tasks from his "to do" list to complete each week.	
With what **materials or conditions**?	
Given a list of responsibilities from his mentor teacher, Jasper will complete 5 tasks throughout each week.	
Measurable: How well must the skill be performed? (Criteria)	**Achievable:** What modifications or accommodations are needed for success? Making the time?
Jasper will check in with his mentor teacher at the end of each week so that his mentor teacher can verify completion.	Jasper may need to organize time to complete his to-do lists each week. Jasper placed the list in small slips of paper in a jar. He randomly picks out a "to do" before or after school.
How will the skill be **measured**? And **how often**?	Any **additional research**? People to talk to?
Mentor teacher will check in weekly.	Meet with mentor to build checklists and completion lists.
Relevance: Why is meeting this goal important?	**Timely:** What is considered mastery for this goal?
Jasper is interested in applying for a job at this school district so he wants to finish his placement with a positive impression.	Completing all 15 tasks within 4 weeks.
What other assessments or data will help assess progress toward the goal?	What are the next steps in this goal area?
Confirm with mentor teacher/ University Supervisor for completion.	Identify 15 tasks for next placement.

 **Chapter Recap.**

Learning Your Tendency to Meet Expectations
- Internal Accountability—You can depend on your intrinsic motivation to get things done.
- External Accountability—Often focuses on the needs of others first

How Do The Four Tendencies Relate to Teacher Collaboration?
- Most people are Obligers (meet external accountability, resist internal accountability); Always meet the needs of others first. If you continue to neglect your needs, you will eventually burn out
- Upholders (meet internal accountability, meet external accountability). Can appear to be rigid and inflexible because they like to meet their routines and goals.
- Questioners (meet internal accountability, resist external accountability). Does not follow arbitrary rules or guidelines. Asks many questions to build understanding.
- Rebel (resists internal accountability, resists external accountability). Focus on their identity. They cannot be made to do anything, but will do anything they put their mind to.

How Do People's Tendencies Impact Collaboration?
- Kaycee (Obliger) shapes her goals around the accountability of others. She is learning to say no more often so she can say yes to her dream job.
- Simone (Upholder) sees that others do not follow to-do lists and schedules like she does. Giving students accountability and clear expectations has helped her classroom management.
- Jasper (Rebel) identifies as an athlete and teacher who likes to make learning fun. He has a priority of becoming a coach in the school where he student teaches now, so this is motivating him to make some changes in his routine.
- Quentin (Questioner) needs to understand the reason and figure out the best choice before he moves forward with decision-making. He is learning to consult with others so that he does not overanalyze his decisions.

How do Tendencies Impact Collaboration
- **Obligers**—Use group work for accountability; Put things on the schedule
- **Upholders**—Make plans for schedule changes; Explain your boundaries
- **Rebels**—Shape goals around your identity; make deadlines and choices
- **Questioners**—Make your own opinion for rules; consult with an expert if you cannot make a decision

 **Collaborative Thinking.**

Questions to ask your mentor/peers

What is your tendency? and what traits are accurate?
What are your strengths when working with others?
What are some traits you value in the people you work with?

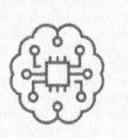

Technology Checkpoints.

Happiness Project: Podcast (Gretchen Rubin and Liz Craft) share backed by science research for happiness and productivity in your professional and personal life.
4 Tendencies: A personality profile that categorizes people into tendencies. The 4 tendencies are Upholders, Questioners, Obligers, and Rebels.
gTasks: A Google app that lets users create to-do lists and manage tasks.
www.GretchenRubin.com: This website from the creator of the 4 Tendencies model, dives deeper into those tendencies and how to use them for your benefit. There is a library full of resources available on the site as well.
Minutes Notetaker: You can use this AI tool to record meetings and have minutes created out of the recording.

Teacher Decision-Making.

How do you feel about shifting your focus to creating goals for working with others? Take a minute to reflect on your self-care and classroom management, are you able to keep up with your goals from Parts I and II? You do not have to make a goal for this chapter. Outline the areas from Parts I and II where you see enough progress so that you can make space for collaboration in the following chapters.

Next Steps.

What is working? . . .

What is not working? . . .

What do I need? . . .

What am I proud of? . . .

What do I need to let go of? . . .

 **Weekly Reflection.**

Use the space below to jot down some notes here to brainstorm some good ideas you have had in your free time. Listen to me remind you that you have this, and I believe in you. I am encouraging these minor changes because you are a quality educator, and students need teachers like you in the field for years to come. You got this!

12

Working with Administrators

Chapter Outline

Shadowing My Elementary Principal	226
The Roles of Administrators	226
School-Wide Management Systems	231
Administrative Goals	235

I would be remiss to write this chapter without mentioning my elementary principal and first mentor in education, Mr. Gabrielson (or to me, Uncle Harry). Growing up, I spent a lot of time with my Uncle Harry and Aunt Chris. Our families would often spend time together. When I was with Uncle Harry, I felt like I was with a local celebrity. He truly impressed me with his ability to always address students and their parents by name outside of the school setting. To this day, he can call former students by name and recall the exact stories of them being in his office. Every connection was meaningful, and people knew that he cared.

When I observe in the schools, I look for administrators with his leadership qualities. He was a positive presence to teachers, students, and his community for 30 years. What impressed me the most was that he lived right next to the community baseball field and the Borough pool. He lived publicly and worked in his garden in the summer months, waving to kids and congratulating them on their baseball efforts. He took time to get to know the families. And by living in a common part of town, I always thought he would be a target for vandalism, such as house egging or tire slashings, by students who felt they were treated unjustly. But this was never an issue. He was fair, and by being fair with his colleagues, families, and students, he was respected.

Shadowing My Elementary Principal

One of my most memorable summers of childhood was the summer of 1993, the summer before I would enter fifth grade. I went to work every day with Uncle Harry in the brand-new Elementary building. This would be the first of 2 years I would get to attend this fantastic high-tech location. Because all the finishing touches were happening, I was "hired" to help him prepare each classroom for the new school year. I was not quite sure of all his responsibilities at that point in my life, but looking back, helping teachers set up bulletin boards was not necessarily one of them. He was there each day, and he was involved in the day-to-day responsibilities of his teachers. It did not end there; he trained with his teachers on new state initiatives. Mr. Gabrielson was also seen at lunch duty to keep an extra eye on students in their free time. Oh, how embarrassing to have a family member near my lunch table. Secretly, I hoped he would come over and address me personally because he was my uncle, and I was so proud to observe how respected he was in my school and community.

Thank you for humoring my reflection on one of my first mentors, but it is in this story that I highlight some key skills to look for with effective administrators. Through these colorful details, you can identify quality administrators to work with in your career. You may see yourself as a leader, which has enlightened you to pursue this role as you continue your education. Uncle Harry always wanted me to get my certification in administration, but I do not think I could live up to it. Despite this, it is essential to recognize the habits of effective leaders, which often predict the success of the school and the likelihood of staying in the classroom. Here we are, back to my goal. Yes, believe it or not, the effectiveness of your building principal(s) is a likely predictor of your success (DeMatthews, Knight, & Shin, 2021). So, how will you know this? This chapter outlines key skills to start looking for in your school building and ways to build an effective relationship with your administrators. From this, you will get ideas for good questions in your interview so that you will be able to determine if you are a good fit with the administrators at the building. Yes, you are interviewing them, as much as they are interviewing you.

The Roles of Administrators

In most buildings, you will have a lead teacher. This is typically a veteran grade teacher or point person for your content. Then you may have an assistant principal who is your go-to person for submitting lesson plans. In larger school districts, there may be several assistant principals. The lead principal will oversee the assistant principals, and these assistants will have divided jobs within the school building or possibly across school buildings. These assistants may be assigned specific tasks, such as attending IEP meetings, addressing behavior issues, and setting assessment goals. You are responsible for knowing the principal who is assigned to your situation. Principals are busy, as you will read in the following pages, so it is your responsibility to ensure you are sending your email questions to the right person.

© iStock.com/Nataliia Nesterenko.

Inclusive and Culturally Responsive Practices.

The following are some considerations to observe in your building principals. Administrators need to create multiple pathways and opportunities for students to achieve academic and social success. Building administrators need to provide access for teachers and staff to communicate with families in their first language. The first language of learners and their families should be present in the school setting.

Overall Responsibilities

In my recent years of working with principals, I have always been impressed when they know all the details of what is happening in their building. From volunteers to student teachers, they know who is in their classrooms. This is not a threat; it is simply bringing to your attention that your interview and recommendation letter are happening every time you enter your building. I have even had principals specifically report the lack of eye contact and wet noodle handshake they received from one of my teacher candidates on the first day of school. You may not want to work in this building for the rest of your life, but remember that the educator world is like getting into Greek life. In fraternities and sororities, you have to pledge your loyalty to the group. You are required to go through a hazing process that may include menial tasks so that you can go above and beyond to prove yourself to others. There is a similar honor code when veteran educators look out for each other. In their opinion, they can determine what is best for the students in the school. So, if you regularly leave early, teachers and principals will pass this information along to members of other school districts. This is a gentle reminder that people observe how you carry yourself daily. Educators share a camaraderie, and believe me, you want to be the student teacher that they are bragging about at meetings. In education, you must show up daily as though you are being interviewed. Refer to Part I with your notes about self-care goals. You need to take care of yourself outside of school to be ready to perform when you get to school each day.

Some of the principal's responsibilities include meetings, observations, addressing emails, and making phone calls. However, you should see them walking the halls and interacting with their faculty and students. You need to notice the teachers' interactions with the administrators. How do teachers talk about their administrators when they are not around? It is essential to know that when you have a problem, you have an administrator willing to listen to you. Similarly, observe how the administrators interact with students. Do students respect the school rules and the authority figures in the building? If students respect their principals, they will likely be respectful in the classroom to limit behavior infractions (PSEL, 2015). Does the principal value your content or expertise? If you are in special education, does the principal understand the roles and responsibilities you have in your job? Will they know that your lesson plans are going to look different?

 **Think About It.**

What times of the day do you see the principal present throughout the school day? What events is he/she seen at after school? Is there mutual respect between administrators and faculty? How do the administrators interact with students?
?

?

© iStock.com/Paper Trident.

Playing Fair

To be clear, fair is not equal, and equal is not fair. I like to think that being an administrator is a never-ending game of "whack a mole." Principals have responsibilities in the building, but sometimes they must drop everything and attend to emergencies. When responsibilities like approving services for students with identified disabilities arise, the principal does not have a roster or a play sheet. Principals need to understand the students' individual needs and know how the legal system can determine the support required for those students (Bateman & Cline, 2019). The consistent decision-making on most days shows true administrators' character. This can help determine if the principal has your best interests at heart.

Inclusive and Culturally Responsive Practices.

Building Culture: This is a makeup of the values, beliefs, traditions, attitudes, and behaviors that contribute to the overall daily environment in a building. All members of the building contribute to the building culture.

© iStock.com/skeeg.

Something you need to observe is the building culture. The building culture comprises the people who interact within the school setting. A positive school culture determines whether teachers and students thrive (Muhammad, 2009). This culture includes families, teachers, staff members, and students. The first consideration is the administrators' role when working with teachers and staff. Some principals are hired directly from a teaching

© iStock.com/Ralf Hahn.

position in that building and move down the hall into the principal's office. This can affect their ability to establish themselves as the new authority figure in the building. Does the principal always hang out with a group of teachers? Does he or she show favoritism with specific faculty members? You must recognize if teachers feel comfortable approaching their administrators for support. It is the administrator's responsibility to shape building culture. If a teacher is unhappy with their role in the building, will the principal work with the teacher to adjust placements? Look for signs based on the decisions made throughout the school year. Is there a focus to keep the same teachers happy, or does everyone in the building have a voice?

Making Big Decisions

All decisions should be made in the best interests of the students. The students are your customers. Similarly, do the principals have favorite students? Are there separate social groups within the building, or can you find the principal intermingling with all teachers and connecting with various students? Can all students complete a range of hobbies to express their interests? Do administrators value student athletes, or do they recognize that it is important for them to give time and attention to the students who need it most? One way to acknowledge this is by observing how the principal spends their time. Do principals attend all activities or only focus on particular interests? Does the principal allow instructional time so students can see their peers perform in the school play? Do they distribute the budget among projects and activities, or is there a focus on one area?

Think About It.

Do the administrators show favoritism to specific faculty, students, or activities? What groups are focused on with the social media sites? Public announcements? School Newsletter? How do parents, teachers, and students talk about the principals in the building? Is the budget allocated to support many interest areas?
?
?
?

School-Wide Management Systems

Another role for principals and administrators is to handle complex decision-making. Principals need to be able to make a range of choices, from when to cancel school due to a weather emergency to how to implement positive school-wide behavior practices. They get to make big decisions on school reform and focus on implementing large-scale formats for the school. Observing the administrators' philosophy and school-wide focus for decision-making is essential. Good leaders should be able to delegate responsibilities. When the principal must make decisions beyond the scope of his or her expertise, the principal should be able to consult with other experts within the school faculty to speak in the best interests of the school community.

Inclusive and Culturally Responsive Practices.

Administrators are responsible for identifying institutional practices, policies, and norms that may be harmful to historically underrepresented groups. Have a presence at these meetings to identify the advocates for students and learn ways to engage in efforts to rewrite policies, change practices, and raise awareness for equitable classrooms.

Crisis Management

Oftentimes, there will be known unknowns within a school community. I always address these topics with my students, and I stress that I hope they never experience a school crisis in their lifetime, but statistically, this is not likely. In recent years, school administrators have had increased responsibilities when addressing the effects of mass casualty (Horton et al., 2023). They have felt the impact of natural disasters, student suicide, and school tragedy. These events can occur with unexpected tragedy and loss. The school has various systems in place to assign responsibilities and ensure the school remains operational when an unexpected teacher death or a natural disaster closes the school for multiple days. The principal is responsible for being the leader and model for teachers and students. It is essential to understand the administrators' responses to these events during these times. Does the principal pull the community together? Do they rely on experts to support them with things beyond their control? Are teachers supported during these situations?

Positive Behavior Interventions and Supports

How do administrators implement Positive Behavior Interventions and Supports (PBIS)? The school principal helps to frame the school-wide set of needs and rules. This includes targeted rules for transition times and noninstructional locations. Some of these examples include hallways, bathrooms, lunchrooms, and so on. Downtime is the most frequent offender of misbehavior. Administrators play an essential role in providing professional development and holding teachers accountable for implementing each phase of the school-wide management system (Scaletta & Hughes, 2022). Reinforcement must be consistent, and oftentimes, the administrators are involved with repeat offenses. Administrators should be a part of these behavior management teams, collecting and examining the data to make ongoing decisions. The administrators must also understand the role of special education regarding disciplining students with identified disabilities. You will be an asset to your school's PBIS team. Be sure to observe and provide insights on your school's PBIS. Below are some ideas for you to check on and contribute to your school's PBIS team. Add some of your own ideas.

© iStock.com/AnnaSivak.

 **Add your Ideas.**
How You Can Contribute to PBIS

Get involved with Data Collection
Survey students to identify motivators
Collect community donations
- Coupons for a slice of pizza
- Time at the local ice skating rink

Have High school involvement for cross-age experiences
- Observe in the Science Lab
- Get your nails painted by a trade school technician
- Have lunch with an athlete

Observe other teachers to make sure you are implementing skills with fidelity

-
-

 **Inclusive and Culturally Responsive Practices.**

Understand that students with identified disabilities have exceptions to behavior management within their disability. This is called the Manifestation of their Disability.

Positive Interactions with Administrators During Your Student Teaching Placement

Just as you should see your administrators throughout the hallways and classrooms, you should be seen throughout the school day. This means you prepare for your classes before and after school so that you can be available to volunteer. This is just a reminder to Obligers, focus on saying yes to the activities you enjoy, and say "no" once, for two times you have already said "yes." For example, you should have already played a sport if you are going to coach that sport. You do not have extra time to search, "How to be an effective coach," and "Why can the goalie use her hands in soccer, but nobody else can?" Below is a list of responsibilities and activities you should be seen doing throughout your placement.

 **Add your Ideas.**
Checklist of things Administrators should see you doing during your placement.

Assist a club or after-school activity
Attend training for a new curriculum (Ask ahead of time. Sometimes these occur in the summer)
Teacher Duties during Prep:
- Bus
- Lunch
- Suspension
- Recess

Go to extracurricular events (plays, musicals, competitions, sports)
Attend a School Board Meeting
Parent–Teacher Organization Meeting (so much can be explained here)
Attend Community Events (Town Parades or City Festivals)

-
-

This chapter provides detailed information about administrators and how they can impact your career. Remember, this is your opportunity to practice and learn the skills required to be an effective educator. Take the initiative to practice these skills and work with your mentor teacher and university supervisor to get feedback. Just like the importance of teaching in front of students, it is also critical for you to take opportunities to collaborate with your colleagues and learn how to make improvements through these interactions with adults. Additionally, this is a reminder not to be afraid to ask questions to your administrator. Suppose you make a mistake in an interview or observation. Ask, "How could I have done that differently?" or "What skills do I need to work on?" Remember that administrators are there to support their teachers, especially new teachers. Find opportunities to show off your skills as a lifelong learner. Take on an engaging role in your school community.

 **Add your Ideas.**
Interactions you should be having with Administrators by the end of your placement

Actively participating in IEP meetings—not just observing
Use data to drive decisions (Behavior management forms, progress monitoring updates, etc.)
Communicating with special education teachers about accommodations/modifications
Maintaining a confident, composed tone when dealing with challenging behaviors
Asking for support (and documenting it) rather than going silent

-
-

Unless you are familiar with the schools you are interested in working at, you may not know the answers to the questions asked throughout the chapter. Nevertheless, you need answers to some of these questions. One meaningful way to learn more about the leaders where you work is to ask questions during the interview process. As they test you to see if you fit the job, you must also know if the people you work for match your teaching philosophy. Below are several questions for your consideration during the interview. You can select some of these questions that matter to you and ask them when the interviewers want to know if you have any questions. You may have some questions of your own. Add your ideas at the bottom.

 **Add your Ideas.**
Questions to ask Administrators During your Interview

If I were to ask several teachers about your role as a leader, what would they say?
Describe the mentoring process in my first few years of teaching.
When a new teacher is effective, what does that look like to you?
What is a red flag you see during student placements?
How involved are you in parent meetings regarding difficult situations, and what do you expect the teacher to handle?

-
-

Administrative Goals

How are you making connections with your administrators? Did you make any instant changes that have improved your interactions with the administrators in your building? If this is your case, lovely. Take the next step into Chapter 13 (Other Colleagues) and know that you can always connect back here and set clear goals for yourself. That is fine if you are not ready to commit to writing and collecting data on that goal. Remember, if you face a difficult situation that requires working with the administrators in your building (and before a job interview), please revisit Chapter 12 for some ways to work with the building principal(s).

Does this topic spark your interest? What are the strengths of the principals in your building, and how can you improve your relationship with these individuals? Remember, the more positive relationship you have with your administrators directly correlates to job satisfaction. The relationships you build with others take time. So, do not get frustrated if the principal does not recall your name when you run into her at the school musical. These connections take time. Prepare yourself to be consistent and think about manageable adjustments you can make for the rest of your placement. After you review the sample goals from these student teachers, proceed to the end of Chapter 15 to develop your own goals.

Jasper Is Staying Beyond the Bell

Our rebel has changed his tune. Jasper has just learned that there will be a track and field coaching position open in the spring. Though this is not baseball, coaching is a dream that fits right into the image Jasper has of himself when he thinks about his career in teaching. While thinking about his image and showing up, Jasper recognizes that he does not want to be seen as a teacher who is only in the building from bell to bell. He knows that this can be perceived as lazy and disinterested in teaching. Jasper will start coming to school earlier and leaving 30 minutes after the teacher's dismissal.

Jasper's Chart

Baseline Data	Making SMART Goals				
	Monday	Tuesday	Wednesday	Thursday	Friday
Arrival	5 minutes late	On time	30 mins early	On time	30 mins early
Departure				Left Early for practice	

Specific: What is the Target Behavior?	
Jasper will arrive 10 minutes early and leave 45 minutes after dismissal.	
With what **materials or conditions**?	
Each week, Jasper has 10 opportunities to arrive early and stay late.	
Measurable: How well must the skill be performed? (Criteria)	**Achievable:** What modifications or accommodations are needed for success? Making the time?
Jasper will arrive 10 minutes early and leave 45 minutes after dismissal, during 80% of the work week.	Find a new practice time Have materials ready before bed Bring materials to work on at the end of the day
How will the skill be **measured**? And **how often**?	Any **additional research**? People to talk to?
Daily	Work with the coach to find another time to practice on Thursdays
Relevance: Why is meeting this goal important?	**Timely:** What is considered mastery for this goal?
Jasper would like to show that he is responsible and dedicated to the program, by spending more time in the building before and after school.	Jasper will meet this goal once he has met this timeline before and after school for 80% of the time for 4 consecutive weeks. He is looking to reach his goal within 6 weeks.

What other assessments or data will help assess progress toward the goal?	What are the next steps in this goal area?
Record the times on the office clock and write times on the desk calendar.	Jasper will next work on getting to work earlier.

Quentin Limits Questions to the Principal

Quentin is placed at a large high school with four assistant principals. He recognizes that his questioning can be off-putting in meetings and especially during an interview. Over the next 4 weeks, Quentin will prepare and interview with a different assistant principal each week.

Quentin's Chart

Making SMART Goals	
Baseline Data	
Quentin's mentor teacher tallied how many questions Quentin asked during several meetings.	
Meetings with Quentin	**# of Questions Quentin Asks**
Parent Meeting	||||| |||
University Supervisor Meeting	|||||
9th Grade Field Trip Meeting	|||||
Specific: What is the Target Behavior?	
During a 20-minute interview, Quentin will limit himself to asking 4 questions to the interviewer.	
With what **materials or conditions**?	
Given a 20-minute practice interview	
Measurable: How well must the skill be performed? (Criteria)	**Achievable:** What modifications or accommodations are needed for success? Making the time?
With each interview, Quentin will limit himself to asking 4 questions to the principal.	Quentin will prepare a note sheet to write down and organize his thoughts before, during, and after the interview. He will send a follow-up email for feedback.
How will the skill be **measured**? And **How often**?	Any additional research? People to talk to?
With each interview Quentin will tally how many questions he asks. He can verify this data with each principal.	Before starting the interview process, Quentin will go to the Academic Success Center at his University for interview preparation.
Relevance: Why is meeting this goal important?	**Timely:** What is considered mastery for this goal?

Quentin wants to improve by prioritizing his questions to others, especially during the interview process.	He will complete 4 interviews over the course of 4 weeks.
What other assessments or data will help assess progress toward the goal?	**What are the next steps in this goal area?**
Quentin will record the interview and tally the questions to keep track.	He will work on tallying his number of questions while he is in meetings.

 Chapter Recap.

Impact from my elementary principal

Rank of administrators
- Lead teachers—responsible for grade level or content decision-making
- Assistant principals—Could divide behavior plans and teacher accountability; may work across schools
- Know who is responsible for your situation

Overall responsibilities of the principals
- Principals pay attention to the details of the building
- They will notice you and how you carry yourself
- Principals responsibilites—meetings, observations, emails, phone calls, discipline, etc.
- Take note how admin is received
- Student/ teacher/ parent interactions

Consider how the administrators contribute to the building's culture

Observe the big decisions administrators are expected to make
- Look for equity in the interests of the student
- Observe how the principal spends their time

School-wide management system
- Handle complex decision-making
- Observe philosophy for decision-making
- How do they delegate and consult

Administrators managing crisis situations
- Know the protocols
- Look for supporting the teachers and pulling the community together

PBIS—Understand the framework and mission for school-wide plan
- Rules for transition and noninstructional areas
- Need professional development to support
- Consistent reinforcement and clear expectations
- Know that specialists like special education teachers will have specific responsibilities

Refer to chart "Questions to ask principal"

Positive interactions to have with administrators while you are student teaching
- Ask questions administrators are there to support teachers, especially new ones
- Be seen
- Volunteer for extracurricular activities
- Collaborate with colleagues
- Be an active participant in meetings

Collaborative Thinking.

Questions to ask your mentors/peers
What are some ways you learn more about your administrators?
What did you learn by interviewing your building principal?
In what ways do you show up to add your presence around the building each day?
What do you look for in a good leader?

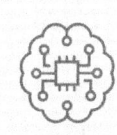

Technology Checkpoints.

National Policy Board for Educator Administration: An organization of groups creating and promoting a set of standards for teachers and educational leaders.
www.pbis.org/school: This website has information and resources on implementing PBIS at the school-wide level.
TeacherKit: The TeacherKit app is used as a classroom management tool, allowing the user to track attendance, behaviors, participation as well as communicate with the parent/guardian at home.
www.Swis.org A PBIS app, the SWIS Suite is used by educators and administrators to track behaviors and make decisions based on the data provided.
AI; Interview practice and feedback: By using AI prompts, you can create practice interview questions and receive feedback based on your answers. You can use prompts to create different scenarios and questions relating to the scenario. This can be helpful for job interviews, parent conferences, and team meetings.

Teacher Decision-Making.

Working positively with your building administrators is another key to your success. Review the things that administrators are observing about you and look for the effective administrator practices highlighted in this chapter. Remember that showing up every day to student teach like it is your job interview can be exhausting, so stay observant with managing your self-care. Consider the areas where you see enough progress to make space for collaborative relationships in the following chapters.

Next Steps.

What is working? . . .

What is not working? . . .

What do I need? . . .

What am I proud of? . . .

What do I need to let go of? . . .

Weekly Reflection.

Take a minute to Use the space below to jot down some of your accomplishments during student teaching. You are making progress. I am reminding you that you have this, and I believe in you. I am encouraging you to highlight new relationships you have made with your colleagues because you are a quality educator, and administrators need teachers like you in the field for years to come. You got this!

13

Colleagues, Paraprofessionals, and Other Support Staff

Chapter Outline

Scenario in the Classroom	241
Strategies for Working with Everyone	250
Scaffolding for Teamwork	254
What to Do When It Is Not Working Out	258
Collegial Goals	260

Scenario in the Classroom

Though you are the student teacher in the building, all school community members currently have slight superiority over you. I bet you know and feel this. However, make sure to practice your interactions with all school community members. As the administration checks in on your successes, other teachers, paraprofessionals, and even the secretary observe how you mesh in the school community. Remember how I started this part by comparing entering education to pledging for Greek life. It may be just the profession, or the fact that you have the responsibility to educate the future; most of the people in your school community are ensuring you are a good fit. No pressure, right? So it is only fair to remind you that it is essential for you to treat all members of your school community with respect.

When you have mutual respect, they will support you when you least expect it. For example, one day I was meeting with a mentor teacher, the paraprofessional chimed in to give an example of how well my student teacher was doing with one of the students. When I shared the story with my student teacher, she was shocked that the paraprofessional noticed. Do not forget the secretaries either. They are typically the first faces you see when you walk into the building. I often greet the secretaries with a hello and some small chitchat. A secretary once told me, "That girl in Mrs. Orr's classroom, I hope we can keep her, she is a good one." On the flip side, she was also not afraid to share that I needed to check the attendance log for a student who left early several days that week. Just another reminder to take care of yourself so you can be your best self when you get to school each day. If you need to reshape some of your self-care goals, review Part I to make some progress.

Collaborating with Others

In this chapter, I will provide an overview of the professionals working in most school buildings. Hopefully, you have taken some time to connect with your tendency to learn how to work to your advantage to complete tasks. There is another benefit to the four tendencies. If you understand the tendencies of the people you work with, you can use this to your advantage when collaborating with others. As a friendly reminder, this only works if you have the person take the short "Four Tendencies Quiz." You can presume a person's tendency based on their outward behavior. However, the motivation behind their actions truly determines an individual's tendency and their motivation to complete tasks. Below is a chart describing the four tendencies in another context of considerations when working with others.

 **Add your Ideas.**
Below are considerations when working with colleagues who have other tendencies. Be sure to add some ideas that work for you when working with other tendencies.

Working with an Upholder
- Don't be offended by their rigidity
- Share "to do" lists
- Keep up with your promises to them
- Give them clear expectations and purpose

-
-

Working with an Obliger
- Balance how much you ask them to do
- Remember Obligers cannot hold each other accountable
- Be cautious if they shift into rebellion
- Align an effective accountability partner

-
-

Working with a Questioner
- Provide research for your choices
- Give a rationale for your deadlines
- Give them a time limit to decide
- Convince them to try something new as "an experiment"

-
-

Working with a Rebel
- Frame your requests around their identity
- But do not address them as "rebels"
- Don't take it personal
- Use "first, then" statements
- Do not feel urged to provide rewards

-
-

© iStock.com/Visual Generation.

Your Mentor Teacher Is Your Guide

The first relationship you must take care of is with your mentor. This is like a co-teaching relationship. You must know the expectations and your role in the classroom. Have regularly scheduled check-ins with your mentor to avoid discussing only problems. Below is a chart for you and your mentor teacher to review and "SHARE" to ensure that you are on the right track in meeting their expectations. Take some time in the first week to compare your "SHARE" notes. Ask clarifying questions. Be sure to understand your mentor, and ensure your mentor understands your answers. Refer to this chart regularly to ensure you meet your mentor's expectations.

 **Add your Ideas.**
Share your ideas with your Co-Teacher and or Mentor. Discuss how to move forward with your differences

Sharing Hopes, Attitudes, Responsibilities, and Expectations

Directions: Take a few minutes to individually complete this worksheet. After completing it individually, share the responses with your co-teaching partner by taking turns reading the responses. Do not use this time to comment on your partner's responses—merely read. After reading through the responses, take a moment or two to jot down any thoughts you have regarding what your partner has said. Then, come back together and begin to share reactions to the responses. Your goal is to either (1) Agree, (2) Compromise, or (3) Agree to Disagree

1) Right now, the main HOPE I have regarding this co-teaching situation is:
___

2) My ATTITUDE/philosophy regarding teaching students with disabilities in a general education classroom is:
___

3) I expect to have the following RESPONSIBILITIES in a co-taught classroom:
___

4) I expect my co-teacher to have the following RESPONSIBILITIES:
___

5) I have the following EXPECTATIONS in a classroom, with regard to:

(A) Discipline ___
(B) Classwork ___
(C) Materials ___
(D) Homework ___
(E) Planning ___
(F) Modification for individual students ___
(G) Grading ___
(H) Noise level ___
(I) Cooperative learning ___
(J) Giving/receiving feedback ___

(K) Other ___

SHARE Worksheet SOURCE: Murawski, W. W., & Dieker, L. A. (2004). Tips and strategies for co-teaching at the secondary level. *Teaching Exceptional Children*, 36(5), 52–58.

Co-Teaching as a Partnership

Co-teaching is often referred to as a marriage (Murawski & Goodwin, 2014), but if you have yet to experience marriage, I want you to be able to connect with the partnership concept as it relates to you. A partnership is viewed as a relationship with a small number (in co-teaching, typically two) of people working together to meet a common goal. For example, you and your roommate share the responsibilities of keeping your apartment clean so that your landlord returns your security deposit. In your case, you and your sibling are the primary caregivers for aging parents, and you both are looking to make sure they can live comfortably at home. You may already be an entrepreneur and have started a business partnership with the goal of making $5,000 in profit next year. Notice that in all of these relationships, people are working together to meet a common goal.

The co-teaching format is similar to the examples listed above in that both teachers are working together to meet common goals for their students. There are benefits to co-teaching, as teachers working together in the same classroom report more job satisfaction and opportunities for professional growth (Weiss & Brigham, 2000). So here I go again, focusing on skills that will bring you joy in teaching. I had the opportunity of working in an enjoyable co-taught classroom with Mr. Larry Harp; this was my favorite class setting. The main reason I left this positive classroom experience was to pass along the benefits of this inclusive co-teaching experience. Larry and I co-planned, co-taught, and co-assessed the students in our inclusive National, State, and Government courses.

You should be equal partners, but the responsibilities for partnerships are rarely 50–50 (Brown, 2021). This means that all duties are not split evenly at all times. There are times you will have to show up more than your colleague. Just as one day you may have to go to work even when you are not feeling your best. These are check-ins you should have with your co-teacher or mentor regularly. In other instances, you may have expertise in a content area, and it is more logical for you to take the lead in preparing the lesson. Hopefully, you will be able to complete the "Share" so that each of you can identify your strengths when working together. Both teachers should be seen as equal partners in the eyes of the students. Neither of you should be viewed as glorified babysitters. The charts on the next few pages can also be helpful for you and anyone you work with in the classroom. The first chart is a sample, and you may use these ideas. The second chart includes options for you and your co-teacher or mentor to brainstorm and create compatible tasks simultaneously. These shared responsibilities can also apply to other adults in your room (i.e., paraprofessionals, volunteers, etc.). Review these documents with the other adults in your room and add your ideas on what works best for your situation. As you continue with this chapter, you will learn skills for effective meetings and delegation of responsibilities that you can apply to your collaborative relationships in the classroom.

© iStock.com/Rudzhan Nagiev.

Skills and Behaviors for Student Teaching

© iStock.com/gmast3r

Think About It.
Notice that both teachers are always doing something related to the lesson.

If one of you is doing this . . .	The other can be doing this . . .
Lecturing	Modeling note-taking on the board/overhead
Taking Role	Collecting and/or reviewing last night's homework
Passing out papers	Reviewing directions
Giving instructions orally	Writing down instructions on board
Checking for understanding with large heterogeneous	Checking for understanding with small heterogeneous group of students
Circulating, providing one-on-one support as needed	Providing direct instruction to whole class
Prepping half of the class for one side of a debate	Prepping the other half of the class for the opposing side of the debate
Facilitating a silent activity	Circulating, checking for comprehension
Providing large-group instruction	Reviewing homework
Running last-minute copies or errands	Monitoring a large group as they work on practice materials
Reteaching or pre-teaching with a small group	Reading aloud quietly with a small group, previewing upcoming information
Facilitating sustained silent reading	Proctoring a test silently with a group of students
Reading a test aloud to a group of students	Providing suggestions for modifications, accommodations, and activities for diverse learners
Creating basic lesson plans for standards, objectives, and content curriculum	Also facilitating station or groups
Facilitating stations or groups	Conducting role-play or modeling concept
Explaining new concept	Considering enrichment opportunities

Adapted from the source: Murawski, W. (2009) *Collaborative Teaching in Secondary Schools : Making the Co-Teaching Marriage Work!*, Corwin Press

 **Add your Ideas.**
Talk with your Co-teacher or Mentor teacher and discuss what each other could be doing.

If one of you is doing this . . .	The other can be doing this . . .
Lectures	
Writes on board	
Reviews timelines or dates	
Assigns homework	
Reviews for a test	
Gives a new vocabulary	
Gives a test	
Teaches complex information	
Takes roll	
Reviews homework	
Disciplines a student	
Circulates around the class	
Leaves to copy materials	
Reads aloud	
Gives Silent Sustaining Reading time	
Creates cooperative learning groups	
Creates rotating stations	
Assigns differentiated work	
Gives directions	
Identifies standard to address	
Works with small group	
Writes on overhead	
Collects classwork	

Three things that we will do to ensure parity in the classroom are:

1) _____

2) _____

3) _____

Reprinted from Collaborative Teaching in Secondary Schools: Making the Co-Teaching Marriage Work! by Wendy Murawski, Thousand Oaks, CA: Corwin, www.corwinpress.com. Reproduction authorized only for the local school site or nonprofit organization that has purchased this book.

Productive Relationships with Paraprofessionals

You may be fortunate enough to have additional support personnel in your classroom. Especially if you are in a special education classroom, you will more than likely have support staff in your classroom throughout the entire day. Depending on the needs of your students, you may have several adults in your classroom. Managing several adults can be just as complex as supervising the students. You will be able to monitor how your mentor navigates this responsibility. Below is a chart of various types of classroom support staff. This is just a general description of their duties. Add your ideas for additional tasks your paraprofessionals could be required to do in your classroom.

⊕ **Add your Ideas.** Various support staff who could be in your classroom and their responsibilities.	
Nurse's Aide- Will follow to each class and focus on medical, dietary, and safety needs. Typically assigned to one student through their IEP	Assure student takes medicine Administers and enforces specialized food diet Supports with transporting classroom materials Transports student in-between classes Provides toileting support
Behavior Aide- Has detailed expectations to focus on the needs of student based on his or her behavior concerns. Typically assigned to one student through their IEP.	Collects behavior data Document communication log Redirects student Implements elopement procedures Take students for breaks as needed
Learning Support Aide- Can be assigned to one or several students in the classroom. Sometimes, this support staff is hired by the school district	Reads tests to students Implements testing accommodations Initiate independent work for struggling students Provide scaffolding Keeps students on task Monitors stations with previously learned material Support students during science labs
Grade Level Paraprofessional This individual can be assigned to work with several teachers throughout the school day. Typically, the school district hires this support staff.	Shared among all grade-level teachers Complete clerical duties Follows assigned student(s) to classes Assigned during reading/math to support small group instruction
Others?	

Depending on whether your support staff is hired by your school district or contracted through health insurance, you will have a different level of responsibility for these adults. When you start teaching, your paraprofessionals will likely be older than you. This can be an awkward dynamic for young individuals who are just building their confidence as new teachers. Nevertheless, remember, you are the expert in your role. Additionally, your paraprofessionals will have strengths and attributes that you can rely on to help your classroom run smoothly. Find out what their strengths are so that you can capitalize on getting their help in the classroom. Building good connections is the backbone of helper relationships. People are more inclined to help someone who is kind and shows appreciation. You should refer to the skills in the remainder of this chapter, including regular check-ins and effective use of time. Consider using this chart specifically to get to know the paraprofessionals in your classroom.

 **Add your Ideas.**
Interviewing your Paraprofessional.

1. Describe what you do during a typical day at school.
   Instructional and noninstructional times
   Preparation activities
   Interactions
   Locations
   Comfort level and appropriateness

2. Describe what you do if/when you encounter difficulties working with a student.
   How procedures were developed
   Level of effectiveness

3. Describe your interactions with school personnel and families in relation to your student(s).
   People
   Types of interactions
   Instructional and noninstructional times
   Team meetings—participation, input, valued
   Comfort level and appropriateness

4. Describe any training you *initially* had related to your job.
   Appropriateness, relevancy
   Sufficiency
   Payment

5. Describe any training you had after working for a while.
   Appropriateness, relevancy
   Sufficiency
   Payment
   Additional training needed

6. Describe the skills and personal characteristics required for your job

7. Describe the hardest and easiest parts of your job, and why they are the hardest and easiest.

8. Describe what would help you do your job better.

9. Describe anything that gets in the way of doing your job well.

Adapted from: Biggs, E. E., Gilson, C. B., & Carter, E. W. (2016). Accomplishing more together: Influences to the quality of professional relationships between special educators and paraprofessionals. Research and Practice for Persons with Severe Disabilities, 41(4), 256–272.

Strategies for Working with Everyone

Before we shift topics to families and school communities, there are many additional adults in your school building who are vital to the daily functioning of the school. These are the individuals who see your students daily. Your students need to see you modeling respect for these adults by showing appreciation for their jobs. For example, "Everyone, fill out your lunch menu. Mrs. Clites loves it when we get our food orders in on time." You may not interact with them often, but over time, you can add collaborative helpers who are making your job a positive experience. Introduce yourself to these people and learn more about what they do. Avoid meeting people when you need them in an emergency. This is not a complete list of individuals or what their job entails. I have included a line to write down the names of these people and add your ideas on ways they can help you during your placement.

⊕ Add your Ideas.
More professionals in your school community

Additional Staff and their responsibilities	Tips for collaborations and ways they can help you
Custodian(s) _____ _____ _____ Responsible for daily sanitization and garbage cleanup.	Teach your students to clean up after themselves. "It is not Mr. Jacob's job to pick up your papers." Share extra treats for the night staff. Thank them when they respond quickly to an urgent cleanup. • •
Maintenance Worker(s) _____ Daily upkeep of the building	Maintenance workers will complete inside and outside tasks like cutting grass, seasonal landscaping, and snow removal. They will also prepare fields and facilities for sporting events. • •
Lunch Servers _____ Collects food orders Meal preparation and clean up Serves meals to students Cleans and sanitizes tables Organizes payments and free-reduced meal documentation	Consider ordering pre-packaged meals for trips Make allergies and food restrictions well-known They can help on days you forgot your lunch or when you have a student who skipped breakfast. • •

Specials Teachers _____ _____ _____ _____ Teachers specializing in noncore subjects (gym, music, art, etc.)	Be on time for these classes (pick up and drop off) Set an expectation for your students' behaviors while they are with that teacher. Follow up with the teacher on students' behavior. Note students who do not thrive academically but shine in other areas. Incorporate these interests in the content you teach.
Technical Support Person A teacher specialist who is trained in audio and visual equipment. This person can provide support and training on technology glitches.	Ask questions about technology issues before they become a problem. Send a follow-up "thank you" to your Tech person when they provide support. Remember, they have day-to-day responsibilities that are beyond your emergency. • •
Technical Trades Teachers _____ _____ Teachers work with students who have decided to major in job-trades areas instead of a college track.	Give tasks to the woodshop teacher. Ex. Have students make signs as gifts for your teachers. Incorporate classroom rewards with their services. Ex. Students have a pizza party from food services. Utilize services for students in need. Ex. Go to the beautician for students to get their hair brushed.
Class Grandparents _____ A district program where retired individuals come to support teachers and students during the school day.	Give meaningful tasks. Incorporate their strengths in your lessons Pair with student(s) who have not made connections yet.
School Nurse _____ Responsible for the health and safety of students in the school. They will distribute prescribed and as-needed medications.	Keep band-aids and ice packs in your classroom to avoid excess trips to the nurse's office. Follow up with the nurse regarding students who ask to visit the nurse regularly. • •
_____	

Inclusive and Culturally Responsive Practices.

Work with educational professionals to find ways to incorporate the experiences of all students in your teaching materials, assignments, curriculum, and other educational services.

Regular Check-Ins

When you work regularly with your mentor teacher, you should share your lesson plans and project ideas well in advance, so you have time to get feedback and make changes. When working with paraprofessionals, you should have scheduled check-ins to discuss their daily responsibilities. You need to avoid requesting meetings just to talk about problems. Whoever you work with each day should have regular daily or weekly check-ins. Why? You do not want to meet only when there are problems. It is crucial that you are clear about your expectations of others and that you understand what is expected of you. You can also talk about changes in your students' schedules or new classroom management plans you want to try. By having these regularly scheduled meet-ups, you give each other time to discuss what is working and what is not working. So, when there is an issue, you do not have to be the one to send the email or hear, "Can we have a meeting to discuss some issues we are having?" Because at that point, a problem could have been prevented.

© iStock.com/Visual Generation.

Think About It.

Who have you built relationships with around the school building?
What are some examples of ways you have been a helpful colleague?
Now is your chance; if you have not met many of the people mentioned in this chapter, it is time to get out there.

?
?

Even brief meetings should have an agenda. It is easy to get off topic if you meet each Monday and discuss the updates on "The Bachelorette." Time is precious when you are in the school building, and you need to make the most of it. I worked with one co-teacher, and our meetings turned into his vent sessions about the challenges one of our students is having. However, during this time, we could also have been planning our lessons for the following week or talking about ways to manage her behavior. To avoid this, I sent out a quick email agenda that I can use each week to keep our conversations on track. Below is the notetaker that I use for meetings. You can personalize this and make it your own.

Add your Ideas.
Agenda Chart to use for note-taking and accountability.

| Attendance: | Date: |
| Location: | Time: |

Agenda: Who is accountable and when

Old Business:

Next Check-in:

Informal Communication

Your professionalism is still being evaluated even when you are not in meetings or in front of your students. Be sure to scan the school for a good professional mentor. Many times, this was not my student teacher's mentor teacher. During my college class, I often heard, "I love my mentor; she is the best, but I am not a fan of her gossip." These informal conversations can sometimes occur in the staff lounge or during lunch. Be sure to avoid gossip at all costs. Sometimes teachers can have these conversations to get the scoop on your opinions. These interactions go back to school culture. It is unhealthy for teachers to thrive when focusing on the negatives about students and their colleagues. Read some tips below on avoiding school drama and gossip, and add some of your ideas on avoiding school gossip.

 **Add your Ideas.**
Limit your informal conversation which can lead to gossip.

Avoid your opinion about people (families and colleagues) who are not in the room.
Do not share stories that your students share, unless someone could be in a harmful situation.
If lunchtime becomes a gossip session, use the time to meet with students.

Responses when you are asked to spread gossip:
"I have not been around long enough to form an opinion on that person."
"I do not have the data to support that issue."
"I do not know the facts, so I am unsure what is relevant."

-
-

Scaffolding for Teamwork

When working in groups, it is crucial to have a layout and clear expectations of each other. Although you are adults, it is important to establish clear rules for how you will work together and who is responsible for what activities. This next section is a framework for working regularly with partners and groups. Each theme fits into pitfalls that individuals have when working in groups. First, I will review four factors that determine the success of a team, with examples for you to connect with when working with others. Then I will discuss strategies you can put into place to avoid common misunderstandings when working in groups.

 **Think about It.**

	Definition	Considerations
Goals	Share your goals for the group. Reach an agreed-upon shared common goal for the task. (Use SHARE for a group project).	Everyone in a partnership will not have the same goals. Reach an agreed-upon common ground for your project and move forward. Be honest!
Roles	Determine roles based on expertise and have clear expectations for who is responsible for each task.	Do not judge how others complete the task if it is not your role. It is okay even if it is not how you would do it. Delegate!
Communication	Use clear communication in and out of meetings. Be sure that you understand your colleagues by asking clarifying questions.	Listen to others during the brainstorming process. If you do not understand what someone is saying, ask about it!
Time	Respect the time of your peers by showing up and being present during meetings. Make good use of time by determining what needs to be done as a group and what can be delegated into independent tasks.	Start on time, this will send the message that everyone needs to get to the meeting on time. Identify what each person can do independently.

Shared Measurable Goals

The most successful teams in sports and groups alike have shared goals and a straightforward way to measure those goals (Friend & Cook, 2007). It is essential to recognize that you need regular team meetings to discuss your goals and track progress. This only works if you are honest about the goals you want to achieve from the project. So, how does this transfer into the classroom? Think about seventh-grade teams working on increasing students' attendance rates before the end of the school year. However, the principal would like a 95% passing rate on the state tests. Yet, the special education teacher and the reading specialist would like to identify 10 more kids for special education services. Each teacher has different goals for the students and their classrooms. Each person is working on various data with other goals. This team needs to work together to allocate resources and expertise to focus on appropriate goals for this school year.

Roles and Responsibilities

Know your roles, and each person has appropriate responsibilities based on their expertise, such as increasing the performance of the seventh-grade students. Each person is approaching the problem with a different focus and solution. The individuals on this team need to discuss which goals are essential for the overall success of the students in this grade. During this time, balance sharing your role and being open to new ideas. Suppose you are the special education teacher looking to collect data for evaluations. In that case, you may be the expert who can present the teachers with some strategies to help them encourage daily attendance. As the principal, they are looking for the special education teacher to reinforce the truancy rules and brainstorm different ways to get students to school on time.

Clear Communication

Effective communication (refer to LAFF; active listening in Chapter 14). During the communication stages, it is important to brainstorm and allow people to share ideas. Ask questions for clarification. Give positive feedback on the ideas you like. Give a set amount of time to discuss topics and brainstorm. Either reach a consensus or vote on the next steps. Before you move forward to the following steps, it is essential to agree upon a standard method of communication that everyone uses when you are not meeting as a group. For example, you may build your documents on a shared drive and use text messaging to give updates. Recognize and respect the method of communication the group uses.

Inclusive and Culturally Responsive Practices.

Observe communication between and among colleagues. Look for learning communities and spaces that are inclusive and free of negative comments or actions that subtly and often unconsciously or unintentionally express a prejudiced attitude toward your peers or students. Before going into meetings or conversations, think about ways you can validate others' opinions.

Emails are an effective means of communication. Once upon a time, email was the most common communication between colleagues. Now, people are less likely to check and communicate through email. School districts provide teachers with an email address; therefore, teachers and staff are expected to check and respond to emails promptly. What is timely? Most educational professionals will say 24 hours, depending on the urgency of the details. Be aware that this can be the primary form of communication for your colleagues, so you should check your email regularly for important updates. Some other teachers may not use texting and may be more inclined to visit or leave a note in your mailbox. Though it can be challenging to balance, you will have a few colleagues who are hard to reach. They may respond quickest through a visit to their classroom during their prep period. One thing to always consider is that email is legal documentation. Before you hit submit, consider if you would be comfortable with this email displayed in court. Email can be used to document meeting notes and clear accountability expectations. It may be frustrating on your part, but as the new teacher, there will be times when you need to go out of your way to communicate consistently with other professionals. When using email, be clear, concise, confidential, and factual. Below are additional tips on using email with others in the school.

 **Add your Ideas.**
Recommendations for Emails

- Reread the email aloud
- **Email is legal documentation**
- Double-check if you need to "Reply All"
- cc: your mentor in emails that include parents and colleagues
- DO NOT WRITE IN ALL CAPITALZ IT WILL NOT CATCH MISPELLLINGS
- Have a signature to explain your role and save time on your greetings

-
-

Effective Use of Time

Make good use of time. Show up on time and make good use of the time while working together. Respect each other's time by giving your attention to the meetings. You can be more productive with brief, regularly scheduled meetings versus longer meetings where participants can get sidetracked. This is where an agenda can come in handy. Decide what needs to be hashed out as a group and what can be assigned as delegated responsibilities. Not all problems can be solved in a day, and each person on your team has different timelines, schedules, and obligations. Determine what can be done as a group and what tasks can be delegated independently. Use effective communication methods discussed above to provide check-ins and updates regarding progress. Remember that the Obligers of your group will need an accountability partner.

 **Think About It.**

Have any colleagues or friends completed the "Four Tendencies Quiz?" How has learning about their tendency helped you to work with them? Have you shared details about your tendency with others, which has helped you work more collaboratively? How is your communication with others in your building? Describe some examples of people whom you should be meeting with regularly. What topics should be discussed?
?
?
?
?

What to Do When It Is Not Working Out

So you are actively listening, planning, and preparing, yet there is still someone difficult to work with. Despite your efforts at collaboration, you may have colleagues, mentors, or parents who are difficult to work with. Remember you are at the beginner status of Greek life, and each day you are proving yourself despite your expertise and experiences. You are required to go through a hazing process that may include being nice to difficult people. The first step is to consider why the individual may be exhibiting challenging behavior in the situation. Just like your students, you cannot control adult behavior or their responses. But their actions may not be about you. What is important is to recognize what the person is doing to escalate the conversation. First, identify these difficulties so that you can help the individual and limit stressful interactions which can contribute to your burnout (Rivedal, Cichocki, & Chung, 2023). Below is a chart that identifies possible reasons why individuals present themselves in a confrontational manner.

Think About It.
Types of Difficult People with Examples of their Behaviors

Types of Difficult Individuals with Descriptions of their Behaviors	Example of Behavior with Colleague and Student's Family Member
Dependent Clinger is an individual with multiple and increasingly frequent requests and needs.	**Colleague:** Always asks you to review the details of your lesson plans and edit their work. **Family:** Always asks you to put their niece Rosalba in a group with her friends to avoid drama.
Entitled Demander is needy, controlling, and intimidating to obtain whatever services they believe they deserve.	**Colleague:** Needs you to complete menial tasks like photocopying. **Family:** Needs you to call after lunch each day to report what Lamar ate independently.
Manipulative Help-rejector is never helped by any support offered and has new problems continuously.	**Colleague:** Does not like the ideas the team created for homecoming week and is spending the weekend working on new decorations **Family:** Does not like the new reading series their son has to read for homework or the books you selected from the library.

Self-Destructive Denier Engages in deleterious behaviors despite any recommendations.	**Colleague:** This peer is not ready for graduation and making decisions about job interviews, so she stays up late and does not come to work on time. **Family:** Refuses to sign permission to evaluate because they feel their daughter's behavior and learning difficulties are due to the challenging teaching strategies and peer conflict she is facing.
Adapted from: Rivedal, D. D., Cichocki, M., & Chung, K. C. (2023). Dealing with difficult people and why it matters. *Plastic and Reconstructive Surgery, 152*(5), 923–928.	

Next step is practicing what to do when dealing with difficult people. Many components of effective practices are already skills that you have read about throughout the chapters. Remember to show up to these situations as your best possible self. Perhaps you are going into a meeting with a family who is historically "Entitled Demanders." You can prepare for this meeting and set up your agenda for success. But sometimes you just may have your colleague drop into your lunch break, presenting you with her "Dependent Clinger" needs. These encounters may catch you by surprise, but Rivedal and colleagues (2023) have steps for these conversations that can help you to have positive outcomes. Below is a table to help walk you through the steps of dealing with difficult people. There is not always one set way to handle difficult people, so be sure to reflect and add your ideas as they relate to your circumstances. This may also be a skill you observe as modeled by your mentor teacher.

⊕ Add your Ideas.
Positive approach to de-escalating a conversation with a difficult person.

Steps	What and why this is helpful
Take deep breath.	This adds oxygen to your blood stream which is calming. Think about your most effective breathwork. • •
Take a moment to pause.	Try counting to 10 slowly and silently; this slows your thoughts. Refer back to Chapter 5 to identify which mind-centering technique works for you. • •

Separate the person from their behavior.	Say "the behavior that this person is exhibiting is difficult," by placing the label of difficult on the behavior rather than the person, may help approach the situation with empathy. Remember to LAFF. • •
Be open, honest, and supportive. Show genuine concern, empathy, and sincerity.	Gestures of empathy help you to connect with the person with the difficulty. • •
Turn inward. Introspection helps you to learn from your difficult encounters.	Be mindful, which entails focusing on the present moment and remaining nonjudgmental. • •
Adapted from: Rivedal, D. D., Cichocki, M., & Chung, K. C. (2023). Dealing with difficult people and why it matters. *Plastic and Reconstructive Surgery, 152*(5), 923–928.	

Collegial Goals

Now that we are getting to the collaboration priorities, there is so much you could work on. I am here to remind you to take small steps toward progress. The upcoming goals are a two-part series to help Kaycee have productive weekly meetings with her grade-level teachers and fellow Obligers. If you are unsure where to begin, review the sample goals below. Remember to start with your baseline data. After examining the goals provided by the student teachers, please navigate to the end of Chapter 15 to formulate your own collegial goals.

Kaycee Has an Agenda

Kaycee has learned that having productive meetings requires an agenda. She shared with the other first-grade teachers that she has an assignment to lead weekly grade-level meetings for 20 minutes each week. She promises they will be productive and on task. They will have these meetings replace the 40-minute-long biweekly meeting during their prep periods. She has pointed out that they will take up the same amount of time. They must meet weekly and follow the agenda. Currently, the teachers are on task for 5 minutes of the meeting. Most colleagues either show up late or leave early for this meeting. Therefore, all the work falls back on Kaycee and her mentor to build resources on their own time. After reviewing the meeting agenda, Kaycee and her mentor thought this could be a great way to get things done in their planning meetings.

Kaycee's Chart

Making SMART Goals	
Baseline Data Kaycee and the other teachers only stay on topic for 20 minutes during a 40-minute planning meeting.	
Specific: What is the Target Behavior?	
Kaycee and her first-grade teachers will get through 90% of the agenda that is prepared before the weekly, 20-minute first-grade planning meeting.	
With what materials or conditions?	
During a 20-minute meeting, Kaycee will check off each topic that is discussed and addressed during that meeting.	
Measurable: How well must the skill be performed? (Criteria)	**Achievable:** What modifications or accommodations are needed for success? Making the time?
3 reminders or expectations in a 30-minute period.	Plug 3 reminders or expectations into each lesson plan.
How will the skill be measured? And how often?	**Any additional research? People to talk to?**
Kaycee will print off an agenda and cross off each item that is addressed during the meeting.	Email the first-grade teachers to get agenda items before the meeting. Send the agenda to the first-grade teachers in advance.
Relevance: Why is meeting this goal important?	**Timely:** What is considered mastery for this goal
By spending planning time on task the teachers will not have to spend their own time completing the tasks that were not discussed.	This goal will be mastered once she has 2 straight weeks of completing 90% of the task agenda items.
What other assessments or data will help assess progress toward the goal?	**What are the next steps in this goal area?**
Kaycee will chart item completion directly on the agenda. Colleagues will share feedback on the progress they are making.	Once they meet this goal, they will focus on other areas of meeting strategies.

Simone Is Checking In

After learning more about "The Four Tendencies Framework," Simone thought it would be a good idea for the individuals she works with to take the "Four Tendencies Quiz." Simone discovered that her co-teacher, Dr. Harkins, is an Obliger. Her paraprofessional and mentor teacher are both Obligers. Simone reviewed the details of the Obliger, which is someone who needs accountability to get things done. Dr. Harkins is also more inclined to be a "people pleaser" and complete others' tasks before completing her own. After reviewing this framework, she has learned she needs to balance her responsibilities with her colleagues better. She and Dr. Harkins agreed that they need to spend more time planning. They follow the agenda form included in this chapter, and they delegate responsibilities and deadlines at the end of each meeting.

Simone's Chart

Making SMART Goals	
Baseline Data Simone followed her mentor's planning routines, and she never met regularly with her co-teacher, Dr. Harkins.	
Specific: What is the Target Behavior?	
Simone and her co-teacher will meet once a week for 40 minutes.	
With what materials or conditions?	
Given Friday afternoon planning time, Simone and Dr. Harkins will take 40 minutes 1x/ week to plan.	
Measurable: How well must the skill be performed? (Criteria)	**Achievable:** What supports are needed for success? Making the time?
40 minutes of engaged and on-task behavior	Take turns making an agenda
How will the skill be measured? And How often?	**Any additional research? People to talk to?**
Each week, the pair's notes and resources will be posted on the agenda/ meeting notes.	Ask the mentor teacher to join when she is included in the lesson. Have a backup plan for emergencies.
Relevance: Why is meeting this goal important?	**Timely:** What is considered mastery for this goal
Consistent planning will help to meet the goals of collaboration.	On-task 40 minutes/week 3 out of 4 weeks in a row.
What other assessments or data will help assess progress toward the goal?	**What are the next steps in this goal area?**
Teachers will share feedback on what is working and what needs improvement.	Once the co-teachers meet the goal, they will discuss adding more colleagues or another day.

 **Chapter Recap.**

Meeting expectations in the classroom
- Treat all members of the school with respect

Collaborating with others; Working with the 4 tendencies
- Upholders—identify and meet their expectations, they may be rigid and stick to timelines and "to do" lists
- Obligers—Balance your requests, cannot count on other Obligers for accountability, watch out for rebellion
- Questioner—give timeline and rationale for decisions, try new things as "experiments"
- Rebel—Do not be offended by their behaviors or feel the need to provide rewards, frame your requests with how they identify themselves

Your mentor teacher is your guide. SHARE to make clear expectations of each other

Co-Teaching is a partnership
- SHARE expectations
- Partnerships are not 50–50
- Neither person is a babysitter, identify other responsibilities while the other is leading the lesson

Productive relationships with paraprofessionals
- Know the contracted expectations of your paraprofessional
- Interview them for strengths and preferences

Strategies for working with everyone
- Get to know the responsibilities of the support staff. Get to know them.
- Have regular check-ins with people you work with daily
- Informal Communications
- email is documentation
- avoid gossip

Scaffolding for teamwork
- Find common ground for shared measurable goals
- Know everyone's roles and responsibilities
- Provide clear and positive communication in preferred format
- Have an agenda and use everyone's time effectively

What to do when it is not working out. Step 1: Identify who you are working with
- Dependent Clinger—has many needs
- Entitled Demander—Controlling and needy
- Manipulative Help-Rejector—Help never works, always has new issues
- Self-Destructive Denier—Avoids recommendations

Step 2: De-escalating a conversation
- Take a breath to add oxygen to your blood
- Pause and use some breathwork
- Show honest empathy
- Focus on the moment and be nonjudgmental

 **Collaborative Thinking.**

Questions to ask your mentor/peers

Ask your teachers about approaches they use when working regularly with others in the classroom.

What are the ways you built more productive meetings?

What strategies do you have to work well with others in your content area or grade level?

What are some engaging activities you implement leading up to the holidays?

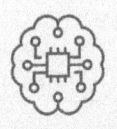 **Technology Checkpoints.**

Resources—Be A Funky Teacher: The resources section on the Funky Teacher Website provides links to highly engaging and fun educational sites that help "bring the funk" into learning.
Minute App (Takes notes for meetings): Use this app to take notes during your meetings so you can stay engaged while not having to worry about note-taking.
www.2TeachLLC.com: 2Teach is a website focusing on inclusion and co-teaching. You can find co-taught elementary and secondary lesson plans as well as books and other products about inclusion and co-teaching.
SurveyMonkey.com: complete interest surveys and compile data from your colleagues.
Doodlepoll.com: Find agreed-upon dates and times for meetings for large groups of individuals.

Teacher Decision-Making. Yes, many moving parts are happening in this part of the book, and your semester. You have built more collaborative relationships with your colleagues. I hope you can embed some of these skills from each chapter into your daily routines. As former habits creep back into your schedule. Focus on what really matters. It is what you do on most days that counts.

Next Steps.

What is working? . . .

What is not working? . . .

What do I need? . . .

What am I proud of? . . .

What do I need to let go of? . . .

Weekly Reflection.

Use the space below to jot down some notes here. Write down some of your collaboration success stories. You are making a difference. Listen to me telling you that you have this, and I believe in you. I am encouraging these minor changes in the school community because you are a quality educator, and students need teachers like you in the field for years to come.

14

Collaborating with Families

Chapter Outline

Continue Weekly Ongoing Communication	268
Making Family Goals	279

So, you have already read over the essential tools for engaging with many people in your school community. However, connecting with families can also predict the success of your engagement with your students. Learning more about your families and the cultural differences can help you to differentiate your instruction and work more collaboratively with families. Educators need to: (a) listen to family stories, (b) avoid assumptions based on stereotypes, and (c) disconnect their own family experiences from the family experiences of their students (McConnell & Murawski, 2017). One way to learn more about your families is to have them complete surveys and incorporate questions within your course content. You can include family members as volunteers and guest speakers in your class based on the expertise they can bring to your class instruction. Continue with this chapter to learn more ways to consult with your students' first teachers, their family members.

Inclusive and Culturally Responsive Practices

In some familial formats, there is a multigenerational hierarchy of authority. Consider how students refer to family members beyond their parents. In some family structures, children are encouraged to question authority figures, whereas in other cultures, educators are highly revered and students will not question adults. It is essential to understand this dynamic with your students. This will play a significant role in how classroom management practices and family communications are handled.

Continue Weekly Ongoing Communication

Family dynamics look very different from what they were 40 years ago. You cannot assume that there is a traditional mother and father household. With increased blended families (cross-generational families, single-parent households, etc.), teachers need to improve their efforts to communicate with families. By understanding the family dynamics in your students' homes, you can better communicate appropriately with families to learn more about your students. Ongoing communication with families is a meaningful way to send details about your class and important updates they need. When you communicate with families, let them know how they can communicate with you. It is ideal to have several communication options to suit each family's needs (e.g., Remind, school phone, email, Class Dojo). Use your weekly or monthly newsletter to share important reminders. View the sample newsletters below to find ways to encourage ongoing communication with families. Be sure to identify how families would prefer to be notified by you, and model that respect. Document in a chart and refer to it when you need to communicate.

Newsletters

Though you have various options, you have alternatives to your private cell phone and social media platforms. Once parents have access to this form of communication, students may also assume that it is appropriate to use these platforms to communicate with you too. Create this boundary with your students now. I defined this "gray area" at the beginning of Part III. You should only use communication methods supported by your school district. These platforms are typically monitored to protect you and your students.

Elementary School Newsletter *Week of September 22* Volume 2, Issue 4		
Dear Families, We've had a great month full of growth, smiles, and learning! As the seasons begin to change, so do the opportunities to explore new ideas, stories, and friendships. Thank you for your continued support in helping our students thrive—both in and out of the classroom!		
With gratitude, **Ms. Kaycee Kim**		
Date	**Event**	**Details**
Sept. 24 (Wed)	Early Release Day	Dismissal at 12:00 p.m.
Sept. 25 (Thu)	Picture Day	Uniforms or neat attire please!
Sept. 26 (Fri)	Popsicle Party for Perfect Attendance	During Lunch
Oct. 1 (Tue)	Family Reading Night	6:00–7:00 p.m. in the Library

Student Shout-Outs Maia—For helping a new student find her classroom! Matteo—For reading 100 minutes this week at home!
First-grade Classroom News: Our class planted bean seeds and are watching them grow. We're writing personal narratives—ask your child to tell their story!
Learning Tip of the Week: Try a "10-minute cleanup" after homework time. Let your child take charge of organizing their backpack and workspace—it builds responsibility and confidence!
Health and Wellness Flu season is coming! Remember: Wash hands frequently Keep kids home if they have a fever
Volunteers Needed: Sign up in the front office (or let me know if you can help) at our Fall Festival (October 22)!

Sample Middle School Newsletter
Week of October 14–18, 2025 Principal: Mrs. Townsend | **Volume 3**
Dear Families, Fall is here, and our students are finding their rhythm. From science labs to music rehearsals, we're seeing curiosity and creativity shine. Thank you for staying involved in your child's learning journey. We encourage you to check grades weekly and reach out to teachers with questions.
Let's keep the momentum going! **Mr. Jasper Green**

Date	Event	Time
Oct. 15 (Wed)	Parent–Teacher Conferences (Early Release)	1:00–6:00 p.m.
Oct. 16 (Thu)	Sixth-grade Field Trip—Science Museum	Depart at 9:00 a.m.
Oct. 18 (Fri)	Fall Dance—Sponsored by Student Council	6:30–8:30 p.m. (Café)
Oct. 25 (Fri)	End of first Quarter	

September Character Trait: Responsibility
Seventh Gr Ava—Turned in every homework assignment and helped a peer with organization.
Eighth Gr Miles—Demonstrated leadership during group English presentations.
Academic Highlights
- **Reading Challenge Update:** Sixth graders have read 1,200 books this semester! Let's reach 2,000 by Thanksgiving!
- **Math Club** meets every Thursday after school in Room 303—new members welcome!

Counselor's Corner
Middle school can be overwhelming—remind your student it's okay to ask for help.
Our counselors are available daily for check-ins.
Tip: Try a 5-minute breathing break together at night or in the morning—it helps calm the brain and improves focus!

> *Highschool Newsletter*   Week of September 7, 2026 Principal: Mr. Seymour | Issue: #4 |
>
> We're already a month into the school year, and we're proud of the hard work and energy your students bring each day! Please take a moment to read through the latest updates, reminders, and celebrations.
>
> Warmly,
> Mr. Quentin Questions (student teacher)
>
> Upcoming Events
> Date   Event   Time
> Sept. 8 (Tues)   Senior College Planning Night   6:00 p.m. (Café)
> Sept. 9 (Wed)   Picture Day—All Grades   During English
> Sept. 11 (Fri) XC Red White and Blue Invite   7:00 p.m.
> Sept. 18 (Fri)   No School—Teacher In-Service   All Day
>
> September Mr. Questions Principal Investigators:
> Science: Natalia P. (11th Grade)—Leadership in lab safety.
> Science: Warren (11th Grade)—MVP partner, tutored partner who was in hospital for 1 week. Congrats! Your positive contributions are noticed and appreciated.
> Academic Corner
> Progress Reports will be emailed by Friday, September 18. Please check your Infinite Campus account.
>
> Tutoring Available after school on Tuesdays and Thursdays from 3:00–4:30 p.m. in Room 149G.
>
> Wellness Tip of the Week
> Sleep Matters!
> Teens need 8–10 hours of sleep to stay focused and healthy. Consider winding down with screen-free time 30 minutes before bed.
>
> *Reminders*
> *Attendance: Call the front office to excuse absences.*
> *Dress Code: Please review the updated guidelines in the Student Handbook.*
> *Clubs: Club Rush continues during lunch in the courtyard through Wednesday.*
>
> If you'd like this turned into a printable flyer, a Google Docs format, or made more grade-specific (e.g., for seniors only), let me know!

Positive Phone Calls

Beyond the newsletter, parent phone calls, or individualized messaging, teachers can provide families with specific student details. You should know that families may associate any teacher, not just you, with their previous negative school experiences (Baker et al., 2016). Though their experiences are not your fault, you must maintain ongoing communication to have family members as allies. It may take time to get a working number or an email response. Try again. Many times, you could be avoided because of previous negative school experiences. Once again, it is not about you. Building positive relationships with families takes multiple connections beyond a parent–teacher conference or yearly IEP meeting. Families will be more responsive when you tell them good things about their child (Bonner, Warren, & Jiang, 2018). As discussed in Chapter 10 regarding students' behaviors, you will quickly learn which students require more support. Try to have positive conversations first, so families will be more receptive when you need to discuss more difficult topics.

Communicating with families will give you more details about life outside of school. Learning more about families and their backgrounds can help you use those details in your lessons and help your students connect with the material. Refer back to Chapter 10, regarding various surveys families can fill out for their child(ren). You can learn many details by talking with families. See the sample "Communication Log" below to add your ideas on communication. You can save your emails in a folder or even take screenshots of messages from a phone app to keep for your records. As mentioned previously, any documented communication can be used in court. This can be helpful evidence to show your efforts when working with families.

© iStock.com/lioputra.

Add your Ideas.

Family Communication Log.

Date Time	Student	Family member	Summary points	Outcomes/ follow-up
8/22	Doug	Gram June email	Dad/ is unable to pick up Doug. He needs to ride the bus	Note posted on the board
9/16	Slone	Called Reggie (stepdad)	S. is doing much better with homework by only doing the even problems	Revisit in 3 weeks

LAFF Don't CRY with Families

Ongoing communication can lead to open conversations with family members about their concerns about their child. Let me be the first to tell you. You do not need to have all of the answers. When considering parents, they would rather you listen, than make them false promises. Families would rather know they are heard (McNaughton & Vostal, 2010). Active listening is an approach often taught to management professionals. McNaughten and colleagues have developed a model of active listening strategy, LAFF Don't CRY (LAFF), for teaching professionals that has proven effective for communication skills for various educational professionals. Teachers have reported feeling more confident communicating with colleagues and families after learning LAFF. Those watching the videos feel that teachers using LAFF have stronger communication skills. Below is a sample of the steps, along with an example conversation (Vostal et al., 2015).

Inclusive and Culturally Responsive Practices

A Teacher Employs LAFF During a Conference With a Parent

LAFF Steps	
Listen, empathize, and communicate respect	Parent: My son, Ethan is having trouble in his math class. He's gotten a D or an F on the last three quizzes. **Teacher: That must be frustrating. I appreciate you coming in to talk with me.**
Ask questions	Parent: He really struggles with his homework each night. **Teacher: May I take notes so I can be sure to remember all of your concerns?** Parent: Sure that's fine. **Teacher: What does Ethan say?** Parent: Ethan says he can't keep up with the teacher in class, so he doesn't understand what he is supposed to do without help. **Teacher: Let's talk more about the homework; what do you see when Ethan is working at home?** Parent: Sure, that's fine. He gets some of his homework done in resource room, but by the time he gets home he's confused again. He works through the example problems, but he can't figure out where he's making mistakes.
Focus on the issues	**Teacher: I want to make sure I have got all this, so I'd like to check my notes with you. You are saying that he has struggled on the last three tests; he can do his homework at school when he has help, but he really struggles at home. Have I got it? Is there anything you would like to add?** Parent: Yes, our nights are getting pretty frustrating. We try to help him, but that's not working very well.
Find a first step	**Teacher: As a first step, I'd like to meet with his math teacher. I want to find out what he is missing. I will call you by Friday and we well will make a plan for next steps.** Parent: Thanks for listening. I wasn't sure quite what to do, but I'm glad I came in.
A Teacher Demonstrates **CRY** Behaviors During a Conference With a Parent Don't CRY Parent–Teacher Conference	

Criticize people who aren't present	Parent: My son, Ethan, is having trouble in his math class. He's gotten a D or an F on the last three quizzes. **Teacher: Ethan has Mr. McDonald, a first-year teacher. He may not be familiar with Ethan's accommodations.**
React hastily and promise something you can't deliver	Parent: Ethan had a first-year last year! Why should he have to suffer because there is so much turnover? **Teacher: That is really frustrating. You know, there are other algebra sections, other teachers. Maybe I can switch Ethan to a more experienced teacher.** Parent: What is going to happen about the low quiz grades he's already gotten? Why should Ethan get bad grades because things are so disorganized?
Yakety-yak-yak	**Teacher: I understand how important grades can be. My daughter is applying to colleges and she is under so much pressure.** Parent: But what are you going to do about Ethan? Perhaps I should talk to the principal about our problem.

Adapted From: McNaughton, D., & Vostal, B. R. (2010). Using active listening to improve collaboration with parents: The LAFF don't CRY strategy. *Intervention in School and Clinic, 45*(4), 251–256.

After practicing this strategy with your peers, consider implementing it when communicating with families. Below is a sample chart to help you determine if you can complete all the steps. You can create a chart to fill in the commonly asked questions. It is important to practice using these steps and notes before implementing the strategy with family members. Through practice, you will feel confident in using this strategy when communicating with others. Remember that you have been chatting for years without a formal template, so learning to ask more questions versus going directly to a hopeful solution will take time. This approach can be used whenever someone comes to you with a problem. If you are an Obliger, it is crucial not to overpromise how to help someone struggling. Be sure to ask questions and rely on the resources available at your school to support families. For example, if Julio is always late for school because his grandma cannot get him out of bed, picking him up for school is not your job. Whose job is it to get students to school? You could add his report to a truancy officer. Ask questions first.

Collaborating with Families

© iStock.com/simplehappyart.

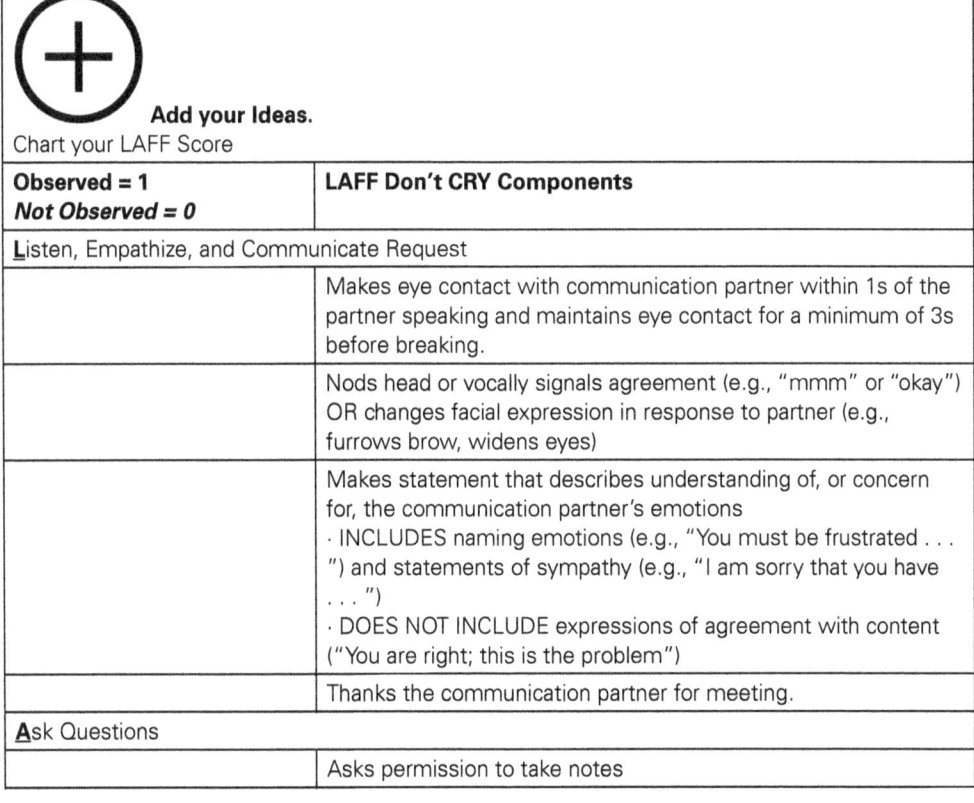

Add your Ideas.

Chart your LAFF Score

Observed = 1 *Not Observed = 0*	LAFF Don't CRY Components
Listen, Empathize, and Communicate Request	
	Makes eye contact with communication partner within 1s of the partner speaking and maintains eye contact for a minimum of 3s before breaking.
	Nods head or vocally signals agreement (e.g., "mmm" or "okay") OR changes facial expression in response to partner (e.g., furrows brow, widens eyes)
	Makes statement that describes understanding of, or concern for, the communication partner's emotions · INCLUDES naming emotions (e.g., "You must be frustrated . . . ") and statements of sympathy (e.g., "I am sorry that you have . . . ") · DOES NOT INCLUDE expressions of agreement with content ("You are right; this is the problem")
	Thanks the communication partner for meeting.
Ask Questions	
	Asks permission to take notes

	Asks **at least 3** open-ended questions • INCLUDES any question related to the situation brought up by the partner. Examples include: "Who is affected by . . . ?", "What does it look like when . . . ", "Where does . . . ?", "When did this . . . ?", "Why do you think . . . ?", "How does this situation . . . ?" • INCLUDES questions that ask for a description of a recent event related to the concern (i.e., more details based on a previous response). • DOES NOT INCLUDE questions that can be answered by "yes" or "no" OR questions that ask for information that was already given (e.g., partner stated concern about the career choice within a student's transition goal and the question asks "What are you concerned about?")
	Clarifies a statement from the partner (e.g., "Are you saying that . . . ?") OR makes paraphrasing statements (i.e., putting the other's words in the participants own words to verify something).
Focus on the issues	
	Reads aloud notes taken during the meeting and asks for corrections/additions
Find a first step	
	Describes a concrete plan to gather more information
	Sets a timeline by which the next communication will occur
Don't **CRY**	
	Does Not makes statements that **C**riticize others (either the communication partner OR those who are not present)
	Does Not **R**eact hastily and promise something s/he can't deliver
	Does Not **Y**akkety-yak-yak (i.e., make statements) about other situations that may or may not be comparable to the partner's concern
	= **TOTAL COMPONENTS OBSERVED**
Adapted From: Vostal, B. R., Mrachko, A. A., Vostal, M., & McCoy, A. (2021). Effects of group behavioral skills training on teacher candidates' acquisition and maintenance of active listening. Journal of Behavioral Education, 1–20.	

Think About It.
What questions do you ask families when they come to you with a problem? Do you quickly resort to problem solving? What are some instances where you can practice active listening?
?

?

Providing Resources Is a Two-Way Street

Parents are known as a child's "first teacher." A misleading point that my younger student teachers often assume is that family members always know how to help their child(ren) learn. As children get older, family members are less likely to help their child with schoolwork due to the complexity of the content (Pressman et al., 2015). This does not mean that the family does not care about their child's education. Plus, having a different cultural experience does not mean the student is at a deficit. There needs to be a shift in mindset for educators. It is our duty as educators to empower all parents to recognize the assets they have to their own children's education (Souto-Manning & Swick, 2006). Refer to Chapter 7, Responsibility = Respect to review the MAPS survey.

If you have already administered the survey, you can review the answers again to gain a deeper understanding of what was shared from a family perspective. Find ways to bring students' interests, cultures, and languages into the classroom. Diversity must be recognized as a resource in the school. On the same token, you see these students daily, so you do have a perception of how these students interact and learn. Does the family have any obvious needs to support their child(ren)? Find ways to collaborate with  families so that providing resources is a two-way street for you and the family members. This is a winning combination with positive outcomes for the students.

Inclusive and Culturally Responsive Practices

Just because a family does not have the level of involvement you expect, does not mean they do not care. Just because a family makes different educational decisions than you would hope does not mean they do not care. Get to know family members and their goals for their child. Sometimes, a family's beliefs or cultural upbringing may lead them to make choices that are different from your experiences.

When you learn more about families and their experiences, you can also learn how they can be an asset to your school community. As you know about the various expertise of your school family members, you can recruit family members to build support networks to provide resources for each other. For example, in the special education community, parents have strong advocacy groups to help each other through the challenges of parenting a child with disabilities. There are many ways to build a community of resources both within and beyond your school community. Get involved in your community to discover how it can work for you. Below is "Epstein's Framework for Types of Involvement" to consider various ways families can build partnerships with their school community.

 **Add your ideas.**

Epstein's Framework for Types of Involvement

6 different types of involvement families may be interested in	Examples of how a school might address and support this type of involvement	What is something you could add to your school?
Parenting: Help from families establish home environments to support children as students.	Develop family support programs to assist families with health, nutrition, and other services; consider specific needs of children with disabilities.	Become familiar with nutritional support. Share parent information resources. Connect parents with support groups. • •
Communicating: Design effective forms of school-to-home and home-to-school communication about school programs and children's progress.	Develop a regular schedule of useful notices, memos, phone calls, newsletters, and other communications; consider that not all parents read or speak English.	Make a template with a newsletter containing updates and resources. Personalized updates via phone and written communication. • •
Volunteering: Recruit and organize parent help and support.	Create a family room or center for volunteer work, meetings, and resources for families; have materials in different languages.	Survey families for their availability and talents. Designate a parent room with space for volunteering and shared resources with contact information. • •
Learning at home: Provide information and ideas to families about how to help students at home with homework and other curriculum-related activities, decisions, and planning.	Provide information for families on skills required for students in all subjects at each grade; have a list of possible adaptations for individuals who are special learners.	Video clips on how to work on new skills. Shared strategies to support homework routine.
Decision-making: Include parents in school decisions, developing parent leaders and representatives.	Implement active PTA/PTO or other parent organizations, advisory councils, or committees for parent leadership and participation; ensure that diverse families are not left out and that meetings are accessible to all.	Promote PTO/PTA involvement and leadership. Endorse parent involvement at the district level. • •
Collaborating with the community: Identify and integrate resources and services from the community to strengthen school programs, family practices, and student learning and development.	Share information on community activities that link to learning skills and talents, including summer programs for students with and without special needs.	Connect with the local library to share summer educational opportunities. Share summer camp scholarship opportunities for socialization and childcare. • •

Adapted from Epstein, J. L. (2019). Theory to practice: School and family partnerships lead to school improvement and student success. In *School, family, and community interaction* (pp. 39–52). Routledge.

Making Family Goals

How is your communication with families? Did you make any instant changes as you read this chapter to increase clear communication with families? If so, fabulous. If this is good enough for you, move on to the last topic, and know that you can always return here and set goals for clear communication and collaboration with family members. If you are not ready to commit to writing a goal, remember where to come when you need to increase your active listening.

Are you feeling like you need to take steps to collaborate more with families? Then what do you like, and what needs to change? Remember that you are taking more time to build relationships with your students' families. If you need to make connections with a family, this might be a good place to create a goal for yourself. Just remember that building relationships with family members takes time. Students who struggle academically often experience more complicated relationships with teachers, and their families commonly have similarly difficult relationships with school staff. This may not change in 1 week. What is realistic for you to work on for the next month? After you review the student teachers' goals for inspiration, continue to the end of Chapter 15, where you can outline your own family communication goals.

Kaycee Actively Listens

Kaycee is intimidated by talking to family members about their student(s). Yet, she recognizes that family engagement is a part of her job. She likes the idea of active listening to allow the family to focus on their issues. Kaycee acknowledges that she likes to be the problem solver, so she must practice asking questions and finding a first step. She will practice the LAFF strategy once a week with her roommate, mentor, and collaborative teachers in the building. She will take their feedback and reflect on the improvements she needs to make in these conversations. She will fill out the "LAFF chart" to determine how many steps of the active listening strategy she has addressed.

Kaycee's Chart

Making SMART Goals	
Baseline Data	
Specific: What is the Target Behavior?	
Kaycee will use the "LAFF chart" once a week to assess how many points she has earned during a practice active listening conversation.	
With what materials or conditions?	
During a conversation once a week	
Measurable: How well must the skill be performed? (Criteria)	**Achievable:** What modifications or accommodations are needed for success? Making the time?

Earn 13 of the 15 points from the LAFF chart.	Use the LAFF notes sheet to take notes.
How will the skill be measured? And how often?	**Any additional research? People to talk to?**
She will collect the data once a week when she practices the active listening strategy.	Get feedback from others each time she practices a conversation.
Relevance: Why is meeting this goal important?	**Timely:** What is considered mastery for this goal
By increasing points on the active listening approach colleagues and family members will be more receptive to these conversations.	This goal will be mastered once she has earned 13 points she may begin using the strategy with families during meetings and conferences.
What other assessments or data will help assess progress toward the goal?	**What are the next steps in this goal area?**
Notes will be taken on the feedback after the active listening conversation.	She will then move to having conversations with families.

Quentin's Investigative Report

Quentin enjoys the connections he is making with students by having principal investigators (PIs) each week. He wants to build this with ongoing communication with families. He has an email communication that goes out to the family of each student during the week the students are PIs. He identifies the most common methods of communication to reach out to families via mail, class text, and voicemail. After reviewing baseline data, Quentin only communicated with 10 families during his first 8 weeks in the classroom. His goal is to follow up with a family using their preferred contact information to share a positive report.

Quentin's Chart

Making SMART Goals	
Baseline Data January—4 family contacts February—4 family contacts March—2 family contacts	
Specific: What is the Target Behavior?	
At the end of each week, he will follow up with the family of my PI (6 total families) using their preferred contact information to share a specific praise about the student.	
With what **materials or conditions**?	
At the end of each week, use a family member's preferred contact.	
Measurable: How well must the skill be performed? (Criteria)	**Achievable:** What modifications or accommodations are needed for success? Making the time?

At the end of each week, he will make 2 points of contact to attempt to reach out to the PIs from each class (3 classes = 6 total family contact).	Set aside time each Friday to make these contacts. Make a note of positive interactions to share.
How will the skill be **measured?** And **how often?**	Any additional research? People to talk to?
Quentin will have a calendar and a chart to check off the PI and contact information.	Ask for preferred contact information from family in "Take Home Survey."
Relevance: Why is meeting this goal important?	**Timely:** What is considered mastery for this goal?
He wants to get opportunities to have positive interactions with families. From this, he may learn more about the students and their families.	By keeping a weekly rotation, this task will be completed after his 10 weeks of student teaching.
What other assessments or data will help assess progress toward the goal?	**What are the next steps in this goal area?**
Quentin will check off when he chats with family members and record in a communication log.	Once Quentin meets this goal, he will then work on incorporating these connections with the students.

These are just examples. Remember to frame your goal around your baseline data. Refer to the "Technology Checkpoints" examples to find ways to measure your goal. Perhaps you just want to send home a newsletter regularly. That is lovely. Whatever your efforts, I applaud you for becoming a teacher who makes a positive impact. Please continue to the next topic for Relationships and Collaboration: Healthy Relationships. Remember to have clear communication, actively listen, and collect data to measure your progress. Keep going. I believe in you and your ability to do great things, and you got this!

 Chapter Recap.
Continue Weekly Ongoing Communication
- Newsletters through paper copy and electronic versions
- Include: health and education tips, important dates, student highlights, questions to ask your students
- Target individual positive communication with families each week
- Updates of "students doing good" calls, emails, or texts
- Log your communication

LAFF Don't CRY with Families (refer to chart for details)
- Ask questions do not jump to solutions
- Take notes to document and give you time to think
- Know your zone of control
- Active listening can apply to colleagues and students

Epstein Framework for involvement (see chart)
- Refer to parent survey to identify how families can be involved

Providing Resources is a Two-Way Street
- Families are children's first teacher
- They will need support at different stages, and tips for academic content

Add families' cultures to your classroom
- Share parent networks
- Learn family resources in your community

Collaborative Thinking.

Questions to ask your mentors/peers
What are some approaches you have used to get to know your family members better?
What are the different ways that you can get family members to contribute to your class community?

Technology Checkpoints.

Parentsasteachers.org: Parents as Teachers recognizes and supports the idea that parents are children's very first teacher. This website has training and other resources to help encourage that idea.
Bloomz: Bloomz is a parent and school communication app that combines all lines of communication from the district level down to one-on-one with a teacher.
Remind: Remind provides a safe communication tool between educators, students, and parents. Without providing mobile numbers, Remind enables you to text students or parents/guardians.
Appletree: Appletree Schools offer free education to pre-k aged kids in the Washington, DC area.
Mykiddo: An app designed for daycare caregivers and parents/guardians to help communicate with ease.
Pacer.org: PACER is focused on helping children with disabilities advocate for better educational opportunities. This website has videos and training on assistive technology, IEP and 504 planning and preparing for adulthood.
CASEL.org: SEL advances educational equity and excellence through authentic school-family-community partnerships. SEL can help address various forms of inequity and empower young people and adults to co-create thriving schools and contribute to safe, healthy, and just communities.
CEC's Initial Practice-Based Professional Preparation Standards: These standards are for special education teachers. They outline the knowledge and skills needed for early childhood education of students with special needs.
Parent Center for Resources: There are 100 of these centers across the United States. They provide training, information, and resources for parents of children with disabilities.

Teacher Decision-Making. Are these steps working? Are you seeing the benefits? Make sure that you are making modifications and adaptations to make more improvements in the classroom, without making it more difficult. Take a minute to reflect on your collaboration. In what areas do you need to grow? Add some deep breaths to your day and recognize the changes worth making for your overall health.

Next Steps.

What is working? . . .

What is not working? . . .

What do I need? . . .

What am I proud of? . . .

What do I need to let go of? . . .

Weekly Reflection.

Use the space below to jot down some notes or draw a picture of a glowing moment in your week. Highlight something that is helping your day go well. Picture a great day. Hopefully, with slight changes to your collaboration and relationships, you will decrease stress and increase joy in your student teaching experience. Keep going, you got this!

15
Healthy Relationships

Chapter Outline

Building Friendships	286
When Friendships Mix	287
Defining Gray Area	288
A Workplace with Gray Areas	289
Being a Novice Teacher While Avoiding Gray Areas	290
Avoiding Gray Areas When You Are the Role Model	292
In Closing	295
Healthy Relationship Goals	295

This last chapter outlines two components of relationships. One is the healthy relationships you need to maintain with your family and friends while you are working. You need to have people you trust and vent to, along with hobbies that you can use to de-stress. Be sure to regularly check that you are in healthy relationships in your personal life (Ghasemi, 2022). Make this a priority. The other consideration is making sure you are not using misleading behaviors in your relationships with students and your school community members. It needs to be addressed because it happens too often.

> **Think About It.**
> Where do you want to work? Near your college? Near home? Any place where you get hired? Who are the people you would like to live near? Family? Friends? Your partner?
> ?
>
> ?
>
> ?

Building Friendships

If you are new to your school district and community, you will have an added challenge of making new friends. One positive thing is that this can be a new way to build healthy habits and new friendships. You must start building a social network, just as you would to organize your classroom. How you spend your time outside of school will affect your overall happiness. If you need to, review your notes from Part I. With many of these activities, you can put yourself out there and strike up a conversation with the people around you. Do not be tempted to doom scroll to avoid conversation. Self-care has become such a focus in the work community that there may be clubs and after-school activities for you to join. Obligers, you will be more successful with accountability partners, so consider joining a club or a class where you have scheduled time to show up. Below is a list of activities that you could consider doing to make new friends.

 **Add your Ideas.**
Circle some activities that you can do to meet new people in your community.

- Visit a dog park
- Join a gym and take a new class
- Visit the library and join a book club
- Volunteer at a local place of worship
- Join a bike meet-up
- Take an art class or workshop
- Attend a community festival or a block party
- Go to an open mic or trivia night

-
-

© iStock.com/Nataliia Nesterenko.

When Friendships Mix

You need to find positive ways to work together with your colleagues. According to the "American Time Use Survey Research," you spend an average of 15 hours a week with your colleagues (US Bureau of Labor Statistics, 2024). Perhaps you plan on working where you grew up, so you are familiar with the teachers and families that make up your school community. With the benefits of familiarity, you must set up boundaries for your public interactions that students and their families can see. However, you may recall the story I shared about my uncle often seeing his school community members in public. He was always viewed as a public figure with a positive reputation. It needs to be recognized that though you are an adult, you need to identify a balance of living your life publicly. Not just physically out in public, but what could be posted about you on social media? If you have not already, it is time to consider your boundaries for public spaces and social media. Like it or not, you are held to a higher standard than individuals in other professions within your community (Keshmiri, Jambarsang, & Mehrparvar, 2023). Your clothing, hobbies, and behaviors reflect your character. Below is a checklist for you to complete regarding things to think about as you are a public figure in your school community.

⊕ Add your Ideas.

How am I presenting myself to others?

Considerations	Your Thoughts
What are some habits or hobbies that may harm your reputation as a teacher? What are some new hobbies that you could explore?	
What places do you visit that could reflect negatively if your students and families saw you? Where else could you go to replace this location?	
Look at your online presence. What are some photos or comments posted about you that should be removed to preserve your character?	

© iStock.com/Visual Generation.

Defining Gray Area

I am using the term "gray area" to define relationship behaviors and interactions not clearly understood by **those in the relationship** or **outside observers**. Teachers are in vulnerable roles with students and mentors, and can fall victim to unclear relationships. This could make a teacher vulnerable to the perception of a questionable situation, which could lead to an inappropriate relationship. This has been known to occur with adult teachers and students when the adult teacher spends extra time with one student who may require more help and attention. Through this support, an imbalance of power develops between these individuals. This can also happen in the workplace when more experienced teachers mentor novice teachers. Your first step is to focus on healthy relationships outside of the workplace. Next, avoid this gray area by setting boundaries at work. In this section, I will refer to a few of my experiences and highlight ways to avoid the gray area as defined above. The National Association of State Directors of Teacher Education and Certification, NASDTEC (2015), has updated its Model Code of Ethics for Educators (MCEE) to give teachers a framework that highlights ethical guidelines for the classroom. Below are the five principles. Please become familiar with and review the examples provided, and add some of your ideas as they relate.

 **Add your Ideas.**

Model Code of Ethics for Educators

Principle I: Responsibility to the Profession
The professional educator is aware that trust in the profession depends upon a level of professional conduct and responsibility that may be higher than required by law. This entails holding one and other educators to the same ethical standards, including but not limited to:

Staying current with professional development.

Avoiding public behavior that discredits your professional ethics.

Collaborating respectfully with colleagues, even when you have differing opinions.

-
-

Principle II: Responsibility for Professional Competence
The professional educator is committed to the highest levels of professional and ethical practice, including demonstration of the knowledge, skills, and dispositions required for professional competence. Along with but not limited to:

Differentiating instruction based on student data and evidence-based practices.

Recognizing when you are unfamiliar with a topic and seek help or further training.

Using evidence-based assessments aligned with standards and learning goals.

-
-

Principle III: Responsibility to Students The professional educator has a primary obligation to treat students with dignity and respect. The professional educator promotes the health, safety, and well-being of students by establishing and maintaining appropriate verbal, physical, emotional, and social boundaries. Some examples include: Respecting students' confidentiality of personal and academic information. Ensuring equal access to learning. Do not show favoritism. Recognizing and responding to signs of student trauma or abuse. ● ●
Principle IV: Responsibility to the School Community The professional educator promotes positive relationships and effective interactions, with members of the school community, while maintaining professional boundaries. This includes the following examples: Maintaining ongoing communication with families. Supporting school-wide programs and initiatives. Keeping conversations among other teachers and colleagues positive. ● ●
Principle V: Responsible and Ethical Use of Technology The professional educator considers the impact of consuming, creating, distributing, and communicating information through all technologies. The ethical educator is vigilant to ensure appropriate boundaries of time, place, and role are maintained when using electronic communication. This includes, but is not limited to: Using school social media for posting student work (with permission). Reporting cybersecurity risks and maintaining password security. Teaching and modeling responsible digital citizenship in class. ● ●
Adapted from: National Association of State Directors of Teacher Education and Certification (2015). Model Code of Ethics for Educators. NASDTEC.

A Workplace with Gray Areas

This section has probably taken me the longest to write on paper because the topics are sensitive and critically important to your career. As the teacher, you are an adult. You need to prioritize healthy adult relationships outside the workplace to avoid getting into a misleading "gray area" with a student or colleague. Your professionalism and relationships at school can determine your career. You need to protect yourself and be reflective of your interactions and how others could perceive them. This gray area is a factor from two angles. First, as a novice teacher, you will be relying on mentors within the school to help you with developing teaching strategies. Additionally, you will be seen as a role model to your students. At times in your career, you may find yourself working with students who are close in age, or despite the age gap, they may try to connect with you as an adult. Both of these topics are sensitive and can be challenging to address. Throughout this section, I will highlight considerations to help you avoid this gray area from both perspectives.

Inclusive and Culturally Responsive Practices.

Consider your friends who are in other professions. It is common practice for them to go out to lunch and have adult beverages. You have different expectations as a teacher; you need to show up each day neatly groomed with professional attire. The expectations in your field look different than other professions.

Being a Novice Teacher While Avoiding Gray Areas

In some situations, I talk about a gray area that cannot be measured or defined in relationships. Just know that it is critical to keep professional boundaries now and throughout your career. I have seen very talented teachers and administrators lose their jobs (and even more) because of inappropriate relationships with colleagues at school. This is not just relevant for age differences. Gray interactions with colleagues can occur even later in your career when you are working with someone who has more administrative power. When implemented effectively, having a mentor in your building helps to limit stress and burnout (Haidusek-Niazy, Huyler, & Carpenter, 2023). Sometimes mentors are designated through your school district; other times, there may be individuals that you naturally connect with because of their knowledge and expertise. For example, you may regularly work with the technology support staff because the class computer is constantly glitching, or she wants you to pilot the new technology materials in your lessons. It is important to be aware of the perspective that others can see when they observe you regularly working with other adults in the building. Later in this chapter, I will share how this unknowingly happened to me, and ways to create clear boundaries with those you work with.

On the next page is a chart with some examples of actions that could be perceived as "gray areas" while you are a novice teacher. There are also alternative options in the right column that you could do to replace those actions. Add some of your ideas that you have or advice you have received on this topic.

 **Add your Ideas.**
Possible Actions in the "gray area" with colleagues and Alternative Options

Actions that could be considered a "gray area"	Alternative options
<ul><li>Always having lunch with one person</li><li>Colleague regularly confides in you with personal information</li><li>Accepting suggestive compliments from a colleague</li><li>Sharing hugs</li><li></li><li></li></ul>	<ul><li>Ask others to join your group</li><li>Find a trusted resource that can provide appropriate support</li><li>Address the colleague on the inappropriateness of the comments</li><li>Ask first, or give high fives</li><li></li><li></li></ul>

When I Was in the Gray Area as a Novice Teacher

In my first year of teaching, I dropped a colleague off after work. I thought I was doing him a favor. In context, this teacher was in his 50s, so I thought nothing of it. I later learned that his wife, and my colleague, speculated about our relationship. I was flabbergasted, and then her recent unfriendly interactions started to make sense. To handle this situation, I had a wonderful boss who vouched for me, stating that this was not within my character at all. Next, I followed up with my colleague to explain to him what his wife was discussing with our colleagues about our relationship. Fortunately, this situation did get cleared up with no repercussions. However, from this experience, I now avoid having other people in my car.

© iStock.com/Olga Kurbatova.

Avoiding Gray Areas When You Are the Role Model

Questionable relationships do not just occur between adults. As a teacher, you have to have clear boundaries with your students, regardless of your age or age difference. There is an increase in students reporting being sexually victimized by school staff (Jeglic et al., 2022). You can assume the actual rate is higher due to the number of undocumented cases to protect the confidentiality of minors (Abboud et al., 2020). This section uncovers more difficult situations and what contributes to teachers getting into a "gray area." Students can sometimes be misled by your mentorship, where the student may view your actions and kindness as a consensual relationship (Deering & Mellor, 2011).

Ways to Avoid the Gray Area When You Are the Role Model

I have always stressed the importance of modeling professionalism. I started teaching at the high school level when I was 21. I needed to be recognized as an adult role model, not a high school student. I ensured that I dressed professionally and kept a respectful boundary with my students. People who know me well know that I am not a hugger. Being in a profession where I have often been close in age to my students has forced me to put up boundaries to avoid this close physical contact with students. As a supplement, I often ask questions about the things my students care about and give specific praise on a job well done. I make myself available in the common areas in our office space. Students must not get the wrong impression from my kindness in the situation. This will, of course, look different if you work with younger students. If something feels wrong, it probably is wrong. This can be challenging to address. It is best to think about these situations, have plans to remove yourself, and report when this occurs. Remember to document any events in which you were in a questionable situation. You should include the date, time, location, and context of what happened. Please add some of your ideas that you have experienced, and ways to address these situations.

⊕ Add your Ideas.
Possible Actions for Role Models in the "gray area" with Alternative Options

Actions that could be considered a "gray area" with students	Alternative options
Students regularly confide in you with personal information Hugging older students Contacting students on social media	Find a trusted resource that can provide appropriate support Ask first, or give high fives Only use school communication that is monitored
• •	• •

When I Was a Role Model in the Gray Area

Similarly, I started working at the college level before I was 30. So again, I found myself within a close age range of my students. I was having a post-observation meeting in my office with a 20-something male student teacher, and a colleague came and opened the door. Afterward, she told me, "At your age, it is probably best that you never have a closed-door meeting with male college students." It is 12 years later, and I always leave my door open when meeting students. In these instances, I was not thinking of how others could perceive my actions, and at the time, I did not even realize that I was in the gray area.

© iStock.com/Overearth.

© iStock.com/simplehappyart.

Reporting Someone in the Gray Area

This is quite the heavy chapter, which has been vital to my moral stance on professionalism. As much as I want you to enjoy your job, I also want you to recognize your responsibility as an adult and professional to be a mandated reporter. Please remember this section and refer to it when you are questioning your behavior or the behavior of others. In many stories of inappropriate teacher behavior, it started with two people in a gray area. Some examples include one individual who had abused their power, or an individual who was vulnerable to the kindness of others. Oftentimes, gossipers share that they had speculations about the individuals. Meaning, someone knew about the situation and it could have been stopped. You are a mandated reporter. Know the protocols for your school and document your concerns. Remember, your number one priority is protecting students. I applaud your efforts in taking this role seriously.

However, I cannot close this book with such a complex topic. I need to end with my sense of humor and a list of professional conversations I have had with principals, mentors, and pre-service teachers over the past 15 years. I keep this list and add it to my "Professionalism Presentation" anytime my college students go into the classroom. Please note I took the time to tell you what to do instead of what not to do. For example, "avoid tobacco products in the school parking lot." It is safe to assume that a school principal called me because a student teacher was spitting snuff in the school parking lot, then coming back into the classroom with granules in his teeth. Feel free to add your stories of professional considerations.

 **Add your Ideas.**
Professional Expectations for Teachers

Avoid suggestive words about drugs, alcohol, or sex on your clothes
No under garments should be exposed while you are teaching
Chin test: make sure that the top of your shirt touches your chin
Wash your hands well after getting a bar stamp
Keep social media contacts private from students
Get your rest at home, not during student teaching
Keep any nicotine products at home. The school parking lot is considered a drug-free zone.
Use school email to communicate with students (cc: your mentor teacher and parents with sensitive topics)
Use a school-approved App for communication when you are an extracurricular coach.
Get approval to post your students on the school's social media
Post your students on the school social media, not your personal account
If you wear jeans on dress-down day, please avoid rips, rhinestone pockets, or any type of shorts.

-
-

In Closing

Cheers to you for taking the time to learn about building healthy relationships with the professionals you will work with throughout your career. You have made it to the end of the book. You are choosing to develop positive relationships with your colleagues and families. You have learned that the importance of clear communication and effective relationships with your colleagues is essential. Take time this week to make more connections with the faculty and staff in your school building. Remember to start small; you can always add on when you meet your goal. Are there improvements? Did you make a goal for yourself? Did you meet that goal? Continue to think about the areas of collaboration in this part. What do you need to continue to focus on?

You have so many teacher decisions to make in a day. Take these changes in stride with your efforts to become a teacher who continues to make progress. Take a minute to congratulate yourself. You have taken the time to work on yourself, so you can be a better teacher who is ready for class each day. Next, you worked on ways to build connections with your students and enhanced strategies for your classroom management. Lastly, you worked on skills and techniques to effectively plan and communicate with your school community. Cheers! Celebrate your success. Recognizing all you have accomplished while reading this workbook and working in the schools is important. By reaching this stage, you've shown your dedication and potential as an educator. I believe in your ability to share both your love for working with students and your passion for the content you teach. I am confident you will succeed, and I hope you continue to feel the same excitement and fulfillment in your work 20 years from now as you do today.

Healthy Relationship Goals

Do you have some areas where you need to work on your relationships? Are you thinking about skills you need to improve? I appreciate that you are making this a priority. Some of these chapters may not be a focus for you now. If you are all set with healthy relationships, great! As always, you can revisit if you need to refresh your reminders to target your relationships. After you review the sample goals from these student teachers, proceed to the end of Chapter 15 to develop your own healthy relationship goals.

Jasper Gets Digitally Literate

Jasper used social media to share stories and communicate with students. At his midterm meeting with his mentor teacher, he learned he was in a gray area by sharing personal contact information with students. Jasper realized that he had to be a model of digital literacy. He determined it would be best to delete all personal social media pages with students and use a professional webpage for job applications. Jasper and the library teacher started a digital literacy club with his middle school students. Each week, they co-teach and

© iStock.com/Rudzhan Nagiev.

help their middle school students develop digital literacy skills. They help students post social media highlights of students and school activities on the school webpage.

Making SMART Goals	
Baseline Data 80% of the students who attended post-socially appropriate artifacts each week.	
Specific: What is the Target Behavior?	
In each class, Jasper will incorporate an interest-area topic or activity that connects with students' interests.	
With what **materials or conditions**?	
Weekly, Jasper will co-teach 6–8 students in a 40-minute digital literacy lesson.	
Measurable: How well must the skill be performed? (Criteria)	**Achievable:** What accommodations are needed for success? Making the time?
80% of the students in attendance will submit a professional post.	Prepare a 20-minute co-taught lesson with the librarian.
How will the skill be **measured**? And **how often**?	Any **additional research**? People to talk to?
The librarian will check the number of posts each week.	Collaborate with the librarian to understand and review digital literacy skills.
Relevance: Why is meeting this goal important?	**Timely:** What is considered mastery for this goal?
Jasper has learned the importance of modeling professionalism with digital literacy.	Jasper will increase to 100% once he has reached this goal.
What other assessments or data will help assess progress toward the goal?	What are the next steps in this goal area?
Take group attendance. Review and document the details shared.	Students will add posts about digital literacy on social media sites.

Kaycee Is Framed for Favoritism on Social Media

As a people pleaser, Kaycee was spending time outside of school with a veteran teacher. She looked up to him as a mentor, and he gave her solid advice about the profession. They would regularly go for drinks and trivia. When her peers were student teaching in the same building, she saw a picture of the veteran teacher and her, that others had shared on social media. This immediately created rumors about Kaycee getting favoritism for the upcoming job opening. Someone posted, "Now we know who is getting the job." Kaycee learned that spending time outside of work is a gray area. She now only goes out socially with veteran colleagues when her peers are included.

Making SMART Goals	
Baseline Data Currently, Kaycee meets weekly with a veteran teacher in social settings.	
Specific: What is the Target Behavior?	
100% of the Kaycee will only go out with veteran teachers if 1 or more of her peers are included.	
With what **materials or conditions**?	
When asked to go out in social settings, she will only go if peers are included.	
Measurable: How well must the skill be performed? (Criteria)	**Achievable:** What modifications or accommodations are needed for success? Making the time?
100% of the time outside of the school setting.	Collaborate with peers to join events.
How will the skill be **measured**? And **how often**?	Any **additional research**? People to talk to?
Each week Kaycee will reflect on her previous week and attempt to make plans with her same-aged peers for the following week.	NA
Relevance: Why is meeting this goal important?	**Timely:** What is considered mastery for this goal?
Meeting this goal is vital to Kaycee because she wants to have healthy working relationships with her peers and does not want to be in the gray area in any social relationships.	Kaycee will perform this consistently until the end of her placement.
What other assessments or data will help assess progress toward the goal?	What are the next steps in this goal area?
Kaycee will calculate on her calendar.	Kaycee will review training skills and tips on what to avoid.

Chapter Recap.

It is important to build a social network for hobbies and downtime
- Find activities you can attend to meet new people

Be sure to protect your image in public and on social media

Interactions not clearly understood by those in the relationship or outside observers can be considered a gray area.

Teachers are held to a higher accountability

Being a novice teacher while avoiding gray areas
- Be clear with your relationships of older and senior members of your building.

Ways to avoid the gray area as a novice teacher
- Limit meeting with others one-on-one
- Have professional social media
- Correct suggestive comments

Avoiding gray areas when you are the role model
- Be clear with your relationships with students
- Meet in public areas and in groups

Reporting someone in the gray area
- You are a mandated reporter
- There is no rationale for a teacher having a relationship with a student

In Closing
- Focus on making progress
- In an emergency refer to your first aid kit
- Share your success with others, share your success with me
- Keep going, you got this!

 **Collaborative Thinking.**

Questions to ask your mentors/peers
What are some ways you met new friends in a new area? How do you balance your relationships with family and friends outside the classroom?
How do you maintain appropriate connections with your students?

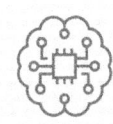

Technology Checkpoints.

NPBEA 2015 Professional Standards for Educational Leaders (PSEL): A set of standards created for teachers and educators. They outline a wide range of topics including ethics, equity, and school improvement among other things.

https://www.understood.org/: A nonprofit website that has free resources and information on ADHD, dyslexia, dyscalculia, language disorders, and written expression disorder. There are topics ranging from school support, parenting children with these learning needs, and signs to watch for.

Poverty Simulation: This is an immersive experience where the user assumes a role of someone experiencing poverty. The simulation helps give you a sense of the realities people experiencing poverty face.

ClassDojo: In the classroom, Class Dojo is a classroom management tool that allows the teacher to award points for positive behaviors. Outside of the classroom, Class Dojo allows for parents to get regular updates.

Flip.com: Free app with safe online spaces for students to share their ideas through video, messaging, and recording.

Remind: Remind provides a safe communication tool between educators, students, and parents. Without providing mobile numbers, Remind enables you to text students or parents/guardians.

SportsYOU: Another safe communication app geared toward coaches, parents/guardians, and players.

commonsensemedia.org: Partnered with Project Zero at Harvard, designed with developmentally appropriate lessons to address media balance, well-being, privacy, digital drama, hate speech, and security with social media literacy across all grades.

beinternetawesome.withgoogle.com: Internet Keep Safe Coalition offers lessons and adventure games to practice online safety skills. Pear Deck created flashcards and presentations support this curriculum.

Teacher Decision-Making.

Congratulations, you have completed the book, and you have made progress. If you look at the data you collected, you have evidence of growth. As you move forward, what are the skills you need to continue to keep track of? What are the skills that have just become new habits? Think about what will best serve you and your goals to be a teacher who continues to make progress. My goal is to help you continue to make progress and, hopefully, with slight changes to your collaborative approach, and increase your active listening in your school community. I believe in you and your ability to do great things, and you got this!

Next Steps.
What is working? . . .
What is not working? . . .
What do I need? . . .
What am I proud of? . . .
What do I need to let go of? . . .

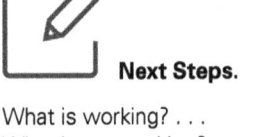**Weekly Reflection.** Use the space below to jot down some things you are grateful for in your school community. Remember, it is about progress. Review your data to highlight your glow and grow moments. Listen to me tell you, "You have got this, and I believe in you." I am encouraging these minor changes because you are a quality educator, and students need teachers like you in the field for years to come. "Keep going." Please feel free to share your success stories with me. Share your progress on Instagram. Tag me: @dr.mcconnell.s_progress

Making SMART Goals

Baseline Data	
Specific: What is the Target Behavior?	
With what **materials or conditions**?	
Measurable: How well must the skill be performed? (Criteria)	**Achievable:** What modifications or accommodations are needed for success? Making the time?
How will the skill be measured? And how often?	Any additional research? People to talk to?
Relevance: Why is meeting this goal important?	**Timely:** What is considered mastery for this goal? **Timeline:** When would you like to achieve this goal?
What other assessments or data will help assess progress toward the goal?	What are the next steps in this goal area?

Making SMART Goals

Baseline Data	
Specific: What is the Target Behavior?	
With what **materials or conditions**?	
Measurable: How well must the skill be performed? (Criteria)	**Achievable:** What modifications or accommodations are needed for success? Making the time?
How will the skill be measured? And how often?	Any additional research? People to talk to?
Relevance: Why is meeting this goal important?	**Timely:** What is considered mastery for this goal? **Timeline:** When would you like to achieve this goal?
What other assessments or data will help assess progress toward the goal?	What are the next steps in this goal area?

Making SMART Goals

Baseline Data	
Specific: What is the Target Behavior?	
With what **materials or conditions**?	
Measurable: How well must the skill be performed? (Criteria)	**Achievable:** What modifications or accommodations are needed for success? Making the time?
How will the skill be measured? And how often?	Any additional research? People to talk to?

Relevance: Why is meeting this goal important?	**Timely:** What is considered mastery for this goal? **Timeline:** When would you like to achieve this goal?
What other assessments or data will help assess progress toward the goal?	What are the next steps in this goal area?

Making SMART Goals

Baseline Data	
Specific: What is the Target Behavior?	
With what **materials or conditions**?	
Measurable: How well must the skill be performed? (Criteria)	**Achievable:** What modifications or accommodations are needed for success? Making the time?
How will the skill be measured? And how often?	Any additional research? People to talk to?
Relevance: Why is meeting this goal important?	**Timely:** What is considered mastery for this goal? **Timeline:** When would you like to achieve this goal?
What other assessments or data will help assess progress toward the goal?	What are the next steps in this goal area?

Making SMART Goals

Baseline Data	
Specific: What is the Target Behavior?	
With what **materials or conditions**?	
Measurable: How well must the skill be performed? (Criteria)	**Achievable:** What modifications or accommodations are needed for success? Making the time?
How will the skill be measured? And how often?	Any additional research? People to talk to?
Relevance: Why is meeting this goal important?	**Timely:** What is considered mastery for this goal? **Timeline:** When would you like to achieve this goal?
What other assessments or data will help assess progress toward the goal?	What are the next steps in this goal area?

References

Abboud, M. J., Wu, G., Pedneault, A., Stohr, M. K., & Hemmens, C. (2020). Educator sexual misconduct: A statutory analysis. *Criminal Justice Policy Review*, *31*(1), 133–153. https://doi.org/10.1177/0887403418806564

Ahmady, S., Khajeali, N., Kalantarion, M., Sharifi, F., & Yaseri, M. (2021). Relation between stress, time management, and academic achievement in preclinical medical education: A systematic review and meta-analysis. *Journal of Education and Health Promotion*, *10*, 32. https://doi.org/10.4103/jehp.jehp_600_20

Ahsan, A., Khan, M., & Siddiqui, R. N. (2012). The healing power of prayer in Islam. *Indian Journal of Positive Psychology*, *3*(2), 168.

Archer, A. L., & Hughes, C. A. (2010). *Explicit instruction: Effective and efficient teaching*. Guilford Publications.

Baker, T. L., Wise, J., Kelley, G., & Skiba, R. J. (2016). Identifying barriers: Creating solutions to improve family engagement. *School Community Journal*, *26*(2), 161–184.

Banks, J. A. (2021). *An introduction to multicultural education* (6th ed.). Pearson.

Bateman, D., & Cline, J. (2019). *Special education leadership*. Routledge.

Benedetti, M. G., Furlini, G., Zati, A., & Letizia Mauro, G. (2018). The effectiveness of physical exercise on bone density in osteoporotic patients. *BioMed Research International*, *2018*(1), 4840531.

Berman, M. G., Jonides, J., & Kaplan, S. (2012). The cognitive benefits of interacting with nature. *Psychological Science*, *23*(12), 1437–1442. https://doi.org/10.1177/0956797612437426

Berman, M. G., Kross, E., Krpan, K. M., Askren, M. K., Burson, A., Deldin, P. J., ... & Jonides, J. (2012). Interacting with nature improves cognition and affect for individuals with depression. *Journal of Affective Disorders*, *140*(3), 300–305.

Biggs, E. E., Gilson, C. B., & Carter, E. W. (2016). Accomplishing more together: Influences to the quality of professional relationships between special educators and paraprofessionals. *Research and Practice for Persons with Severe Disabilities*, *41*(4), 256–272.

Billingsley, B. S., Bettini, E. A., & Williams, T. O. (2019). Teacher racial/ethnic diversity: Distribution of special and general educators of color across schools. *Remedial and Special Education*, *40*(4), 199–212.

Bissell, K., Chou, S., & Dirks, E. (2024). Elite but struggling: Mediated narratives of women athletes and mental health disclosures. *Journalism & Communication Monographs*, *26*(1), 4–63.

Bonner, P. J., Warren, S. R., & Jiang, Y. H. (2018). Voices from urban classrooms: Teachers' perceptions on instructing diverse students and using culturally responsive teaching. *Education and Urban Society*, *50*(8), 697–726.

Boveda, M., & Aronson, B. A. (2019). Special education preservice teachers, intersectional diversity, and the privileging of emerging professional identities. *Remedial and Special Education*, *40*(4), 248–260.

Bowden, J., & Sinatra, S. T. (2020). *The great cholesterol myth, revised and expanded relevance: Why lowering your cholesterol won't prevent heart disease--and the statin-free plan that will.* Fair Winds Press.

Brown, B. (2021, August 11). *Brené on strong back, soft front, wild heart* [Podcast episode]. In *Unlocking us with Brené Brown*. Spotify. https://brenebrown.com/podcast/brene-on-strong-back-soft-front-wild-heart/

Brown, P. (2019). When silence is golden. *Early Years Educator, 21*(2), 28–30.

Butler, A., & Monda-Amaya, L. (2016). Preservice teachers' perceptions of challenging behavior. *Teacher Education and Special Education, 39*(4), 276–292. https://doi.org/10.1177/0888406416654212

Cain, K. M., & Dweck, C. S. (1995). The relation between motivational patterns and achievement cognitions through the elementary school years. *Merrill-Palmer Quarterly, 1982*, 25–52.

Carroll, A., Hepburn, S. J., & Bower, J. (2022, August). Mindful practice for teachers: Relieving stress and enhancing positive mindsets. *Frontiers in Education, 7*, 954098.

Carroll, A., York, A., Fynes-Clinton, S., Sanders-O'Connor, E., Flynn, L., Bower, J. M., ... & Ziaei, M. (2021). The downstream effects of teacher well-being programs: Improvements in teachers' stress, cognition and well-being benefit their students. *Frontiers in Psychology, 12*, 689628.

Casses, M. M. (2025). Get Down with Dog: A Yoga Story. Independently published.

Cochran-Smith, M. (2021). Rethinking teacher education: The trouble with accountability. *Oxford Review of Education, 47*(1), 8–24. https://doi.org/10.1080/03054985.2020.1842181

Common, E. A., Lane, K. L., Cantwell, E. D., Brunsting, N. C., Oakes, W. P., Germer, K. A., & Bross, L. A. (2020). Teacher-delivered strategies to increase students' opportunities to respond: A systematic methodological review. *Behavioral Disorders, 45*(2), 67–84.

Deci, E. L., & Ryan, R. M. (2000). The "what" and "why" of goal pursuits: Human needs and the self-determination of behavior. *Psychological Inquiry, 11*(4), 227–268.

Deering, R., & Mellor, D. (2011). An exploratory qualitative study of the self-reported impact of female-perpetrated childhood sexual abuse. *Journal of Child Sexual Abuse, 20*(1), 58–76.

DeMatthews, D. E., Knight, D. S., & Shin, J. (2021). The principal-teacher churn: Understanding the relationship between leadership turnover and teacher attrition. *Educational Administration Quarterly, 58*(1), 76–109. https://doi.org/10.1177/0013161X211051974

De Smet, A., Dowling, B., Hancock, B., & Schaninger, W. (2022, July 13). *K–12 teachers are quitting. What would make them stay?* McKinsey & Company. Retrieved from https://www.mckinsey.com

Dontre, A. J. (2021). The influence of technology on academic distraction: A review. *Human Behavior and Emerging Technologies, 3*, 379–390. https://doi.org/10.1002/hbe2.229

Driedger, J. (2001). Spirituality according to Oprah. *Vision: A Journal for Church and Theology, 2*(2), 41–48.

Dumbaugh, D., & Haunsperger, D. (Eds.). (2022). Building community in the classroom. In *Count me in* (Vol. 68). American Mathematical Society.

Ennis, R. P., Royer, D. J., Lane, K. L., Menzies, H. M., Oakes, W. P., & Schellman, L. E. (2018). Behavior-specific praise: An effective, efficient, low-intensity strategy to support student success. *Beyond Behavior, 27*(3), 134–139. https://doi.org/10.1177/1074295618798587

Epstein, J. L. (2019). Theory to practice: School and family partnerships lead to school improvement and student success. In C. L. Fagnano & B. Werber (Eds.), *School, family, and community interaction* (pp. 39–52). Routledge.

Flower, A., McKenna, J. W., & Haring, C. D. (2017). Behavior and classroom management: Are teacher preparation programs really preparing our teachers? *Preventing School Failure: Alternative Education for Children and Youth, 61*(2), 163–169.

Friend, M., & Cook, L. (2007). Co-teaching. *Educational Leadership, 64*(5), 48–52.

Fullan, M., Rincón-Gallardo, S., & Hargreaves, A. (2015). Professional capital as accountability. *Education Policy Analysis Archives, 23*(15), 15. https://doi.org/10.14507/epaa.v23.1998

Gao, X., & Yin, H. (2020). The relationship between physical activity and subjective well-being: A meta-analysis. *Journal of Health Psychology, 25*(12), 1934–1947. https://doi.org/10.1177/1359105318768256

Ghasemi, F. (2022). (Dys) functional cognitive-behavioral coping strategies of teachers to cope with stress, anxiety, and depression. *Deviant Behavior, 43*(12), 1558–1571.

Haidusek-Niazy, S., Huyler, D., & Carpenter, R. E. (2023). Mentorship reconsidered: A case study of K-12 teachers' mentor-mentee relationships during the Covid-19 pandemic. *Social Psychology of Education, 26*(5), 1269–1288. https://doi.org/10.1007/s11218-023-09788-w

Harkins Monaco, E. A., Brusnahan, L. L. S., Fuller, M. C., Odima, M. O., & Odima Jr., M. O. (2024). *Disability, Intersectionality, and belonging in special education: Socioculturally sustaining practices.* Rowman & Littlefield Publishers.

Hirshkowitz, M., Whiton, K., Albert, S. M., Alessi, C., Bruni, O., DonCarlos, L., ... & Adams Hillard, P. J. (2015). National sleep foundation's sleep time duration recommendations: Methodology and results summary. *Sleep Health, 1*(1), 40–43. https://doi.org/10.1016/j.sleh.2014.12.010

Horton, D., Spigelmyer, P., Zoucha, R., & Rebmann, T. (2023). Disaster preparedness in K-12 schools: An integrative review. *Journal of School Health, 93*(8), 726–732.

Hsouna, H., Boukhris, O., Abdessalem, R., Trabelsi, K., Ammar, A., Shephard, R. J., & Chtourou, H. (2019). Effect of different nap opportunity durations on short-term maximal performance, attention, feelings, muscle soreness, fatigue, stress and sleep. *Physiology & Behavior, 211*, 112673.

Jeglic, E. L., Clakins, C., Kaylor, L., Margeotes, K., Doychak, K., Blasco, B., Chesin, M., & Panza, N. (2022). The nature and scope of educator misconduct in K–12. *Sexual Abuse, 35*(2), 188–213. https://doi.org/10.1177/10790632221096421

Jennings, P. A., & Greenberg, M. T. (2020). Supporting teachers' social and emotional well-being: Strategies for resilience and effectiveness. *The Future of Children, 30*(2), 55–74. https://doi.org/10.1353/foc.2020.0003

Justus, J. (2023). Using self-monitoring to increase behavior-specific praise in students. School Psychology Review, 52(1), 34–52. This study found that minimal-training self-monitoring interventions led to increased on-task behavior and positive replacement behaviors.

Keshmiri, F., Jambarsang, S., & Mehrparvar, A. H. (2023). Effective components of teachers' professionalism in viewpoints of various stakeholders. *Journal of Education and Health Promotion, 12*(1), 24. https://doi.org/10.4103/jehp.jehp_1565_21

Kirk, J., MacDonald, A., Lavender, P., Dean, J., & Rubin, G. (2017). Can treatment adherence be improved by using Rubin's four tendencies framework to understand a patient's response to expectations. *Biomedicine Hub*, *2*(Suppl 1), 1–12. https://doi.org/10.1159/000484261

Kollerová, L., Květon, P., Zábrodská, K., & Janošová, P. (2023). Teacher exhaustion: The effects of disruptive student behaviors, victimization by workplace bullying, and social support from colleagues. *Social Psychology of Education*, *26*(4), 885–902.

Larson, K. E., Pas, E. T., Bottiani, J. H., Kush, J. M., & Bradshaw, C. P. (2021). A multidimensional and multilevel examination of student engagement and secondary school teachers' use of classroom management practices. *Journal of Positive Behavior Interventions*, *23*(3), 149–162.

Latino, A., Cataldi, J. R., & Fischetti, F. (2021). Mind-clearing matter: Exploring the psychological benefits of nature. *Journal of Environmental Psychology*, *77*, 101689. doi:10.1016/j.jenvp.2021.101689.

Lazenby, R. (2015). *Michael Jordan: The life*. Talent sport.

Leo, U., Persson, R., Arvidsson, I., Håkansson, C., Moos, L., Paulsen, J. M., & Nihlfors, E. (2020). External expectations and well-being, fundamental and forgotten perspectives in school leadership: A study on new leadership roles, trust and accountability. In L. Moos, E. Nihlfors, & J. M. Paulsen (Eds.), *Re-centering the critical potential of nordic school leadership research* (Vol. 14, pp. 209–229). Springer International Publishing. https://doi.org/10.1007/978-3-030-55027-1_12

Levin, B. (2008). *How to change 5000 schools: A practical and positive approach for leading change at every level*. Harvard Education Press.

Mace, F. C., McComas, J. J., Mauro, B. C., Progar, P. R., Taylor, B., Ervin, R., & Zangrillo, A. N. (2010). Differential reinforcement of alternative behavior increases resistance to extinction: Clinical demonstration, animal modeling, and clinical test of one solution. *Journal of the Experimental Analysis of Behavior*, *93*(3), 349–367.

MacSuga-Gage, A. S., & Simonsen, B. (2015). Examining the effects of teacher-directed opportunities to respond on student outcomes: A systematic review of the literature. *Education and Treatment of Children*, *38*(2), 211–239.

McConnell, B. M. (2020). CEC mentorship helping teachers succeed through "first years." This could be you! CEC Convention.

Mckenna, J. W., & Flower, A. (2014). Get them back on track: Use of the good behavior game to improve student behavior. *Beyond Behavior*, *23*(2), 20–26.

McNaughton, D., & Vostal, B. R. (2010). Using active listening to improve collaboration with parents: The LAFF don't cry strategy. *Intervention in School and Clinic*, *45*(4), 251–256.

Michels, N., & Hamers, P. (2023). Nature sounds for stress recovery and healthy eating: A lab experiment differentiating water and bird sound. *Environment and Behavior*, *55*(3), 175–205.

Mohapel, P. (2025). The neuroscience of psychological well-being and flourishing. In P. Jones (Ed.), *Happiness and the psychology of enlightenment* (p. 171). IntechOpen.

Muhammad, A. (2009). *Transforming school culture: How to overcome staff division*. Solution Tree Press.

Murawski, W. (2009). *Collaborative teaching in secondary schools: Making the co-teaching marriage work!* Corwin Press.

Murawski, W. W., & Dieker, L. A. (2004). Tips and strategies for co-teaching at the secondary level. *Teaching Exceptional Children*, *36*(5), 52–58.

Murawski, W. W., & Goodwin, V. A. (2014). Effective inclusive schools and the co-teaching conundrum. In J. McLeskey, F. Spooner, B. Algozzine, & N. L. Waldron (Eds.), *Handbook of effective inclusive schools* (pp. 292–305). Routledge.

McConnell, B. M., & Murawski, W. W. (2017). The importance of partnerships. Murawski, WW ScottK. L.(Eds.), What really works with exceptional learners, 338–355.

Nagro, S. A. (2022). Three phases of video-based reflection activities to transition teacher candidates from understanding to examining practice. *Journal of Special Education Preparation, 2*(1), 28–37.

Nagro, S. A., & deBettencourt, L. U. (2019). Reflection activities within clinical experiences: An important component of field-based teacher education. In T. E. Hodges & A. C. Baum (Eds.), *Handbook of research on field-based teacher education* (pp. 565–586). IGI Global.

National Association of State Directors of Teacher Education and Certification. (2015). *Model code of ethics for educators.* NASDTEC.

National Policy Board for Educational Administration. (2015). *Professional standards for educational leaders 2015.* Author.

Norcross, J. C., Mrykalo, M. S., & Blagys, M. D. (2002). Auld lang syne: Success predictors, change processes, and self-reported outcomes of New Year's resolvers and nonresolvers. *Journal of Clinical Psychology, 58*(4), 397–405. https://doi.org/10.1002/jclp.1151

O'Rourke, C., & Beaudoin, L. (1998). *The McGill action planning system: A planning framework for professionals working with individuals with disabilities.* McGill University.

Paris, D., & Alim, H. S. (2017). *Culturally sustaining pedagogies: Teaching and learning for justice in a changing world.* Teachers College Press.

Park, C. L., & MacKinnon, D. P. (2013). The role of religion in coping with stress: A meta-analytic review. *Journal of Counseling Psychology, 60*(4), 565–578. https://doi.org/10.1037/a0034654

Peeples, K. N., Hirsch, S. E., Gardner, S. J., Keeley, R. G., Sherrow, B. L., McKenzie, J. M., Randall, K. N., Romig, J. E., & Kennedy, M. J. (2018). Using multimedia instruction and performance feedback to improve preservice teachers' vocabulary instruction. *Teacher Education and Special Education, 42*(3), 227–245. https://doi.org/10.1177/0888406418801913

Pfund, G. N., & Miller-Perrin, C. (2019). Interaction and harmony in faith communities: Predicting life purpose, loneliness, and well-being among college students. *Journal of College and Character, 20*(3), 234–253.

Pressman, R. M., Sugarman, D. B., Nemon, M. L., Desjarlais, J., Owens, J. A., & Schettini-Evans, A. (2015). Homework and family stress: With consideration of parents' self confidence, educational level, and cultural background. *The American Journal of Family Therapy, 43*(4), 297–313.

Reichert, C. F., Deboer, T., & Landolt, H. P. (2022). Adenosine, caffeine, and sleep–wake regulation: State of the science and perspectives. *Journal of Sleep Research, 31*(4), e13597.

Rivedal, D. D., Cichocki, M., & Chung, K. C. (2023). Dealing with difficult people and why it matters. *Plastic and Reconstructive Surgery, 152*(5), 923–928.

Robbins, M. (2023). *The high 5 habit: Take control of your life with one simple habit.* Hay House, Inc.

Rossman, M. (2022). Taylor Swift, remediating the self, and nostalgic girlhood in tween music fandom. *Transformative Works and Cultures, 38*(1).

Röttger, S., Theobald, D. A., Abendroth, J., & Jacobsen, T. (2021). The effectiveness of combat tactical breathing as compared with prolonged exhalation. *Applied Psychophysiology and Biofeedback, 46*(1), 19–28.

Rubin, G. (2017). The Four Tendencies: The indispensable personality profiles that reveal how to make your life better (and other people's lives better, too). Harmony.

Ryan, R. M., & Deci, E. L. (2020). Intrinsic and extrinsic motivation from a self-determination theory perspective: Definitions, theory, practices, and future directions. *Contemporary Educational Psychology, 61,* 101860.

Scales III, A. (2024). *Sacred practices of affirmation, meditation and worship.* Albert Scales.

Scaletta, M., & Hughes, M. T. (2022). Administrators' perception of their role in school-wide positive behavior interventions and supports implementation. *Journal of School Leadership, 32*(3), 267–288.

Schön, D. A. (1983). *The reflective practitioner: How professionals think in action.* Basic Books.

Seide, M. (2024). How is talk therapy different from talking to a friend? *Verywell Mind.* https://doi.www.verywellmind.com/how-is-talk-therapy-different-from-talking-to-a-friend-5181588.

Shechter, A., Quispe, K. A., Mizhquiri Barbecho, J. S., Slater, C., & Falzon, L. (2020). Interventions to reduce short-wavelength ("blue") light exposure at night and their effects on sleep: A systematic review and meta-analysis. *Sleep advances: A journal of the Sleep Research Society, 1*(1), zpaa002. https://doi.org/10.1093/sleepadvances/zpaa002

Sherod, R. L., Jones, J. S., Perry, H., & Oakes, W. P. (2023). Precorrection: Empowering teachers and families to support students in varied learning contexts. *Preventing School Failure: Alternative Education for Children and Youth, 67*(2), 91–97. https://doi.org/10.1080/1045988X.2023.2181302

Shintani, R. (2025). The Sleep-gratitude connection: Positive thinking for restful nights and better health. *Critical Debates in Humanities, Science and Global Justice, 5*(2), 127–138.

Shirrell, M. (2021). On their own? The work-related social interactions and turnover of new teachers. *American Journal of Education, 127*(3), 399–439.

Simonsen, B., Freeman, J., Kooken, J., Dooley, K., Gambino, A. J., Wilkinson, S., VanLone, J., Walters, S., Byun, S. G., Xu, X., Lupo, K., & Kern, L. (2020). *Classroom Management Observation Tool (CMOT).* University of Connecticut. Retrieved from: https://nepbis.org/classrooms-data-tools-resources/

Sinek, S., Mead, D., & Docker, P. (2017). *Find your why: A practical guide for discovering purpose for you and your team.* Penguin.

Souto-Manning, M., & Swick, K. J. (2006). Teachers' beliefs about parent and family involvement: Rethinking our family involvement paradigm. *Early Childhood Education Journal, 34*(2), 187–193. https://doi-org.pitt.idm.oclc.org/10.1007/s10643-006-0063-5

Stansberry Brusnahan, L., Maguire, E., Harkins Monaco, E. A., Leckie, A., Bailey, S., & Fuller, M. (2023). Leading with an equity lens: Addressing the intersection of racism and ableism in public schools. *Teaching Exceptional Children, 55*(5), 302–313. https://doi.org/10.1177/00400599231173073

Steele, D., & Whitaker, T. (2019). It is important to catch kids being good – and recognize them for it – because students need attention … and they will get it, one way or another. In D. Steele & T. Whitaker (Eds.), *Essential truths for teachers* (1st ed., pp. 90–90). Routledge. https://doi.org/10.4324/9780429022029-52

Stevens, K. B., & Lingo, A. S. (2013). Assessing classroom management: The umbrella approach. *Beyond Behavior, 22*(2), 19–26. https://doi.org/10.1177/107429561302200205

Sugai, G., & Horner, R. (2009). Responsiveness-to-intervention and school-wide positive behavior supports: Integration of multi-tiered system approaches. *Exceptionality, 17*(4), 223–237. doi: 10.1080/09362830903235375

Talbott, S. (2021). *Mental fitness: Maximizing mood, motivation, & mental wellness by optimizing the brain-body-biome.* Turner Publishing Company.

Tang, Y. Y., Holzel, B. K., & Posner, M. I. (2015). The neuroscience of mindfulness meditation. *Nature Reviews Neuroscience, 16*(4), 213–225.

Tebow, T., & Gregory, A. J. (2022). *Mission possible: Go create a life that counts* (1st ed.). WaterBrook.

US Bureau of Labor Statistics. (2024). BRS 2024 Tables: U.S. Bureau of Labor Statistics. https://www.bls.gov/brs/data/tables/2024

U.S. Department of the Interior & The White House. (2015, February 19). *Let's get every kid in a park.* [Press release]. https://obamawhitehouse.archives.gov/blog/2015/02/19/lets-get-every-kid-park

van der Helm, E., Gujar, N., & Walker, M. P. (2010). Sleep deprivation impairs the accurate recognition of human emotions. *Sleep, 33*(3), 335–342. https://doi.org/10.1093/sleep/33.3.335

Vanderkam, L. (2011). *168 hours: You have more time than you think.* Penguin.

Vanderkam, L. (2022). *Tranquility by tuesday: 9 ways to calm the chaos and make time for what matters.* Penguin Publishing Group.

Vostal, B. R., McNaughton, D., Benedek-Wood, E., & Hoffman, K. (2015). Preparing teachers for collaborative communication: Evaluation of instruction in an active listening strategy. *National Teacher Education Journal, 8*(2), 5–14.

Vostal, B. R., Mrachko, A. A., Vostal, M., & McCoy, A. (2021). Effects of group behavioral skills training on teacher candidates' acquisition and maintenance of active listening. *Journal of Behavioral Education, 31*(4), 679–698.

Walker, M. (2017). *Why we sleep: Unlocking the power of sleep and dreams.* Simon and Schuster.

Walker, V. L., Lyon, K. J., Clausen, A. M., Chen, J., & Smith, H. H. (2023). Video performance feedback and video self-monitoring to improve systematic instruction implementation for pre-service teachers. *Journal of Special Education Technology, 38*(2), 174–186. https://doi.org/10.1177/01626434221102524

Wang, X., Husu, J., & Toom, A. (2025). What makes a good mentor of in-service teacher education?—A systematic review of mentoring competence from a transformative learning perspective. *Teaching and Teacher Education, 153,* 104822.

Weinstein, A. A., van Aert, R. C. M., Donovan, K., Muskens, L., & Kop, W. J. (2024). Affective responses to acute exercise: A meta-analysis of the potential beneficial effects of a single bout of exercise on general mood, anxiety, and depressive symptoms. *Psychosomatic Medicine, 86*(6), 486–497. https://doi.org/10.1097/PSY.0000000000001321

Weiss, M. P., & Brigham, F. J. (2000). Co-teaching and the model of shared responsibility: What does the research support? *Advances in Learning and Behavioral Disabilities, 14,* 217–246.

Willis, J., & Willis, M. (2020). *Research-based strategies to ignite student learning: Insights from neuroscience and the classroom.* ASCD, 1.

Worland, J. (2016, March 16). *How meditation helps Katy Perry, Jerry Seinfeld and other celebrities stay focused*. Time. https://time.com/4263202/katy-perry-meditation/

Xi, Y., Li, Q., Zhang, M., Liu, L., Li, G., Lin, W., & Wu, J. (2019). Optimized configuration of functional brain network for processing semantic audiovisual stimuli underlying the modulation of attention: A graph-based study. *Frontiers in Integrative Neuroscience, 13*, 67.

Acknowledgments

In true Bethany fashion, I cannot just name a few people; I need to share my gratitude in themes. I figure I can spread out more free copies that way.

To my teachers throughout my career. I really tried to name-drop the characters through my vignettes, many of you who stood out and taught me so many life lessons. For the people who said, "I don't know if you got this, only you have the ability to know what you need to do to get better at this job." To my dad, who said, "I don't think you have the patience for special education." You are right, Dad; I am "persistent," and because of that, I will always support the students who need it the most. Dad, you are also part of "people who didn't tell me what I want to hear."

To my bosses throughout my career. To my first boss, Barb Shamp, in the halls of Gaithersburg, who told me it's all about "rubbing noses with the whohas" up to Charline Barnes Rowland who told me to "write the book." Even in my college job as a painter, with the days I slept on the job. Thank you for not firing me when I was not my best self. If you don't fire me on my worst day, you get to see that I have so many better days ahead and "I can write the damn book."

To my colleagues throughout my career, thank you. Thank you for humoring my collegiality and not name-bashing or gossiping about me to the students. I hope that on my best days, you will see a positive reflection of "Part III." Liz, thank you for always upholding me as an Obliger.

To my professional women in the workforce. You are cited throughout this book as my homage to giving me some of the best advice in my professional and personal career. You showed up for me in your Zoom calls, Polo messages, emails, research, websites, podcasts, television series (this includes you Ellen DeGeneres and Oprah). You showed up for so many people like me when I needed it the most. For that, I am eternally grateful for the work that you do, and now I know what it means to stand on the shoulders of giants.

To SSEPC for being my home in the professional world. For all of the women who pushed me and helped me navigate how to be a professional in the workforce. These people humored me when I pointed out that most of the "newbies" were women holding accountability for women in work sessions, while "the boys were at the bar." Thank you, Liz, for introducing me to this group.

To all of my mom consultants. As a girl who lost her mom at 5, I have been doing this mom thing with some instincts, reading, and YouTube searches. I somehow got these two kiddos into the teen years. I realized my mom has planted so many moms and cousins to consult along the way. I never got to hear, "you are just like your mother," but what I would like to think is I have been afforded the opportunity to be a buffet mom who gets to pick and choose parenting style tips that work for me. Some of those people happen to be my sisters (Kristy and Erin). DailyTay, I cannot wait for your content when your girls are teenagers.

To my students. I have learned more from you than you will ever know. Some of you I know I connected with more than others. But to the ones I offended—know that I still work to do better because of your feedback: "my tone" and my "face," even the one who said, "it was inconvenient that she was pregnant." Don't worry, I did not have any more kids. That is how seriously I take my student surveys. I am so reflective in my teaching that when I get negative feedback, I make changes to appease the negative comments. Thank you for your patience as I grow as a teacher. I hope you can take something from my class, even if it's how to use a "neti Pot."

Now here are some specifics:

David Bateman, for always being my sounding board for my professional goals. You have made so many amazing contributions to the field of special education. When I earned the PERC Grant, it was the best $200 I ever "won" I know my publication did not have the best turnaround time, but words cannot express my gratitude for you always taking the time to listen to my ideas.

To Derek and Amelia, "it's not about you." But, at the same time, it's all about you. When I told you I was writing a book, you finally saw me as cool. Not that "I wasn't a band-aid doctor" or "I need to tell Mrs. JaQueline that she is a bad teacher," but writing a book is cool. Believe it or not, because of my car ride conversations with each of you, I have had the discipline to write this book. Do you still think I am cool?

Doug, "if you could see you through my eyes, you'd just get better all the time." But after 20 years of marriage, it means that through each chapter, you get to grow up and go through transitions together. I say that we are blessed in that each time we grow up, we still love each other, but more importantly, we like each other too. So we are against the odds. I will keep doing things the right way just as long as you keep doing things my way. Thank you for being "US." We are the letter people, from Kindergarten to Today—You are the Sunshine to my Umbrella.

Index

accountability
   external   206–7
   internal   207–8
   movement   77–8
   virtual   79–80
administrators   225
   goals   235
      Jasper's administrative goal chart   236–7
      Quentin's administrative goal chart   237–8
   making big decisions   230–1
   overall responsibilities   227–8
   playing fair   229–30
   positive interactions with   233–5
   roles of   226–31
Ahaprocess.com   124
AI
   interview practice and feedback   239
   surveys   147
alarms   49
American Time Use Survey Research   287
Appletree Schools   282
attention getters   157

balanced diet   57–8
Banks, J. A.   138
behavior challenges, structure for   116–17
behaviors, for classroom success
   classroom reinforcements   193–4
   classroom umbrella approach   181–4
   class-wide motivation   190–3
   goals   195–7
      Jasper's behavior goal chart   195
      Simone's behavior goal chart   196–7
   positive behavior interventions and supports   184–5
   precorrections   188–9
   teaching of   186–8

behavior-specific praise   115
beinternetawesome.withgoogle.com: 299
biases   133
Biles, S.   96–7
BlackonBlackEducation.com   147
Blinkist   179
Bloomz   282
body scan   102
box breathing, see tactical breathing
brain-centering goals   98–100
brain craves   9
brain juices   7–13
BrainPop.com   179
brainstorm   12
breathwork   90–1
Breethe app   102

calm   102
Canva   165
CASEL.org   282
CEC's Initial Practice-Based Professional Preparation Standards   282
ChatGPT   128
Chopra, D.   92
choral responding   169–70
Class Dojo   124, 165, 299
classroom
   collaborating with others   242–3
   co-teaching as partnership   244–7
   meeting expectations in   241–50
   productive relationships with paraprofessionals   248–50
   your mentor teacher is your guide   243–4
classroom management   109, 112
   connecting with students   112–14
   opportunities to respond and student engagement   116
   rule reminders and clear expectations   114–15

Simone's classroom management goals chart   121–2
structure for behavior challenges   116–17
video self-reflection   117–20
Classroom Management Observation Tool (CMOT)   109–12, 118
classroom reinforcements   193–4
classroom umbrella approach   181–4
class-wide contingencies   191
class-wide motivation   190
   group *versus* group   191
   self-monitoring   192
   teacher *versus* student   190–1
CMOT   127, *see* Classroom Management Observation Tool (CMOT)
collegial goals   260–2
color analogies   41
color coding   24
commonsensemedia.org   299
communication   215, 217
   teamwork   256–7
   working strategies, informal   254
convenience   78–9
co-teaching, as partnership   244–7
counseling   96–8
coupon book   198
courageousconvesation.com   147
crisis management   231–2
cue cards   173–4
culture   113–14
   considerations to classroom   138–40
Curipod.com   124

decision making, administrators   230–1
deep breathing   89, 90
domino effect   43
donorschoose.org   198
Doodlepoll.com   264
dopamine   9, 11
Dreambox.com   124
Dropbox   34

Edutopia   198
emails   256–7
equal education   138
Evernote app   34
Every Kid in a Park (2015)   93
exercise   69–70
   running   70–1
   skiing   71–3
   strength training   74–6
   yoga   73–4
external accountability   206–7

FacingHistory.org   147
families   267
   goals   279–283
      Kaycee's active listening chart   279–80
      Quentin's investigative report chart   280–1
   ongoing communication with   268–78
family survey   131–2
finger representation   173
first-then statements   153
Flip.com   299
Flowcabulary.com   165
food   51–2
   at home   58
   making good choices   56–8
   meal planning   60–1
   out and about   58
   setting fuel goals   61–5
   snacking   58–60
four tendencies   208–10, 222
   impact success of student teachers   211
   Jasper, resisting rules rebel   214–15
   Kaycee, people pleasing obliger   211–12
   people's tendencies impact collaboration   210–11
   Quentin, questions your questions   215–19
   Simone, upholds herself and others   212–13
Four Tendencies Quiz   208, 210, 242
   Jasper's chart   219–20
Freecycle.org   198
friendships   286
   when friendships mix   287
frozen vegetables   57
fuel goals   61–2
   Jasper's chart   64–5
   Simone's chart   62–3
Fullan, M.   207
Funky Teacher Website   264

goals
   setting for more time   30–3
   teamwork   255
   weekly setting   28–9

GoNoodle.com   84, 102
gray areas
   defining   288–9
   novice teacher, avoiding   290–1
   role model, avoiding   292–4
   workplaces with   289–90
Gretchen Rubin Four Tendencies Framework   206, 209
grocery pickups   67
grounding   94
group *versus* group   191
gTasks   35, 222

Habitica   35, 102
hand signaling   172–3
"The Happiness Project"   209, 222
Harkins Monaco, E. A.   113
healthy relationships   285
   avoiding gray areas, role model   292–4
   building friendships   286
   in closing   295
   defining gray area   288–9
   goals   295
      Jasper, digitally literate   295–6
      Kaycee, favoritism on social media   296–7
   novice teacher, avoiding gray areas   290–1
   when friendships mix   287
   workplace with gray areas   289–90
human brain   4, 87
   calming of   90–1
   dusting of   93
   hope for   88–9
   incorporating nature   94–5
   listening   4–5
   listen to relaxing noise   40–2
   organizing   95–6
   piecing together   96–8
   planning   4–5, 7–13
   prepping for rest   39–40
   reflection   4–7
   respond to   4–5
   strength training to   89–90

idea sharing   168
IEP, *see* Individualized Education Plan (IEP)

individuality
   with middle level and secondary students   135–6
   in students elementary   133–5
Individualized Education Plan (IEP)   131
informal communication, working strategies   254
internal accountability   207–8

Jordan, M.   91
journaling   95–6
   Kaycee's journey through   98

Kahoot!   179

LAFF Don't CRY (LAFF)   272–6
Larryferlazzo.edublogs.org   124
Learnningforjustice.org   147
listening, human brain   4–5
log your meals   67
log your water   67
Lose It! app   67

MAPS, *see* McGill Action Planning System (MAPS)
McGill Action Planning System (MAPS)   131
meal planning   60–1
meditation   89–90
meditative stories   92–3
mentors   243–4, 290
mindfulschool.net   102
mindset-like beliefs   6
minimalist phone   35
Mintal sleep tracker   49
Minute App   264
Minutes Notetaker   222
Model Code of Ethics for Educators (MCEE)   288
movement   76–7
   convenience   78–9
   getting your accountability   77–8
   goals   80
      Jasper's work routine goal chart   81–3
      Kaycee's movement goal chart   80–1
   virtual accountability   79–80
   weekly goal setting   79
My Fitness Pal   67
Mykiddo app   282

Nagro, S. A.   118
nap time   44–5
naptime body scan   49
National Association of State Directors of Teacher Education and Certification (NASDTEC)   288
Nationalequityproject.org   147
National Policy Board for Educator Administration   239
nature immersion   93
NearPod.com   179
negative narratives   6
newsletters   268–70
NOOM food app   67
novice teacher, avoiding gray areas   290–1
NPBEA 2015 Professional Standards for Educational Leaders (PSEL)   299

Obama, B.   93
obligers   209, 211–12, 219, 286
ongoing communication, with families   268
   LAFF Don't CRY with   272–6
   newsletters   268–70
   positive phone calls   270–2
   providing resources   277–8
organization   114
Ottavino, A.   94
out-of-school events, participation in   142–3

PACER   282
Padlet.com   179
Panoramaed.com   147
paraprofessionals, productive relationships with   248–50
Parent Center for Resources   282
Parentsasteachers.org   282
partnerships
   co-teaching as   244–7
   responsibilities for   245
Perry, K.   89
phone calls   270–2
Pickerwheel.com   124
planning
   human brain   4–5, 7–13
   for spending your time   24–8
podcasts   102
   bedtime stories   49
poll everywhere/clickers   174, 179

Pomodoro timer   35
Positive Behavior Interventions and Supports (PBIS)   232–3
Positivediscipline.com   165
positive relationships   205
positive visualization   91–2
Post-it notes   6
poverty simulation   299
precorrections   188–9
Principal Investigators (PI)   145
productive relationships, with paraprofessionals   248–50
protein foods   57

questioners   215
questioning   115
quiet opportunities, to respond
   cue cards   173–4
   hand signaling   172–3
   poll everywhere/clickers   174
   whiteboard responses   171–2

Rapid Eye Movement (REM) sleep   38
rebels   209, 214–15, 219–20
reflection
   human brain   4–7
   on spending time with time tracking   24–6
regular check-ins, working strategies   252–3
religious meditations   102
Remind app   6, 282, 299
responsibilities
   administrators   227–8
   for partnerships   245
   teamwork   255–6
responsibility and respect   127–8
   check biases   133
   considerations for happening outside of classroom   140–1
   cultural considerations to classroom   138–40
   family survey   131–2
   goals   143
      Kaycee's after-school activities chart   144
      Quentin's principal investigators chart   145
   individuality in elementary students   133–5
   individuality with middle level and secondary students   135–6
   participate in out-of-school events   142–3

students community   141–2
students survey   128–31
students value   136–8
Responsiveclassroom.org   165
Reticular Activating System (RAS)   5
Rivedal, D. D.   259
running   70–1

scheduling   155
   attention getters   157
   efficient transitions   157–9
   introducing lessons   155–6
   prepare for downtime   159
school-wide management systems   231
   crisis management   231–2
   Positive Behavior Interventions and Supports   232–3
   positive interactions with administrators   233–5
screentime   49
SEL   282
self-monitoring   192
skiing   71–3
sleep
   REM   38
   schedules (*see* sleep schedules)
   self-care routine   37
sleep checklist   49
sleep cycles   38, 39
sleep goals   45
   Kaycee's sleep goal chart   47–8
   Simone's snooze goal   45, 46
sleep monitor   35, 49
sleep schedules   38
   listen to relaxing noise   40–2
   prepping brain for rest   39–40
smartclassroommanagement.com   165, 179
SMART Goals   29
snacking   58–60
social pressure   206
sound color   41
spirituality   88–9
SportsYOU   299
step monitor   84
sticky notes   84
strength training   74–6
student participation
   Kaycee's chatter box goal   175–6
   Quentin's question goal   177–8
   quiet opportunities to respond   171–4
   verbal opportunities   167–71
students
   connecting with   112–14
   elementary, individuality in   133–5
   individuality with middle level and secondary   135–6
   survey   128–31
   teachers *versus*   190–1, 213
   value of   136–8
students community   141–2
student teachers   16–17
   difficulty in finding time   21–3
   four tendencies, impact success of   211
   Jasper   18–19
   Kaycee   17–18
   Quentin   19–21
   Simone   17
SurveyMonkey.com   264
SWIS Suite   239

tactical breathing   90
task
   behavior specific and varied praise   154–5
   consequences   151–2
   engaging and inclusive seasonal activities   159–61
   first-then statements   153
   on-task goals   161
      Quentin's chart   163
      Simone expectations   162
   prepare for unexpected   161
   rules and expectations   149–51
   scheduling each day   155–9
teacher behaviors   15–16
TeacherKit app   239
teachers *versus* student   190–1, 213
Teachervision.com   165
teamwork   254–5
   clear communication   256–7
   effective use of time   257
   roles and responsibilities   255–6
   shared measurable goals   255
Tebow, T.   88
tendency   206
   external accountability   206–7
   internal accountability   207–8

Think-Pair-Share   168–9
time, effective use of teamwork   257
Timetoast.com   147
Tolle, E.   92
turn and talk   170–1

Understood.org   147
upholder   209, 213

Vanderkam, L.   21
vegetables   57
verbal immediacy   113
verbal opportunities, student participation   167
   choral responding   169–70
   Think-Pair-Share   168–9
   turn and talk   170–1
video self-reflection   117–20
virtual accountability   79–80
virtual accounts   84
visual timers   157

wake-up routine   43–4
   nap time   44–5

water   51–2, 56
   "going to the well"   54
   how much to drink   53
   water bottle trend   55
   what counts as   54
water bottle trend   55
weekly goal setting   28–9, 79
whiteboard responses   171–2
Winfrey, O.   92
working strategies
   with everyone   250–1
   informal communication   254
   regular check-ins   252–3
workplaces, with gray areas   289–90
www.GretchenRubin.com   222
www.pbis.org/school   239
www.Swis.org   239
www.2TeachLLC.com   264

yoga   73–4
YouTube   84
   meditative stories   102

About the Author

Dr. Bethany M. McConnell, PhD, has been part of the Pitt-Johnstown community since 2011. She coordinates the special education program and oversees field placements, including student teaching opportunities in New Zealand and Bolivia. She teaches upper-level special education methods courses that focus on classroom management, social-emotional learning, and culturally responsive teaching. Still, she spends much of her time in schools working alongside pre-service and student teachers. She especially enjoys helping future educators set wellness goals, create engaging lessons, and learn how to "work well with others" as professionals. Her experiences in the classroom inspired her to create this interactive workbook to help student teachers reflect, grow, and track their progress for their lifelong goals of teaching. She is married to her high school sweetheart, Doug. They are raising their teenagers, Derek and Amelia, and she is still making progress on work-life balance and using humor in both teaching and parenting.